HEMATOL

THE SCIENTIST AS EDITOR

Guidelines for Editors of Books and Journals

Maeve O'Connor

Senior Editor, Ciba Foundation, London

An ELSE—Ciba Foundation Guide for Editors

A Wiley Medical Publication

John Wiley & Sons

New York/Toronto

JOHN WILEY AND SONS INC
605 Third Avenue, New York, NY 10016

First published 1979 by
PITMAN MEDICAL PUBLISHING CO LTD
PO Box 7, Tunbridge Wells, Kent, England

Library of Congress Catalog Card Number 78-60428

ISBN: 0-471-04932-8

Sponsored by Editerra, the International Federation of
Scientific Editors' Associations, the International Union
of Biological Sciences and the International Union of
Geological Sciences.

ELSE (European Life Science Editors) is the acronym
adopted by the European Association of Editors of
Biological Periodicals.

The Ciba Foundation, London, is an educational and
scientific charity for the promotion of international
cooperation in medical and chemical research.

Editerra is the European Association of Earth–Science
Editors.

Printed and bound in Great Britain

Contents

Preface

Can scientists who become editors stay sane? One experienced observer of the publishing scene thinks that academics who agree to edit scholarly books put their reason at risk: 'To get the single author to write to a deadline is bad enough; to have an academic editor trying to whip-in a dozen prima-donna professors is a recipe for a nervous breakdown.'[1] Editing of this kind certainly has its stresses and strains but it can also be both stimulating and enjoyable. In reality editors in all areas of scholarship probably manage to remain as rational as any of their colleagues. But how can potential editors of scientific books or journals discover what is in store for them, and make the publication path smoother for themselves, their authors and the readers? There are surprisingly few books to which they can turn for advice or information on editing, and among those few books, the only available one on editing scientific publications is addressed to experienced editors of journals.[2] In this book I have therefore set out to give both beginners and more experienced editors a broad view of how multi-author books, conference proceedings and journals are edited, copy-edited, printed and published. It seems appropriate to deal with these three kinds of scientific publication together because they have many editorial processes in common.

The first chapter of this book introduces editing in general terms and outlines the work of editing each of the three kinds of publication. Amongst other things the first chapter describes how to find a publisher, how long it takes for a book to be published, and how books are priced. The next eight chapters deal with the editorial procedures common to books and journals, in more or less the order that the various processes are handled on the road to publication—from guiding authors and keeping track of manuscripts to printing and proofreading. The particular problems of editing conference proceedings and of managing and editing journals are examined separately. The last chapter surveys innovations in scientific publishing, discusses professionalism in editing, and ends with a look at what the future holds for scientist-editors. The ten appendixes include a sample contract with a publisher; sample guidelines for authors, referees, book reviewers and advertisers; and a set of suggestions on references.

The purpose of this book is to describe and discuss the many facets of editing scientific books and journals and to explore the responsibilities of editors towards authors, readers and science itself. I hope that the book, as well as helping editors and copy editors, will prove useful to anyone interested in the scientific publication system as a whole.

1 Editing outlined

Editing is both an art and a craft. The art of any kind of editing lies in knowing which manuscripts to accept outright, which to reject and which to accept in spite of their imperfections. The craft of scientific editing lies in revising and preparing material for publication as promptly as possible and in a form acceptable to readers. But what exactly do scientific editors do? How do they learn to find the best authors or select the best articles for multi-author books or journals? How do they operate a refereeing system? How do they develop a method for revising, or teaching others to revise, the presentation of scientific work? What are their responsibilities to authors, to readers and to science itself? The people most in need of answers to these questions are those who have been enticed into editing by assurances that there is really nothing much to it and that it will not take much of their (unpaid) time. Neither statement is true. Editing is complex, time-consuming, and often exhausting. It can also be absorbing and highly satisfying, as this book will show.

Editors need good judgement, tempered with imagination and intuition, and a wide and sound knowledge of the disciplines covered in their publications. They should be endowed with a firm command of language—perhaps extending to more than one language—and a well-controlled passion for accuracy. They must exercise tact in dealing with authors and commonsense in revising the language or structure of papers. And they must be able to cope with, or arrange for others to cope with, the numerous practical problems of getting typescripts into print and then into the hands of readers.

In general, the aims of scientific editors are to choose the best and most original work available at the time on a particular topic or in a particular branch of science, and to bring that work to the attention of interested readers as promptly as possible, in a form that is both readable and retrievable. Scientific editors, alone or with the help of advisers and assistants, save readers' time and tempers (and some authors' reputations) by rejecting or revising any mediocre, badly presented or misleading work. These aims are the same as those of editors in other branches of scholarship. Scientific editors differ from others perhaps only in requiring a particularly crisp and exact style of writing and in preferring certain conventions and methods of presentation that have come to be regarded as indispensable in science.

The exact functions of scientific editors vary with the fields in which they work. Some of their work is creative, some of it consists of substantive and technical editing, as defined in Chapters 5 and 6, and the rest is administrative. In the less mathematical, more literary fields such as psychology, sociology, archaeology and some parts of theoretical biology, editors are concerned more with assessing the quality of ideas than with improving the way those ideas are expressed. Authors in these fields may even refuse to have their manuscripts edited. When the subject is one in which experimental data or reproducible observations are impossible to obtain, authors are perhaps justified in being less than precise. In the more material sciences, however, certain ways of presenting results and arguments are widely accepted, and systems of nomenclature are continually being proposed, debated and (occasionally) agreed; clarity and conciseness are vital, and logic essential. Editors must therefore be familiar with the standards and usages of their disciplines and be prepared to tighten author's presentations accordingly.

Whether editors obtain material for publication by seeking out the best authors to contribute to a book or by selecting the best manuscripts from the many submitted to a journal, the problems are the same: good authors are rare and prescriptions for success in compiling good scientific books or journals are rarer still.

What, in fact, are the criteria for judging quality? Chase[1] found that, as ranked by 191 successful scientists, those criteria are: logical rigour, replicability of research techniques, clarity and conciseness of writing style, originality, mathematical precision, coverage of significant published work, compatibility with generally accepted disciplinary ethics, theoretical significance, pertinence to current research in the discipline, and applicability to 'practical' or applied problems in the field. In Chase's sample this ranking order varied with the discipline: natural scientists placed more emphasis on replicability of research techniques, originality, mathematical precision and coverage of the published work, while social scientists gave higher ranking to logical rigour, theoretical significance and applied significance.

Even with these criteria as guides, the ability to choose the best work to publish remains an indefinable and elusive talent owing as much to intuition as to a deep knowledge of the subject. Since a talent of this kind cannot be taught, though it develops with experience, the rest of this chapter concentrates on outlining the other aspects of editing multi-author books, conference proceedings and journals. The first section goes into some detail over the editing and publishing of multi-author books, since these do not receive a separate chapter to themselves later, unlike the other two categories, and since some of this first section also applies to conference proceedings—which are of course another form of multi-author book. The three sets of outlines are intended to place the various editorial procedures in context for editors or potential editors of any type of scientific publication.

MULTI-AUTHOR BOOKS

The term 'multi-author books' refers here to books with chapters by different authors on different aspects of a single topic and to collections of review papers such as those in yearbooks and similar series. The principles described apply to textbooks as well, but their planning is not covered in detail. The compilation of a multi-author book can be justified only if the subject is such that one person could not handle it adequately. The subject should therefore be one with facets in many disciplines, or be especially complex, or so new that it is essential for previously unpublished developments in different institutions to be described by the original workers. Monographs, review series and textbooks may all meet these criteria.

Editors of multi-author books have to make sure that the subject is covered adequately and in a balanced way. They select authors so that this goal can be reached, arrange to fill gaps if anyone fails to submit a chapter in time, and edit the text so that the book has unity and a coherent style. They need two almost contradictory qualifications. They must know their subject very well indeed so that they know what kind of book is needed in that area of science and can choose the appropriate authors to collaborate in producing it. At the same time they must be able to put themselves in the place of readers who are not as knowledgeable as the contributors to the book; they must then edit the chapters so skilfully that readers will not only understand the different contributions but also appreciate the connections between the chapters and the structure of the subject as a whole.

Multi-author books may be initiated by a scientist with an idea for a book, or by a scientific society or institution, or by a publisher's 'acquisitions editor' who asks a scientist to do the editing. Before approaching a potential scientific editor, an acquisitions editor makes sure that a market exists for the proposed book. Scientists or a scientific organization with an idea for a book or series of books should themselves examine what competition there is from recently published work, as they will have to convince a publisher that the book or series meets a need and has an assured market in established disciplines or professions. No one should compile a book first and hope to find a publisher afterwards: if publishers disagree with a scientist's assessment of the market the work will all be wasted.

After the initial idea for a book has been mulled over and knocked into shape, therefore, the editor writes an outline of what it will contain and draws up a list of potential contributors. An editor who wants to stay sane keeps the list short: the fewer authors there are, the easier it is to keep in touch with them and the less likely it is that manuscripts will be delivered late, or not at all. For a yearbook or annual review, however, some editors find it advisable to invite more authors than will eventually be needed: then if any authors fail to submit their chapters in time the book can still be produced on schedule, and the chapters received after the deadline can be updated and printed in the next year's volume.

The outline helps to show the editor which kinds of expertise are needed for the various chapters, and the writers may then almost select themselves. But even if the possible authors are an editor's friends (or perhaps especially if they are), their latest work has to be examined critically before they are invited to contribute. Is their knowledge of research developments still comprehensive and sound, or have they turned into overworked administrators? Do they have good reputations for keeping to deadlines? Have their recent papers had to be heavily edited before they could be published?

When contributors are being chosen, editors may be subjected to certain pressures. Formal or informal advisers occasionally make suggestions that are not strictly disinterested. This kind of pressure can usually be recognized easily enough and the editor can be ready to deal with it firmly but tactfully.

Pressure from a sponsoring society may be more difficult to cope with. If the book is one of a series covering a wider field, a sponsoring organization sometimes asks for topics to be included which do not fit into the editor's plans for that particular publication, or the sponsor may ask for certain topics to be excluded because they are to be covered in other books in the series. Or the society may want some of its officers to be invited to contribute even though they are not particularly qualified to do so. Again, editors have to be ready with prompt and tactful solutions to this kind of problem.

Another type of pressure may be felt if a book has two or more editors. Joint editors must discuss the aims and scope of their book in some detail before they approach possible contributors or a publisher. They should be quite sure that they agree completely on what the book is about and to whom it is addressed, what work each of them will do during its preparation, which disciplinary conventions they will use, and what general procedures they will follow. Usually, each editor is responsible for a different section of the book. But to ensure consistency and prevent overlapping of chapters, at least one editor should read all the manuscripts before the material goes to the printer. If co-editors edit each other's chapters in the book, they are probably wise if they agree to exchange comments in writing rather than face to face.

Although the editor of a multi-author book usually asks potential contributors informally at an early stage whether they are interested in collaborating on the book, it is better not to send out formal invitations to write chapters until after certain practical details have been agreed with a publisher. Scientific editors who have to find a publisher will want one who can provide, or at least promise, good production arrangements, attractive presentation, rapid printing, and rapid and efficient worldwide distribution and promotion. Book reviews, publishers' catalogues, publishers' advertisements in journals, and the advice of librarians and of colleagues who are authors or editors can all help when a short list of suitable publishers is being drawn up. Directories of publishers show how well established different publishers are, what agencies they have in other countries, how many books they publish each year and what kind of books they publish (it is no good sending a book on nuclear physics to a publisher specializing in poetry). Publishers who handle perhaps 50 books a year can give a book individual attention, but getting it into print is only the first step: wide distribution is essential too, and small or new publishers may not have the necessary machinery for this.

If a book in English is to be published by a British publishing house which has no branch in the USA, or by an American publisher without a UK subsidiary, the potential editor should ask what arrangements will be made for handling sales in North America or the UK market, respectively. Worldwide publication is not automatic unless the publisher has world rights in a book or arranges to assign certain rights to another publisher who operates in areas not covered by the first publisher.

Another point the potential editor should investigate is who in the publishing house will be assigned to watch over the book during the publication cycle. A publishing house editor normally acts as the scientific editor's contact on all matters to do with the book's production and promotion. A contact of this kind is essential if the scientific editor is not to waste time looking for the right person every time a query arises. And if copy-editing is being done in the publishing house the scientific editor should also find out how much the copy editor will do and arrange to see the manuscripts again after they have been copy-edited but before they are typeset or retyped as camera-ready copy (see Chapters 5 and 6).

For their part, publishers want authoritative and reliable texts, neither too short nor too long, that are likely to reach them in readily publishable form, preferably with some well-known names amongst the authors. European publishers who want to sell books on the American market are happy to see American authors among the contributors and vice versa. Editors looking for publishers should therefore send all those on their short list the outline of the book, the list of potential authors (including a few words about the qualifications of each), and some indication of the book's length, the level of readership and the range of disciplines to be covered. Detailed questions about production schedules, marketing arrangements and so on can be left until a publisher shows definite interest, but it is worth asking at this stage about the total production time and possible price for the book.

Once a scientific editor and a publisher reach an understanding in principle, a formal agreement is negotiated, dealing with some or all of the following: the approximate length of the typescript; the date by which the typescript should be handed to the publishers; the target publication date; royalties or fees; copyright and other rights; responsibility for costs incurred during editing; responsibility for copy-editing; indexing and proofreading; responsibility for libel; arrangements for reprints and free copies; and other matters affecting production, design, promotion and distribution, including sanctions to be invoked if the agreement is broken. A sample contract between a publisher and an editor is shown in Appendix 1.

Before any agreement is signed it is probably wise for new editors to consult a lawyer who knows something about authors' rights, or take advice from colleagues who are experienced editors or authors. Editors who insist on tight production schedules must remember at this stage that they will have to keep their side of the bargain by producing manuscripts promptly at the agreed time. The publisher is unlikely to try to influence the content of a book once the agreement has been signed, but if the book later turns out to be very different in length or scope from what was agreed originally, the publisher has a legitimate complaint and a new agreement may then have to be negotiated.

Most publishers offer editors either a fee or a standard royalty based on either the list price of the book or the net receipts from sales, the arrangement to base royalties on net receipts being more common in the USA than in the UK. In the UK, 10 % of list price is a common royalty on a hardback book, though $12\frac{1}{2}$ % or 15 % may be offered. To produce the same amount as a 10 %, $12\frac{1}{2}$ % or 15 % royalty based on list price, the royalty based on the publisher's actual income from sales would have to be higher—about 15 %, 19 % and 23 %, respectively, assuming an average discount of 35 %. A sliding scale may be agreed by which the royalty increases (or starts) when, say, 1000 or 2000 copies have been sold. On a paperback edition the royalty may be $7\frac{1}{2}$ % of list price, or perhaps only 5 % or 6 %.

Publishers price books, usually, at about five times the production cost per copy (the unit cost), or at a price per page which works out at roughly the same as five times the unit cost. A breakdown of list price might look like this:

Production cost	20 %
Average discount (to booksellers etc.)	35 %
Royalty	10 %
Marketing and overheads	25 %
Publisher's profit	10 %

The publisher makes 10 % profit only when every copy has been sold, and makes no profit at all until a certain sales figure, the break-even point, has been reached.

Editors who have their readers' interests at heart rather than their own often want to know why books are highly priced. The answer is that if the book is in English the publisher has to pay to produce, advertise and distribute the book to a worldwide market, yet the total expected sales may be very small. A highly specialized monograph of interest only to graduate research workers in a limited field of study might sell, say, 500–1500 copies in three years before it goes out of date; a collection of review papers in a series that every library feels obliged to buy may sell 2000–3000 copies; and a textbook for undergraduates may sell anything from 10 000 copies upwards, depending on how wide its appeal is and how long it remains up to date. The comparative cheapness of paperbacks is entirely due to the publisher's expectation of high sales, not to the lower cost of a paper cover: the unit production cost for a paperback is usually very little less than that of the hardback version. Similarly, textbooks or other books with large markets are cheaper than specialized monographs of the same length because the production cost for a large number of copies is not much more than for a small number and the unit cost therefore falls.

Even though the main appeal of a scientific book lies in the quality of its contents, its appearance has a certain importance. Long before manuscripts are ready for the printer, the editor should discuss the design of the book with the publisher or the publisher's designer and ask to see specimen pages showing the style of headings, references, the typeface, type size and so on (see Chapter 8).

When general arrangements with the publisher have been completed, the editor can draw up a timetable for receipt of manuscripts. For a book likely to run to, say 250–400 pages, about 12 months might be a reasonable time between formal invitations going to the authors and manuscripts being sent to be printed. Longer may be needed if authors have to write long chapters or several chapters each, or if the authors have particularly heavy professional commitments which leave little time for writing (but it is better to avoid choosing these as contributors in the first place). With a 12-month schedule authors may be allowed, say, four months for writing their contributions, with reminders about the approaching deadline being sent to them after 10 weeks and again after 15 weeks. If a manuscript fails to arrive the editor decides whether to drop the chapter or find a substitute author who can write it in time. The rest of the 12 months is needed for consultation, editing, revising and writing any introductory or linking material. Depending on the production method, the printer's capacity and capability, the contributors' cooperation and the editor's sense of urgency, publication of the book itself will then take 5–12 months from the time the printer receives the last typescript from the editor: first proofs will be ready in six to eight weeks, or longer; authors may be given—or take—up to four weeks to return corrected proofs; correction of first proofs and production and proofreading of second proofs may take another four to six weeks; and final printing, binding and so on may take six to eight weeks, or longer.

As soon as the timetable for receipt of manuscripts has been drawn up the editor can send formal invitations to contributors. The letters should outline the book and indicate the level of readership the editor has in mind. The editor suggests what each person should write about and how long the chapter should be, gives the date by which a working title and synopsis should be supplied and the date the manuscript has to be ready, and may want to say what action will be taken if the typescript does not arrive in time. The publisher should be named, as should the other contributors, with those who have not yet agreed to contribute being distinguished from any who have already informally agreed to do so. Authors should be told whether secretarial or other expenses will be met, whether a fee or a share of the royalty will also be paid, when proofs (if any) can be expected, and whether a free copy of the book, or reprints of chapters, or both, will be provided by the publisher. If an editor has decided that unsatisfactory chapters will be rejected even though people have been invited to write them, authors have to be warned that the editor reserves the right to do this. If chapters are to be seen by an editorial board or other referees, authors ought to be informed of this too. A form of assignment of copyright (Appendix 2; and see Chapter 3) may be enclosed with the invitation. (See Appendix 3 for a sample letter of invitation.)

The editor also prepares a style guide (see Chapter 2 and Appendix 4) and, before sending it to the authors who accept the invitation, may test its practical value by writing a chapter for the book to the guide's specifications. Alternatively, the editor might ask authors to follow the guidelines of an appropriate journal in the field and simply add a few instructions about specific requirements for the book. Later, when the contributing authors have supplied working titles and synopses for their chapters, the editor distributes these, or a detailed summary based on them, to all contributors.

The editor's main problem in the earlier stages of the preparation of the book will be to get all the authors to deliver a publishable manuscript on time, so that dilatory contributors do not undo the good work of the punctual ones. A draconian solution is to commission a new author if a chapter has not arrived in spite of frequent reminders. If a small amount of money is available for editorial and writing costs, one way of using it is to pay extra secretarial and other fees to help authors who are asked to write a chapter at short notice.

When manuscripts begin to arrive, the editor logs them in (Chapter 3) and checks whether authors have covered the subjects arranged at the agreed length, and whether they have presented their material appropriately for the intended audience, written passages that overlap too much with other chapters, left gaps they were expected to fill or introduced contradictions with other chapters. The editor then revises the content or style as necessary, and writes linking pieces if the subject changes too abruptly between chapters.

When most of the material is ready for the printer, the editor either writes or asks someone else to write a preface or foreword outlining the book and its aims (see p 71). Instead of a preface, or sometimes in addition to it, the editor or one of the contributors may write an introductory chapter setting the scene for the rest of the book in more detail than a short preface allows. Introductions or prefaces, together with any passages written to link different sections, do much to give multi-author books the unity they often lack.

After all the manuscripts have been referred for outside opinion if necessary (Chapter 4), edited and revised (Chapter 5), copy-edited and assembled in what seems a logical order (Chapters 5 and 6), the editor considers the book as a whole once more, to see that it has the required unity and consistency of style. No one wants to receive this sort of review:[2]

> 'What the book lacks is an Editor, and its weakness lies in the . . . absence of coordination . . . There is grave doubt as to whether anyone with editorial authority has read the entire book . . . When cross-references do occur they are often blind: thus Le Grand writes "Chemical structure of rhodopsin and other visual pigments will be discussed by Robson in Chapter 4 of this volume", but the reader will turn to Chapter 4 in vain.'

At this stage, as well as when editing each chapter, the editor must keep the readers clearly in mind. The book has to be made intelligible to the least experienced readers and to workers in other disciplines, but these readers should not be patronized, nor should more knowledgeable readers be given the feeling that the text is over-explanatory. The editor's role is to see that the chapters are on the same level of intelligibility and show authors where over-familiarity with their subject has led them to condense too much, fogging the readers' understanding. In the interests of clarity the editor must be ready to insert subheadings, define symbols and neologisms, and substitute plain language for laboratory shorthand or for the impenetrable prose that is unfortunately far too common in science.

When work on the text is finished, the 'front matter' or 'prelims'—the title page, preface, contents and so forth (Chapter 7)—are prepared and the typescripts are sent to the printer, usually via the publisher (Chapter 7). The publisher will then probably ask the editor to write descriptive blurbs for the jacket and provide other promotion material (Chapter 7). The publisher will want advice on individuals, societies and institutions who might be included in a mailing list of possible buyers (Chapter 7) and a list of journals or people who might review the book (Chapter 7). The editor may also be asked to choose designs and colours for the binding and dustjacket (Chapter 8).

Depending on the production policy agreed with the publisher (Chapter 8), there may be two proof stages, or one, or none. Proofs are dealt with as described in Chapter 9 and a master set is returned to the publisher by the date agreed. If there are two proof stages, authors normally receive only the first but the editor receives the second as well.

As soon as paged proofs are available, the editor either compiles an index or has it prepared by a professional indexer (see p 72–74). Once the index proof has been checked, the editor need only wait expectantly for publication day and the comments of contributors, other colleagues and—eventually—book reviewers.

CONFERENCE PROCEEDINGS

Conference proceedings differ in several ways from other multi-author books, and their editors often face an additional set of problems. The editors may have had no opportunity of influencing the choice of papers presented at the conference, and they may even have their editorial functions thrust on them after a meeting has ended. They then have to try to construct a satisfying book out of several unrelated building-blocks separated by yawning gaps. When this goal is reached it is usually only because the editor has cajoled speakers to produce good manuscripts, rewritten some passages, interpolated linking paragraphs, or written whole chapters to replace missing manuscripts. But many people who have been seduced into editing conference proceedings at a late stage find themselves forced to allow a motley collection of papers to be published, in a book that is later deservedly attacked by reviewers for the unevenness of its contents.

The responsibilities of editors of conference proceedings range from rewriting most of the papers and re-drawing the illustrations to doing nothing more strenuous than giving permission for their names to grace the title page—an unethical practice that should be anathema to any scientist with a reputation to consider. In general, the work of the conference editor depends partly on the size of the conference and partly on how much help and advice the publisher—if there is an outside publisher—can provide. If the sponsoring organization publishes its own conferences but has no regular system for doing so, the editor will probably not only undertake the scientific editing but will also be expected to deal with printers and arrange for marketing and distribution. Another route to publication for conferences is in journals or journal supplements, a solution which does away with some of the criticisms made about the publication of conference proceedings (see Chapter 10).

The aim of most conferences is to generate interaction amongst those who attend them. The aim of the published proceedings is to preserve all worth-while material presented during the meeting and make it available to readers who did not attend the conference. Both sets of purposes should be clearly defined by the organizing committee at the outset and adhered to afterwards, otherwise both meeting and book will be less than adequate. The editor has to recognize the different goals of meeting and book, and work with the conference organizers and with any co-editors in achieving both sets of aims.

For some conferences intended for publication, all speakers are invited by the organizing committee; for others, especially large congresses, anyone who wishes may submit a paper or abstract for consideration by the committee; in a third type, the programme may consist of a mixture of invited and submitted papers. The organizing committee then has to make a number of decisions about publication (see also Chapter 10). Should all papers on the programme be published, or only some? How are papers to be selected for publication? Will they be refereed? By what date must they be submitted? Are full papers, or only synopses, to be circulated before the meeting? In the published book, will discussion sections be included? Who will publish or print the proceedings?

Ideally, the editor is a member of the organizing committee when these questions are discussed. Even if other people choose the speakers, the course of publication runs more smoothly when the editor can see to it that invitations and circulars contain clear and firm general information for authors on the requirements for synopses and manuscripts. Fully detailed instructions are more conveniently given in a separate set of guidelines for contributors. The sample guidelines for multi-author books shown in Appendix 4 can be adapted for conference proceedings.

Publishers who specialize in conference proceedings can help the editor by providing advice about the style guide and by assisting with copy-editing and proofreading. As well as covering the items already listed for multi-author books, the agreement drawn up between the publisher and the sponsoring organization may define what assistance will be provided and make it clear how discussions will be handled, if these are to be published. If the sponsoring organization itself is the publisher, the editor and organizing committee may negotiate an agreement specifying the exact role of the editor in the publication of the proceedings. If, as often happens, points like these are not covered in the formal agreement, they should nevertheless be agreed in writing by those concerned.

Royalties for, and sales of, conference proceedings are similar to the figures given for multi-author books, though conference editors are perhaps more likely to be paid a fee for their work than royalties, and volumes of proceedings rarely, if ever, have such high sales as textbooks.

Once the date for a conference has been arranged, other dates can be fixed around it. These dates depend on what the organizers decide to circulate before the meeting. A good compromise is to send out a programme containing synopses—preferably rather extended, factually informative ones—about three to four weeks before the conference. Speakers should be asked to send these summaries to the editor or organizers some 10 to 12 weeks before the meeting. With repeated reminders, it should be possible to obtain over 90 % of the summaries in time to be printed with the programme. Some organizers make receipt of the synopsis by a certain date a condition of the author being allowed to speak.

In some ways handling a large conference is easier than handling other multi-author books; a would-be contributor who fails to deliver a paper at the meeting, for example, can hardly insist on it being included in the published proceedings. The main problems for the editor therefore lie in obtaining synopses in good time, and perhaps in arranging for the recording and transcription of impromptu papers and discussions.

A particularly important part of the editor's work on proceedings is the conversion of a good oral presentation into a publishable paper if authors have not succeeded in doing this. Where discussions are included, the editor's most valuable contribution lies in preparing them for publication in a way that satisfies both readers and participants (see Chapter 10).

Work on manuscripts for conference proceedings is similar to that on manuscripts for other multi-author books (p 9–10, and see p 118). The main principle of editing conference proceedings is also the same as for other multi-author books: a single intelligence—the editor's—must hold the various parts together in spite of disparities in the scientific level of contributions and in the communicative skills of the authors. For conferences another important principle to follow is that the proceedings must be published quickly if they are to be of any use to readers. This means establishing firm timetables (see p 8 and p 114–115) and keeping to deadlines. Delays in the early stages can easily lead to a volume being out of date before it leaves the binders.

JOURNALS

A journal is, in effect, a third kind of multi-author book, but one that appears weekly, monthly, quarterly, or perhaps irregularly, with most of its contents submitted by authors for their own reasons rather than solicited by editors for theirs. Editors of journals are responsible to the scientific community as well as to their sponsors (often learned societies). At the same time they usually have great freedom in controlling the content and form of what is published. It is this freedom that allows editors to put an individual stamp on their journals, even though many different authors contribute to each issue.

Scientific journals, whether sponsored by learned societies or by commercial publishers, vary from the ultraspecialized to the general, from the rich giant to the impoverished dwarf, and from the academically detached to the politically *engagé*. The scale of the editor's work varies accordingly, but the basic responsibilities remain the same for every kind of journal. Editors must define or re-define the aims and scope of their journals and choose articles and other features congruent with those aims. They have to decide whether to select articles after consulting referees or mainly on their own unassisted judgement. They must determine whether poorly presented but scientifically valuable papers should be published as they stand or be improved before publication—and, if papers are to be improved, whether the work should be done by the editorial staff or by the authors. Editors must also organize an efficient handling system for typescripts and proofs, ensure prompt publication by the most suitable printing method, and cooperate with secondary services (abstracting and title-listing) and data banks in making primary articles readily retrievable. Some editors are also responsible for the efficient distribution, promotion and economic viability of their journals.

Most journals, whoever sponsors them, have an editorial board or committee whose ostensible purpose is to advise the editor on anything and everything to do with running the journal. In practice, boards range from the purely decorative to the strictly functional. Most commonly, board members act as referees or as section editors, or they may recommend other people who would be suitable as referees. When a journal is new, board members well known in their disciplines may be persuaded to write several of its first articles, as an encouragement to other contributors. The only material reward for board members is likely to be a free subscription to the journal: apart from this, publication of their names is the best compensation most journals can offer.

The editorial boards or committees of journals sponsored by learned societies are elected or coopted in the same way as other committees of these societies. If the society is a local or national one, the members of the committee may meet formally once a year or more often, and their duties usually include establishing the policy of the journal.

Members of editorial boards of commercially sponsored journals, on the other hand, are invited to join the board by the editor and publishers, and they may never have any formal meetings at all, still less any discussions of policy. Committee or board members may be asked to serve for a set number of years or for an unlimited term, but a set time is preferable: good advisers can always be asked to serve another term on the board but replacing bad or inert advisers can be difficult if membership is for an unspecified time.

For most journals, but not all, referees help editors to select papers for publication (see Chapter 4). The criteria for selection of papers are those listed at the beginning of this chapter (p 2).

Journal editors also have to decide whether to publish a wide variety of articles and features or whether to restrict the journal to one or two types of section, and they must choose the specifications which apply to each section. The possible sections include:

Original articles: will there be a maximum permitted length or specified form?
Solicited research articles
Short notes, e.g. on methodology: same handling as for full-length articles, or with special arrangements for speedy publication?
Review articles: solicited, unsolicited, or both?
Hypotheses not stemming from the author's own results
Comments on other published papers, without new data
Correspondence
Corrections: how to bring them to the reader's attention?
Editorials: never, occasionally, or in every issue? Linked to articles in the same issue or independent? Political or apolitical? Signed?
Synopses of papers to be presented at meetings of the sponsoring society
Other society business (including presidential addresses and the like)
Guidelines for authors: in every issue?
Book reviews
Advertisements
University and other appointments vacant and wanted

This list seems formidable, but many of the decisions may be simple to make, or may be made by the editorial board, the sponsoring society, or the publishers (and see Chapter 12). The simplest list of what to publish would probably be:

Original, unsolicited articles (or letters, for a 'Letters' journal)
Corrections (otherwise known as Errata)
Guidelines for authors (see below and Chapter 3)

Even this short list can produce problems, as can be seen from Lois DeBakey's book *The scientific journal*,[3] in which experienced journal editors provide guidelines for others, revealing as they do so a wide range of opinion, and even disagreement on certain points. The main questions are: (a) are referees to be used, and if so how are conflicts of opinion between them and the authors to be resolved (see Chapter 4)?; and (b) is the presentation of articles to be improved and, if so, how much and by whom (see Chapters 5 and 6)? On the second point, it is generally recognized that the journal editor's role is to uphold standards, both by rejecting poor articles and improving good ones. *Solicited* articles, including editorials, review articles and book reviews should, however, be edited with a light hand, especially if they are signed—another policy decision that has to be made (see Chapter 12).

Although journal editors may commission review articles and other items, they spend much of their time dealing with unsolicited manuscripts submitted for publication by hopeful authors. The general principles of selection have already been mentioned (p 2) and the mechanics of handling manuscripts are described in Chapter 3. The editor, or the editorial office personnel of the larger journals or organizations, examines each manuscript when it arrives and, if referees are used, decides who is best qualified to assess it (Chapter 4). Occasionally it will immediately be obvious that a paper can be accepted or rejected without being sent to anyone else. If the journal does not use a refereeing system the editor is the only arbiter anyway. Selection there has to be: apart from questions of quality, few journals could afford to publish all the papers submitted.

The work of journal editors and referees is made easier if each journal provides clear instructions or guidelines for authors (Chapter 2 and Appendix 4). Guidelines can never, of course, improve the quality of the research described in submitted papers, but they can influence authors to think more carefully about the style and form of their typescripts. If an author submits a paper that has clearly been prepared without reference to the guidelines, the editor may decide to return it, after first considering the principles discussed in Chapter 5.

Most new editors want to change the format, layout and covers of their journals, but—surprisingly, perhaps—this involves much more than individual taste. Restraints on size, for example, have been imposed by postal authorities and laid down by Standards organizations (e.g. ANSI Z39.1–1967 [4]). Changes should not be initiated lightly. Designers, publishers, printers and librarians have to be consulted and various production methods and the relevant cost factors have to be taken into account (see Chapter 8). Another temptation that must be resisted is changing a journal's title, as this causes endless confusion for the secondary services as well as producing problems for readers, authors and other editors.

Journal editors have to decide who their clients are. If they aim to serve authors they will develop a system that allows either for rapid publication of submitted articles or for equally rapid rejection. If their chief clients are the readers, careful and critical review will be the main aim, together with much editorial work on the accepted articles to make these as comprehensible, interesting and retrievable as possible. To attract readers, these editors will probably encourage Correspondence, Comments on published work, Hypotheses and so forth (see Chapter 12). If they see themselves as committed neither to authors nor to readers as separate groups, but to the advancement of science as such, they may take one of two directions. Either they will demand extensive and rigorous proof of every statement made—and here they will rely heavily on the approval of the referees; or they will decide to publish only the most original work, even when it yields conclusions contrary to the prevailing consensus (or dogma).

In practice, most editors try to serve authors, readers and science: it is a question of deciding with what priorities and by what mechanisms. Of course, the image of 'the reader' as someone who subscribes personally to the journal, opens it eagerly as it arrives and reads it through from cover to cover is old-fashioned, if not mythical. Readers are those who are alerted to individual articles either by a secondary (title-listing or abstracting) service or by their own browsing through the Contents pages of current periodicals in a library. Editors who keep this concept of 'reader' firmly in mind ask authors to add key phrases to their titles, for inclusion on the Contents pages of the journal. They place the Contents in consistent form on one of the outside covers. They arrange for the name of the journal and its volume number and date, as well as the page number, to appear on each page of the journal, so that a full reference is included on photocopied articles or parts of articles. Conscientious editors also draw special attention to Corrections; the unthinking or insecure editor hides them away. The first course of action promotes scientific progress; the second impedes it. Attention to details of these kinds distinguishes the considerate editor active in the service of science from the arrogant or merely conservative arbiter of which articles deserve publication.

Unlike most editors of books, editors of some scientific journals may have to contend with the financial problems of keeping their journals going, as discussed in Chapter 11. Here I need only point out that economic pressures force editors to make their journals as attractive as possible, whether by selecting the best articles and publishing them much faster than any competitors, or by offering a superb and rapid editorial service to those who are not masters of language, or by commissioning informed comment on work being published in the same issue of the journal. If, in these and other ways, an editor can create a superlative product, people are likely to pay what is asked for it—a proposition that may remain true even in times of shrinking library and research budgets.

These outlines already show that editing is not a simple task. The expansion or explosion of the scientific information system that has been in progress since the 1950s has exposed editors of primary publications to increasingly heavy pressures from would-be authors. At the same time editors have had to learn to cope with the requirements of the secondary services and with the problems posed by new techniques of information transmission. To keep the information system running smoothly editors must be stringent in selecting only first-rate original work for publication. They must be punctilious in ensuring that readers can obtain or identify published material as quickly as possible. And, as discussed in the next chapter and in Chapter 5, they should arrange for authors to receive whatever editorial guidance they need and it is practicable to give them.

2 Guiding authors

If finding or selecting the best work to publish is the editor's first responsibility, helping authors to produce good papers is the second. Guidance is provided through guidelines or instructions drawn up for authors to use when they prepare papers, and by the comments that editors or referees make on manuscripts submitted for publication. In their reports or comments on potentially publishable manuscripts, editors and referees usually tell authors where gaps, inconsistencies or other faults lie and indicate how the structure or content could be changed to make the eventual version readable and retrievable. This is defined as substantive, or creative-cum-substantive, editing. It is pictured in action by Dr David Nathan[1] in this tribute to Dr Franz Ingelfinger, former editor of the *New England Journal of Medicine:*

'On several occasions, this contributor, having learned that his opus had actually been accepted, would receive a message to call the *New England Journal of Medicine,* extension 25. Dr Ingelfinger wished to speak to me.

"Doctor, as you know, the *Journal* has accepted your article".

"So I understand," was the cautious rejoinder.

"But the reviewers and the editorial board must have failed to notice that the article is not particularly clear in many areas"—a long pause by the contributor associated with tachycardia and generalized perspiration.

"Perhaps you could come over, and we could discuss the matter."

"It would be a pleasure."

"I'm free this afternoon. Are you?"

"Oh, of course. I'll be right over."

Then would start the process of tutorial: an examination of text, artwork, appropriate legends, abstract. The paper and figures, now in shambles and covered with blue pencil, are returned for reassembly, complete redrafting and, of course, a major improvement in style and thrust.

I often asked myself how he could possibly do it, particularly in fields in which he had no background. It is, I suppose, a mysteriously developed skill in communication. I shall never forget the many hours of training freely given to me by this remarkably devoted man.'

19

Creative and substantive manuscript editing are discussed in Chapter 5. The rest of this chapter is about the kind of guidance provided in guidelines or instructions to authors.

Contributors to a multi-author book, including conference proceedings, are often provided with *guidelines,* while authors submitting papers to a journal are usually expected to read the journal's *instructions to authors.* The terminology tells us something about editorial attitudes to authors. But whatever they are called, are these stipulations really necessary? Don't requests or demands for uniformity force authors to suppress all individuality in their writing? Why should busy scientists conform to numerous rules about apparently trivial matters such as punctuation, capitalization and italicization? Does constancy of format and style really serve science and, if so, how?

Among the many answers to these questions are that not even the strictest editor requires uniformity of thinking, that precision in minor details is essential to credibility in the exact sciences, and that the existence of rules about apparent trivia encourages, or perhaps forces, authors to consider carefully what they want to say and how they should say it. Rules help writers to focus their thoughts on the work in hand by removing time-wasting doubts about minor details and allowing them to concentrate on the essentials of logical structure, clarity and precision. And although good guidelines or instructions will never in themselves cause first-rate papers to be produced, they can do much to smooth the path for authors, editors, typists, typesetters and—eventually—readers.

For *multi-author books,* guidelines for contributors are often drawn up in collaboration with the publisher's staff. Some of the information in the editor's letter of invitation (Appendix 3) should be repeated, including a reminder about the aims and scope of the book. The conventions and terminology to be used are noted, and style guides, textbooks on scientific writing, and dictionaries might be recommended here. Authors should be asked to supply an abstract or synopsis even if it will not be published: writing abstracts helps authors to clarify their thoughts (Ref. 2, p 15), and reading them gives the editor a good idea of how a book will develop. Authors must also receive clear instructions about the form of the typescript: the number of copies needed, the maximum number and size of illustrations and tables, keywords or index terms, and the way references are to be cited in the text and listed at the end of the chapter (see Chapters 5 and 6 for further discussion of the last two items). In biomedical fields, the question of whether experiments were ethically performed has to be included.

Sample guidelines for contributors to a multi-author book are given in Appendix 3, which includes comments on some of the items. These guidelines can easily be adapted for speakers at *conferences,* though some publishers provide their own detailed guidelines on how to prepare conference papers. If a sponsoring organization is its own publisher, the editor should consult the printer about guidelines, as the printing method will dictate the extent and precision of the instructions on how papers are to be typed.

Guidelines for contributors to conferences should make it clear whether speakers are expected to describe original research, review others' research, put forward hypotheses, speculate, or do any of these things (see Chapter 10). A description of the aims and scope of the conference should appear in the circulars publicizing the meeting and can be omitted from the guidelines. A section on discussions should be added if these are to be published, and the differences between written and spoken presentation of papers should be emphasized. Contributors may, for example, be asked to give full details of experimental procedures and so on in the typescript, but it is best to remind them that when they face the audience they should concentrate on a very few main points—clearly and logically connected and judiciously repeated in different ways so that listeners will be able to assimilate them without becoming bored. Although the manner in which people present papers at meetings is not the primary concern of editors, or of this book, the guidelines for contributors to conferences are the place for suggesting that speakers should talk as naturally as possible and look at the audience rather than read every word without once raising their eyes from the lectern. The guidelines should also recommend that before speakers make slides of any figures they submit for publication, those figures should be drastically simplified to give the audience a chance of understanding them (a brief paper by Mary Evans[3] gives good advice on producing legible slides; and see Ref. 4).

A major task of *journal* editors is to establish clearly and concisely what their journals are meant to achieve, what will be included, and what will be excluded. The guidelines for authors should therefore include a statement of the purpose and scope of the particular publication. The guidelines should if possible be condensed into one or two journal pages, printed in the same position in every issue of the journal and included in the list of contents. If the guidelines are not printed in every issue, a reference to the most recent set should appear in every contents list, so that conscientious authors do not decide to follow a carefully preserved but out-of-date version. The guidelines should be similar to those given in the sample for multi-author books (Appendix

4), appropriately adapted for the journal and possibly supplemented with a list of accepted terminology and the conventions of the discipline. A checklist of what authors must send to the editor will also be useful (see Ref. 5, p 60).

The guidelines should be worded and laid out in such a way that authors will realize that these are not trivial or pedantic rules drawn up merely to annoy but a serious attempt to improve communication between them and their readers (see Ref. 6, p 71–78). Editors of new journals should study the guidelines for authors in other journals before they list their own requirements. New editors of well-established journals should take a close look at the journal's current guidelines: these do not carry the eternal weight of the Ten Commandments and should indeed be critically reviewed every year. Conventions change, old terms drop out of use, new areas of study spawn new words, and groups of editors move (slowly enough, to be sure) towards a common policy on these so-called minor matters: individual editors will want to move with them. Common policies on these matters give editors, too, more freedom to concentrate on the essential structure and functions of their publications and a better chance of bringing them out on schedule.

3 Keeping papers moving

Bringing publications out on schedule calls for an efficient processing and progress-chasing system. Authors are seldom amused, or forgiving, if their manuscripts are lost; and editors should know the whereabouts of each chapter or article at any moment in the long trek towards publication. But though the position of manuscripts in space is important, it is their place in the timetable that determines what has to be done about them next. For books, a preliminary timetable is drawn up during the planning stages (see Chapter 1). When the editor predicts the date by which the material will be ready for printing, some publishers provide printing schedules. Others, the realists, distrust long-term forecasts and produce schedules only when manuscripts arrive in their offices. For most journals, of course, regular press and publication dates make continual demands that have to be met with a supply of manuscripts.

In keeping papers moving, editors of books will be engaged mainly in chasing authors, editors of journals in chasing referees. During the preparation of papers and later, during production, editors have to see that copy editors, proofreaders and printers keep to schedule. Efficient secretaries or editorial assistants can cope with all or most of the mechanical chores, but it is the editor who has to make sure that the system is a good one. For many books and for small journals the control system for manuscripts can be kept fairly simple. If manuscripts for a journal are submitted to different members of the editorial board, the editor should arrange for them to follow the same standard procedure on receiving a manuscript.[1]

In a large editorial office, one person should probably be made responsible for logging in and chasing up manuscripts. For all types of publication a wall chart or a log book, ruled for as many columns as circumstances demand, is then the simplest way of plotting progress in such a way that anyone can see instantly where papers are. Movable tags or stickers, coded by colour or shape, are useful refinements for wall charts but fibre-tipped pens or any other handy markers will do.

For a *book*, the editor first decides the order in which the chapters

23

will be printed (the 'running order'); manuscripts are numbered and listed on the chart by number and by the first author's name. Two or three lines are left free at the top for introductory matter ('prelims')—title page, contents, preface, etc. (see Chapter 7). For a *journal,* manuscripts are assigned consecutive numbers as received—'78–10' might be assigned to the 10th manuscript received in 1978. For both books and journals, when manuscripts are received the date of receipt and the number of text pages, tables, illustrations and other items in a paper are recorded, and the editor or an assistant makes the check described in Appendix 5; for journals an estimate of the length of the printed article is also useful. As each step towards publication is completed, the date is entered on the chart or on the correspondence folder for each manuscript, or on both chart and folder.

The steps towards publication include some or all of the following:

(1) manuscript examined by editor, sent to referee(s), returned by referees, sent to author for revision or approval of editorial revision, returned by author (sent again to referees, returned by referees), checked by editor, rejected or accepted;

(2) sent for copy-editing (sent to author for approval of copy-editing changes, returned by author);

(3) sent to printer, first proof received (sent to author if the printer has not done this), returned by author, corrected by editor, returned to printer;

(4) second proof received, returned to printer;

(5) published.

Columns in the log may also be used to show the editorial lag (from receipt of paper to the date it goes to the printer) and the publication lag (from receipt by printer to publication date).[2] For journals, separate charts for every issue can be used to keep track of which articles are in which issue and how many pages remain to be filled.

Printed cards are often used to acknowledge receipt of manuscripts, whether from referees or authors, and to remind referees that manuscripts are overdue. The acknowledgement card for authors should be posted as soon as the manuscript is received and logged in. The card should include the reference number of the manuscript and tell authors that they will hear again from the editor within, say, six weeks, but that if they hear nothing by then, they should write to enquire about the fate of the manuscript.

Although printed acknowledgement cards and reminder cards are useful for the editorial office and acceptable to authors and referees, the editor should preferably send personally signed letters for other purposes—especially when rejecting a paper (see Chapter 5). Efficiency is all very well but no one likes to feel they are dealing with an editor who is a machine rather than a person.

If the publisher of a book or journal is to have full freedom to disseminate the material in various forms, such as microforms and reprints, authors have to assign copyright in their papers to the publisher, sponsoring body or journal (see Chapter 7). For contributors to books the editor can send a form of assignment with the letter of invitation or later, or the publisher may ask individual contributors to sign a contract similar to the editor's (see Appendix 1). For journals the form of assignment is usually sent with the letter of acceptance. The form can usefully include a statement that the author has obtained written permission to reproduce any copyright material used in the paper (see Appendix 2).

Correspondence relevant to manuscripts can be kept in folders or large envelopes prepared for each manuscript and filed in numerical order. For a *journal,* folders could go in a PENDING drawer while referees are considering manuscripts or while manuscripts are awaiting editorial attention. If a manuscript is returned to the author for revision, the folder stays in the PENDING drawer, but if it is rejected the folder is moved to a REJECTED drawer and the correspondence, with one copy of the paper, is kept for at least a year (in case a revised manuscript, on the same subject but with more extensive data, is submitted). When a manuscript is accepted, the folder goes in the ACCEPTED drawer, in a section corresponding to the issue of the journal in which the paper is scheduled to appear. If delays then occur, or on the other hand if it becomes possible to publish the manuscript earlier than expected, the folder is moved accordingly. Once an issue has been published, manuscript folders corresponding to that issue are moved to a BACK ISSUE drawer. The contents of folders for published papers should be kept for a year or more unless space is at a premium: even then, six months is an absolute minimum, as queries arise even after publication.

If correspondence and manuscripts are kept in light-coloured manilla folders or envelopes, a rubber stamp with something like the following design can be used:

	OUT	Remind.	IN		OUT	Remind.	IN
Recd	(Date)			Revd ms from Au			
Ref 1	(Name)	(Date)	___	___	Ref 1	___	___	___
Ref 2	___	___	___	___	Ref 2	___	___	___
Ref 3	___	___	___	___	Ref 3	___	___	___
Rej/Acc	___				Rej/Acc	___		
To Au for revision ___							

(Remind. = date on which reminder sent.)

Not all these spaces will be needed for every manuscript, especially for a book, but this design allows for most eventualities, including the use of a third referee and a second consultation with referees after revision.

If the manuscript is accepted, a second stamp of the following design can be used on the folder, to keep track of the paper's movements to and from the printer:

To printer	_____
Proof 1 recd	_____
Au proof IN	_____
Corr proof 1 OUT	_____
Rev proof IN	_____
Corr proof 2 OUT	_____
Pubd	_____

Where large numbers of manuscripts are being handled, some kind of memory prompter is needed—for example, a large calendar or diary with plenty of space for each date. When manuscripts go out for any procedure that carries a deadline (usually, referees' comments), the reference numbers can be written in on the deadline dates. When manuscripts are returned, the numbers are crossed out if the relevant procedure is complete. At regular intervals, the folders whose numbers have not been crossed out should be examined to see what action—sending reminders, telephoning, etc.—has to be taken. The manuscript numbers are then entered again for a later date, if appropriate. The PENDING drawers, charts and log books should be checked frequently to see that nothing has been overlooked.

As well as a chart or log book, and filing drawers and folders, record cards of some kind are usually needed. For a journal, or for a book with many contributors, two file cards should be made for each manuscript. On one, filed in numerical order, the first author's name and the date of receipt of the manuscript are recorded, as well as the manuscript number. On the other card, filed alphabetically by the first author's name, are recorded the first author's name and address, the names of any co-authors, the date of receipt and title of the paper, the number assigned to it, and the names of the referees (if any) to whom it is sent. (Instead of this file card, a copy of the title page of the paper can be used, with the extra information added as necessary.) When an author or a referee enquires about a manuscript it is easy to find its number quickly from the alphabetically filed card and then discover from the chart or manuscript folder where the paper is.

For a journal using referees another two sets of file cards are needed: one set for topics, with a list of suitable referees for each topic, and one set for referees. On the cards for referees, their names, addresses, telephone numbers and areas of expertise are recorded. When a paper is sent to a referee, the date, the number of the manuscript and the first author's name are entered on the card; later the return date and the action recommended are noted. These cards are a useful source of information about the performance of referees, especially if the editor adds rough assessments of their quality of judgement on each manuscript.

More detailed advice on manuscript control (and other editorial practices) can be found in the American Psychological Association's *Guidelines for APA journal editors*[2] and similar in-house guides.

4 Working with referees

Refereeing of unsolicited articles submitted to journals is the main topic of this chapter. Refereeing of solicited papers for books or journals is dealt with briefly. Alternatives to refereeing are also discussed.

WHAT DO REFEREES DO?

The main function of referees is to advise editors—*not* decide for them—whether papers are suitable for publication *in a particular journal,* and whether the work is original, of high quality, up to date, and described in sufficient detail and clearly enough for readers to follow the argument or replicate the procedures discussed. This system of peer review is usually regarded as the lynchpin of reliable scientific publication, yet there is no rigorous proof of its efficacy[1] and it is attacked for the anonymity that referees often enjoy, for delaying publication, and for being élitist, conservative and conducive to plagiarism. The system is an acknowledgement that not all editors can be polymaths: most need advice about work on the periphery of their specialties, and many have to be rescued either from accepting articles that are brilliant but unsuitable for their journals or from rejecting those that are important but badly written.

Refereeing is commonly thought to be simply a matter of accepting or rejecting papers, but it is more than that. Referees also help editors to educate authors by suggesting improvements in the form and presentation of papers. Most authors respond well to constructive criticism or advice, especially as they usually have to act on it before they can get their work published. The comments they receive from editors and referees may help them when they write their next papers, and in the long run the load on editors and referees should be gradually lightened.

In some countries and disciplines the refereeing system is not as highly developed as in others. Editors who decide to adopt stricter criteria must not suddenly start rejecting every paper that fails to match the new standards. A single unconventional paper may be worth several based on competent and well-presented research. Editors and referees must learn to distinguish between unorthodox but brilliant papers and those containing statements or conclusions that are wrong, trivial or based on inadequate methods.

HOW MANY REFEREES, WHO ARE THEY, AND HOW DO THEY WORK?

Whether editors use one, two, or more referees for each paper is a matter of choice, not an unvarying rule. Two is the commonest number. The more there are, the longer the process is likely to take, unless editors stick to very firm schedules.

Referees may be members of the editorial board (see Chapter 1), associate editors, or others representing the disciplines covered by the journal. Ideally they should know their subject in depth but not be narrowly confined to one topic; be fair to authors and readers alike; have high standards but be generous towards minor flaws; be conscientious but not nitpicking; be prompt in returning manuscripts but not superficial in assessing them; and possess impeccably sound judgement. Such paragons are rare, but with the two-referee system editors can compare one referee's report with another's and gradually identify referees who have many of the good qualities and few of the bad.[2] If this comparison shows that some referees make assessments that are often wrong or prejudiced, the editor should remove them from the journal's list of advisers. Referees who constantly recommend papers that are later justly criticized by readers should be dropped too,[3] since soundness of judgement cannot be taught. Slowness is another incurable habit and referees who hold manuscripts longer than the scheduled time more than twice in succession should also be struck off the list. Prejudice can be compensated for, and fairness encouraged, by the guidance the editor gives to referees (see p 32, and Appendix 6).

The choice of referees does not always fall entirely on the editor's shoulders. Some editors invite authors to take part in the selection. For example, the *Proceedings of the National Academy of Sciences, USA* has a system of 'pre-review' by which authors can submit manuscripts through any member of the Academy who is willing to consider them. If the paper appears likely to deserve publication, the Academy then selects two referees who are experts in the field. If the referees approve of the manuscript, it is forwarded with their comments and those of the Academy member to the Editorial Office, with a recommendation that the manuscript be published. Even if one referee advises against acceptance, the Academy member has the right to recommend that this advice be overruled, and to explain why, if the member and the other referee favour publication. In such cases publication usually follow more or less automatically, although the Managing Editor, and the Chairman of the Editorial Board reserve the right to ask the Academy member to reconsider such a recommendation. Sometimes they may even reject the paper, but this rarely happens. The Academy member's name appears on the published article as 'Communicator' and members therefore take this responsibility very seriously—though they themselves can have papers published in the *Proceedings* without any refereeing, if they wish. The system is particularly suitable for a journal of wide scope, since the editor in effect delegates the choice of referees to someone working in the same field as the author.

In another system, used by the *Journal of Biological Chemistry* and others, all papers submitted go first to the editorial office, where each is assigned to an Associate Editor or to the Editor-in-Chief. The Editor or Associate Editor then assigns the paper to a member of the Editorial Board who is considered especially competent to deal with it, or the Associate Editor may handle the paper directly. The Editorial Board member (or the Associate Editor) may consult referees, if necessary, but does not have to do so. The Board member's decision letter, often with referees' reports or extracts from them, goes to the Associate Editor, who may revise the letter slightly before sending it to the author, usually with any referees' reports. If the Board member has recommended rejection, the manuscript goes to another Board member, or occasionally to more than one, and the procedure just described is repeated. If revision is requested, the author returns the revised manuscript directly to the Associate Editor, not to the editorial office. The Associate Editor has full authority to accept the paper; if this happens, the manuscript goes back to the editorial office, its arrival is recorded and it is sent on to the copy editors before being passed for printing. In this system, authors do not choose the Associate Editors who will handle their papers, though they may express a preference when they submit their papers. Although the system introduces an extra step in handling, it allows the editorial office to spread the work evenly between the available Associate Editors.

Another variant is for a small core of local Associate Editors (say five to seven) to meet weekly or fortnightly to discuss each manuscript and the comments made on it by outside referees as well as by one of the Associate Editors. This system seems cumbersome and liable to lead to superficial judgements taken under pressure of time and personality but where it is used it is apparently much enjoyed by the committee members for its educational value, and it often leads more naturally than other systems to the emergence of a successor to the chief editor when a term of office ends.

WHY DO REFEREES REFEREE?

Refereeing is time-consuming and often troublesome, it provides its practitioners with little public recognition and even less money, and it leaves them open to the charges of conservatism and plagiarism. Yet it is surprisingly easy, especially for an established journal, for editors to enlist referees of high standing. Many scientists look on the work as part of their wider obligation to science. Many even regard their selection as an honour, or at least as potentially useful to their careers. Others agree to be referees for the educational benefits it brings them: they see the most up-to-date information in their subject well before it is published, and they also learn something from reading the editor's comments and those of any other referees who review the same manuscript.

Many people therefore accept an invitation to join a panel of referees with little hesitation. Keeping them happy on that panel is another matter. If the editor understands people's motives for being referees, several things can be done to reward them for their work. One is to publish, at the end of each year, a list of referees who have acted for the journal during the year. Another is to let it be known that appointments to the editorial board—which provide visible evidence of scientific status—are made from the ranks of referees whose work has been particularly valuable. A third way is to keep referees informed about what happens to the manuscripts they work on, sending them copies of other referees' comments and of letters of decision to authors; and if the editor has acted against a referee's advice, a letter of explanation is usually appreciated. These communications take a little time, and increase the costs of photocopying and postage, but the rewards in goodwill are great.

Monetary rewards for referees are rare. Where payment is made it is usually intended to cover not much more than postage costs. Few scientific journals could survive financially if they had to pay their referees at a rate commensurate with the time spent. And, in spite of what some people think, 'commercial' journals are in no better position to pay for such work than are journals sponsored by societies or institutions.

GUIDELINES FOR REFEREES

Since different journals have different specific requirements, it is as well for each to have printed guidelines, such as those in Appendix 6, stating the journal's policy and telling referees what kind of papers to look for and what kind of information the editor wants.[2] Referees should be told:

(1) That they are allowed to refuse to review a manuscript without giving reasons;
(2) That they are the editor's advisers, not the final arbiters;
(3) Whether they should comment on presentation or only on content (to the extent that these can be separated).

They should also be asked:

(4) Do the data support the conclusions?
(5) Do any parts of the paper call for elaboration, clarification or condensation?
(6) Are the title and abstract fully informative and do they accurately reflect the content of the paper?
(7) Are there errors in computation, equations, formulae, derivations, tables, graphs or drawings, or nomenclature?
(8) Is the number of references excessive?

Many journals also provide a standard form, incorporating some of these questions, for referees' reports. The sample form included in Appendix 6 can be suitably modified for different journals. Since not everyone likes these forms, referees should be told whether it is essential to fill them in or whether other ways of commenting are sufficient.

Lastly, referees should be asked not to correspond directly with the authors, and the journal's policy on anonymity of review should be stated (see p 35–36).

REFEREEING PROCEDURES

There are almost as many variations in refereeing systems as there are journals using them, as the procedures already described show (p 29–30). Whatever system the journal adopts, flexibility is recommended: for example, if it is obvious that a particular manuscript needs no refereeing, the editor should simply accept it for publication, or reject it, as the case may be. If this attitude conflicts with the policies of the journal's sponsor, the editor has to try to convince the sponsor of the advantages of flexibility.

Depending on which variant of the refereeing system a journal prefers, the editor deals with manuscripts after their arrival has been recorded and acknowledged (see Chapter 3) basically as follows.

(1) Manuscripts are assigned to one of three categories: accepted, rejected, and for refereeing—the last being the largest category.

(2) Accepted manuscripts are kept for editing and copy-editing (Chapters 5 and 6), and acceptance letters are sent to the authors. Rejected manuscripts are returned to the authors, with tactful letters explaining why they are not suitable for publication in the journal and possibly suggesting other journals to which the papers might be submitted.

(3) From the file cards on referees (Chapter 2), or the editor's memory, one or more referees are selected for each manuscript that is to be refereed. A copy of the manuscript is sent to each referee selected, together with the guidelines for referees and the form for comments (Appendix 6).

(4) If a paper is to go to two referees one of the following four procedures, or something similar, can be used:

(a) A copy can be sent to both referees simultaneously, perhaps after a telephone call to make sure that they are willing and available (see the discussion of delay, p 37–38). When comments arrive they are compared and any contradictions are dealt with as described later (p 34–35).

or (b) A member of the editorial board may be sent two copies of the manuscript and asked to select a second referee or to select two referees. The board member can be asked either to collate the two reviews and draft a letter to the author for the editor's consideration, or to send reviews straight to the editor.

or (c) The manuscript can be sent to one referee and, when the review is returned, the manuscript can be sent to a second referee selected either because the editor wants advice on an aspect not dealt with adequately by the first referee, or because the editor wants to counterbalance what looks like bias in the first review. A copy of the first review may or may not be sent to the second referee with the manuscript, as seems appropriate.

or (d) If only one referee is generally consulted, a variant of 4(a), (b), or (c) may nevertheless be used when a manuscript has too many facets for one referee to cope with.

(5) A referee's review (and the manuscript, if its return is requested) should be acknowledged as soon as it reaches the editorial office. If no review arrives by the date requested, a telephone call or a reminder card is sent to the referee. If the review still doesn't arrive, the editor telephones or cables for an answer, or proceeds without the review, according to the established policy of the journal.

(6) When the editor has read the review(s) and decided whether to accept a manuscript outright, to accept or reconsider it subject to revision, or to reject it, an appropriate letter is sent to the author (see Chapter 5). Constructive suggestions for changes or concrete reasons for rejection are given in the letter. Any abrasive comments by referees are toned down without the basic criticism being removed (and the editor may want to tell the referee why this has been done, as mentioned earlier). Except as noted in (7) below, the referees are sent copies of the editor's letters to authors.

(7) If the author is asked to revise the paper, the editor writes to the referees after the revised manuscript has arrived and a further decision has been made about it. The editor may be able to accept the revised version without sending it to the referee(s) again; but if major revision was requested and the editor cannot judge whether the referees' criticisms have been met, or if the author provides detailed rebuttals of the criticisms, the revised manuscript and the author's comments are sent to one or both of the original referees. When a final decision has been reached, the editor thanks the referees and sends them copies of the relevant letters and comments.

(8) If the author has not replied to a request for revision after about six months, the correspondence is reviewed. It may be worth writing a follow-up letter, as a show of interest in the paper may bring it in even after such a long delay (and see p 55). If no reply appears after another six to eight weeks it is probably safe to assume that the author is not going to produce a revised manuscript. The editor then marks the folder PRESUME WITHDRAWN and moves it out of the PENDING file.

RECONCILING CONFLICTING OPINIONS

If two referees of similar expertise and status disagree about the acceptability of a manuscript or the need for revision, the editor has to find some way of reconciling their verdicts. If the 'negative' referee is criticizing what the paper does *not* do—the approaches to the problem which the author might have used but didn't, the extra experiments which might be valuable but are not needed to validate the conclusions—the editor may choose to disregard the advice, since the referee should simply have judged the paper as submitted. On the other hand, if the 'positive' referee seems to have been superficial and to have overlooked the deficiencies pointed out by the other referee, the editor may disregard the 'positive' decision. If the editor's knowledge of the subject is sketchy, the 'positive' referee may be sent a copy of the 'negative' report (with or without being told who wrote it) and asked to say frankly whether it seems valid.

If there are differences of opinion about revision, the editor is probably the best judge of which suggestions for revision are reasonable. The suggestions should be made as specific as possible (see Chapter 5) and the author should be told which revisions are considered essential, which are not essential but important, and which are optional for acceptability.

Another way of reaching a decision when referees disagree is to send the paper to one or two new referees, after telling them about the reactions already received. The value of increasing the number of advisers is, however, somewhat doubtful. As Ingelfinger[1] points out, referees' opinions are highly variable and there is no reason why the opinion of referee 3 should carry any more weight than that of referee 1 or 2. Rather than obtaining a third review, a better course is to ask a final adviser not to arbitrate but to comment on the reviews as well as on the manuscript. This really should give the editor the information needed to reach a sensible decision.

A fourth method is to follow the dictum: 'If referees differ violently, publish the paper; there must be something exciting in it.'

THE CHARGES AGAINST REFEREEING

In any discussion of refereeing, anonymity is the first aspect attacked. The other main charges are that referees tend to be conservative and élitist, that they delay publication unnecessarily, and that they can plagiarize all too easily.

Anonymity

Most editors decide after careful consideration of the pros and cons that referees' identities should not be made known to the author (Ref.

4, p 12–13). But if a referee firmly believes that reports should be signed, this should be allowed, even if the general policy of the journal is to keep its referees anonymous. Similarly, a referee who insists on remaining anonymous should be allowed to do so even if the journal usually sends signed reports to authors.

The question of anonymity surfaces regularly in the correspondence columns of journals and it is often suggested that, if referees are to remain anonymous, the names of authors should in all fairness be concealed from the referees. The argument is that when referees see the title page they may be biased either in favour of the manuscript or against it, depending on whether the paper comes from a prestigious author or department or from an unknown author at an obscure institution, or (perhaps worst) from a rival in the field. But removing the title page does little to hide the laboratory of origin from knowledgeable referees, or referees may spend more time guessing who the authors are than considering the content of the manuscript.

Ill-feeling is inevitable if referees are outspoken in their criticism of poor work, and referees must be protected from authors' reactions. The editor must, however, also be careful to protect the authors by detecting and suppressing biased and unjustified criticism when it occurs. This does not mean that the criticism should be suppressed when the paper is rejected: editors who reject papers without giving reasons are behaving as though they were infallible; conversely, if they think their reasons will not withstand scrutiny, they have no basis for rejecting those papers. Openness with authors, while hardly the royal road to popularity, is the best policy in the end, even though the cloak of 'confidentiality' under which some editors shelter may seem to protect them from trouble in the short term.

A related question is whether referees of the same papers should be identified to each other. Here, identification probably does more good than harm. It is likely to make referees less prone to carelessness and capriciousness.

Conservatism and élitism

Referees are chosen for their expert knowledge. This very expertise tends to make them partial to a particular way of looking at a subject—although top-flight scientists are (by definition) open to new views and ready to see dogma shattered. Most referees are probably in the very good but not top category, largely because the most senior scientists are too busy to review papers promptly. Editors should therefore watch for excessive conservatism and try to counteract it by accepting unorthodox papers if they seem methodologically sound, even if the referees have advised that the conclusions differ from the current consensus. Instinct, and the general criteria of scientific method, help editors to distinguish unorthodox, sound papers from unorthodox, unsound papers. Outside advice is surely not needed to tell an editor whether the observations are too few to support the conclusions, the statistical methods weak or inappropriate, or the data internally inconsistent. The editor may indeed be more objective than a specialist referee when the results obtained are contrary to cherished current beliefs.

Commentators in various disciplines—for example, Neufeld[5] in physics; DeBakey (Ref. 4, p 18–19) and Pyke[3] in biomedicine—have pointed out that referees tend to be biased in favour of rejection, and they suggest that the editor should compensate for this. Appropriately worded guidelines (Appendix 6) are one way of counteracting this bias.

Delays and plagiarism

Referees are sometimes accused of delaying publication while they incorporate the results or methods of the refereed work into their own research or publications. This of course is conscious plagiarism; it is rare because it is easily exposed and always condemned, however distinguished the plagiarist. Authors who are worried about plagiarism by referees can protect themselves by presenting their work at seminars and conferences before submitting a paper for publication. At these meetings they not only announce their work but may also receive valuable criticism. Another suggestion[6] is that abstracts of submitted articles should be published in an abstracts journal as evidence of authorship of an idea or conclusion. Such a system would, however, be open to abuse by authors, who could stake out intellectual ground to which they had little or no title. In addition, a high proportion of 'abstracts' published before conferences—and perhaps better called 'synopses' in these circumstances—are never substantiated in published articles, either because the authors describe studies that do not survive further work and critical scrutiny, or simply because the authors never find time to finish the work as planned.

Editors can circumvent the problem of plagiarism, as well as the general charge of delay, by insisting on rapid refereeing, say within two to three weeks (though a determined plagiarist could still delay publication by providing a review full of minor criticisms and suggestions for revision). Referees can be asked to return manuscripts *immediately* if they know they cannot meet the deadline or if a particular manuscript is too close to their own current work, or for any other reason, including fear of unconscious plagiarism. Better still, if the journal's budget permits, is for the editor to telephone referees first to make sure that they will accept the manuscript and can do the work within the time specified. Another device is to attach a sticker to the envelope, asking the addressee's secretary to return the packet if the referee is out of town; a covering note to the same effect can be enclosed in case the sticker is overlooked.

Delay can also be reduced by careful choice of referees. On the file card for each referee (see Chapter 3) the time spent on each previously reviewed manuscript should be recorded. The card also shows whether that referee has recently been sent any manuscripts for review, though it will not show how much other work, including manuscripts from other journals, the referee has on hand. A fairer method may be to send manuscripts only to members of the editorial board, with members being invited to join the board on the strict understanding that they will receive no more than an agreed number of manuscripts for refereeing in any one year. Clear, succinct guidelines for the referee to work from also help to reduce delay (Appendix 6). Lastly, referees' time should not be wasted with papers the editor can handle without their advice.

Of course, when authors revise papers they often introduce much longer delays than referees ever do. Some of the criticisms about delay being caused by referees can be forestalled if the date of receipt, including receipt of a revised version, and the date of acceptance are printed in the published papers. Publication of these dates has more implications for claims to priority than may be realized at first (Ref. 4, p 42–48; and see Chapter 12).

ALTERNATIVES TO REFEREEING

The alternatives to a full refereeing system are (a) no refereeing at all—which means selection by the editor alone, with or without improvement of the presentation; (b) refereeing of certain topics only; (c) refereeing of borderline manuscripts only; and (d) refereeing of only those manuscripts that—though clearly acceptable—need expert polishing.

(a) The advantage of using no referees is speed of decision; the disadvantage, the risk of a wrong decision. If an editor's most frequent mistake is to reject good papers, science is not necessarily any worse off: the authors will simply submit their papers to other journals and probably get them published. The first journal may miss some good papers but there may be enough good ones around for this not to matter much.

If an editor's most frequent mistake is to publish papers that are not up to standard, the journal's correspondents will soon comment on this. The editor either learns from those mistakes or decides to consult referees in future.

When no referees are consulted editors are perhaps justified in giving no reason, apart from lack of space, for refusing papers; they are probably not in a strong position to provide expert criticism except in limited areas of their subjects, and to offer an elementary critique of scientific method may be insulting after what has obviously been a hurried reading. Authors who submit manuscripts to journals that do not use referees probably expect summary acceptance or rejection. If papers are accepted, authors are entitled to expect some editorial help with presentation, e.g. clarification or condensation, improvement of terminology or help with illustrations (Chapter 5); if such help is not provided, they may well prefer to send their manuscripts to a 'Letters' journal whose sole purpose is rapid publication.

(b) Refereeing of certain topics only is a useful way of dealing with aspects of the field which lie outside the editor's experience or competence.

(c) Refereeing of borderline papers only is a good way of applying the educational function of the refereeing system where it is most needed. This procedure will cater for manuscripts from inexperienced or scientifically isolated authors who hope to get advice from more experienced workers than those with whom they are usually in contact.

(d) A manuscript that is clearly acceptable on scientific grounds may nevertheless need certain changes in structure or improvements to the presentation. If the editor lacks either the time or the specialist knowledge to make these, a referee from the appropriate specialty can be asked for advice.

REFEREEING COMMISSIONED ARTICLES OR CONFERENCE PAPERS

Everything that has been said here about refereeing unsolicited articles for journals applies in principle to other kinds of publication when referees are consulted, except that the editors must be much more forbearing with invited contributions than journal editors need to be with unsolicited manuscripts. For books, it is probably wisest to have only one, or at most two, advisers or consultants, to whom the editor can explain precisely what the book is aiming at: 'occasional' referees of odd chapters may produce a detailed but useless critique based on mistaken assumptions.

If journal articles, book chapters or conference papers which have been commissioned or accepted in principle seem on arrival to be unpublishable, editors certainly need advice, either to bolster their own opinions or to show them that their first impressions were mistaken. When a referee's guidance is requested in such a case, it should be made clear on which items the editor wants comments, but nothing should be said about the editor's particular misgivings if a truly independent opinion is wanted. If the referee confirms the editor's doubts, it is probably best if the contribution is rejected immediately; if the author is asked to revise the paper, a long and painful correspondence may be started which never leads to a satisfactory conclusion. Instead, the editor should write explaining that the contribution does not fit into the original conception of the book. If possible, some suggestions should be made about where else the paper might be published, so that the author does not feel that too much time has been wasted. Then, for journals or for books other than conference proceedings, another author can be invited to write an article or chapter on a similar but not identical subject, or the editor may write a chapter to fill the gap in a book—taking care not to plagiarize any of the rejected material! Tact, always an asset to an editor, as the next chapter implies, will have to be exercised if the author is not to feel wounded when the book is published.

5 Manuscript editing: creative and substantive editing

Manuscript editing can be separated into three processes—creative, substantive and technical—each of which shades into the next. One person, the editor, may do all three types of work; or a copy editor (sometimes called a subeditor, a manuscript editor or a technical editor), may be responsible for substantive and technical editing after the editor and referees have finished their creative editing work. This chapter is mainly about creative and substantive editing, which call for either the active cooperation of authors or their passive approval. Chapter 6 is about technical editing, in which editors or copy editors prepare manuscripts for the printer, consulting authors over major changes only. Some overlapping of these two chapters reflects the overlap in the work itself. Other editorial responsibilities dealt with here concern the ethics of experimentation, multiple publication and writing to authors.

Creative editing itself consists of three aspects, two of which are not strictly manuscript editing. These two—finding or recognizing the best work to publish, and determining the aims and scope of a publication—are discussed in Chapters 1 and 12. The third aspect consists of pointing out to authors how and where they might reorganize, expand or condense their manuscripts to produce a more logical progression of ideas or give a more effective account of their work. In this educational part of their calling editors may have the help of referees, as discussed in Chapter 4.

Substantive editing means ensuring that authors have said what they want to say as clearly and correctly as possible. It is usually done at the same time as technical editing and includes correcting the grammar and spelling, making minor suggestions about the reorganization, expansion or condensation of the text, and suggesting how titles, key terms, abstracts, statistics, tables and illustrations might be better presented and how style might be revised to give greater clarity and precision.

The rationale for some of these aspects of revision is to be found in the way the scientific information system works. Most scientists keep in touch with new developments by browsing through journals or recently acquired books in libraries, scanning current-awareness publications or comprehensive abstracting journals, talking or writing to colleagues, and attending scientific meetings. Few people subscribe to many journals or buy many books for their own shelves. The current-awareness services rely heavily on the titles of papers, and abstracting services take over, verbatim if possible, the author's abstract printed at the head of the article. Unfortunately, few authors seem aware of the uses to which their titles and abstracts will be put. They visualize readers who scan titles and abstracts and who can immediately read the papers that interest them, which is rarely what happens in practice. Editors therefore have to guide authors to produce informative titles and abstracts.

RESPONSIBILITY FOR REVISION

After editors have examined manuscripts and considered any comments from referees, they decide how much revision should be done, who should do it, and when. If major revision is needed, the manuscript is usually returned to the author with a letter saying whether the paper is likely to be accepted after revision or merely reconsidered for publication. Major revision is heavy work and some authors may prefer to offer their manuscripts to less exacting editors.

If the revision requested is minor, one question is whether copy-editing (that is, substantive and technical editing) should be done before or after the author revises the paper. When copy-editing is done in a central office serving several publications, editors may prefer to return manuscripts to the authors for revision before copy-editing. Other editors may choose to have copy-editing done first, saving both postage and the authors' time.

Editors who do all their own copy-editing may read each chapter or article three times or more after the selection process is complete. The first reading is a general one to see whether and where any major changes in content or structure are needed. At the second reading the editor goes through the paper dealing with the points discussed in this chapter and the next. References, and sometimes other items, are checked separately. The third run-through is for checking the correctness and consistency of the editorial changes to the typescript.

Copy editors deal with the work covered by the second and third readings and with the aspects of technical editing described in Chapter 7.

Editorial changes, normally made in ink for the printer, are better made clearly in pencil on the typescript if the author is going to see the changes. A reasonably legible photocopy can then be sent to the author for checking and revision. Changes are explained in the manuscript margin if the reason for making them is unlikely to be clear. The editor can draw attention to doubtful points with a marginal note: 'Author please check'. In a covering letter the editor may say that some changes are merely suggestions which are not binding on the author but are intended to clarify the meaning for readers unfamiliar with the author's subject.

Where copy-editing is done after the author's revision, major changes made by a copy editor should be either approved by the editor or checked by the author, and queries should be settled before a paper goes forward for printing. This principle of clearing all except trivial changes with authors should be a feature of editorial procedures whenever time and the budget allow. For one thing, if any further changes are needed it is much cheaper if authors make them before typesetting than after. For another, it is the authors who carry responsibility for the content of their papers: editors or copy editors who alter manuscripts can easily falsify the authors' intended message.

There are editors who contend that allowing authors to comment on editorial changes in this way is a dangerous kindness. They regard authors as morally ruthless characters who will stop at nothing to get papers printed in reputable publications. These editors, who protect their readers by being very strict with authors, may be right about workers in their particular fields. Other fields may boast authors of a higher calibre.

Editors also have different opinions about how much work should be done on papers they have accepted for publication. Some editors argue that authors must do all the revision, especially of the style (see section on Improvement of Style, p 48, and that their own part is to give authors general guidance on what changes to make. Other editors, realizing that some authors are either incapable of following general instructions or genuinely have no time to do so, prefer to have papers thoroughly revised in the editorial office. The two points of view have been debated by DeBakey and Woodford.[1] The solution to the dilemma probably lies between the two extremes of no editing and full editing, but all editors must formulate policies on the aspects of revision discussed below.

Structural reorganization

Reorganizing a whole chapter, argument or section ought to be the author's responsibility, but the editor or referees must have good reasons for asking for major reorganization, and they should suggest how it should be done. Afterwards, tables and illustrations may have to be renumbered and references rearranged, or at least checked to see whether they still apply. (The traditional structure of scientific papers—introduction, methods, results and discussion—is discussed in Chapter 12.)

Expansion

If a step in the argument is missing, or if further experimental evidence is needed, only the author can supply the missing material.

Shortening

Shortening an article to a given length may be done by the author but is often better done in the editorial office. If the author is asked to do the work the editor must indicate how it might be done: which sections, paragraphs, tables or illustrations could be deleted, which parts could be condensed, and which marginally relevant theme might be cut out. 'Cut your article by a third and we'll have another look at it' is not very helpful advice for authors. A piece entitled 'The craft of shortening' in *The Lancet*[2] gives useful tips, some of which I borrow and adapt here, with apologies and acknowledgements to the anonymous author:

(1) Shorten the Introduction by cutting out all references to previous work that are not directly related to the work described; citing a review article will probably cover most of them.
(2) Omit details of methods described in other publications. The principles on which the methods are based are often more significant; on the other hand, major modifications must be described exactly.
(3) Do not repeat in the text information provided in tables or legends to illustrations.
(4) Reduce speculation in the Discussion to reasonable, testable hypotheses.
(5) Use the active voice and first person whenever appropriate; they are usually more succinct.
(6) Cut out all flabby introductory phrases such as 'It is interesting that . . .'—and all woolly words of uncertain meaning (see Ref. 3, p 93–98).

The title

A title that conveys the main subject or message of a chapter or article in as few words as possible is important for easy retrieval (Ref. 3, p 46–47). Yet many titles are imprecise or uninformative, and referees comment on them surprisingly seldom. Since editors know more about the use of titles in information retrieval than most authors, editors should have a major say in re-titling chapters or articles where necessary; only if authors produce good arguments to back up their preferences should they be allowed to keep the original version. It is worth remembering that a title in the form of a question or statement has more impact and is easier to understand than a title built around an abstract noun. For example, the titles 'Activities of enzymes in plasma should be measured at 37 °C' and 'Is Dextran 70 a lymphocyte mitogen?' are simple, direct and clear, conveying the authors' meaning far better than alternative forms that lack verbs.

The abstract

Like titles, abstracts too often go unscrutinized by referees and must be carefully edited to make the paper as widely useful and retrievable as possible. Abstracts written in English, for example, are read by thousands of scientists whose mother tongue is not English, or they may be translated by linguists unfamiliar with the scientific content (but see below). For the sake of those users, as well as for English-speaking readers, editors should make sure that abstracts are written in plain and simple terms. The same principle naturally applies to abstracts in *any* language. Above all, jargon—that is, short-cut phraseology intelligible to only a select few—and unexplained abbreviations should be eliminated. And, in contrast to other parts of the text, in an abstract first-person constructions should be changed to the third person, which is considered more appropriate for secondary service usage.

Abstracts were not commonly printed at the beginning of chapters in multi-author books until recently, but the practice is useful for readers. Even in a book in which each chapter reviews a particular area, a descriptive abstract saying what subjects are covered can be extremely valuable. In some books, especially textbooks, a table of contents may be more useful than an abstract at the head of the chapter, though abstracting services do not reproduce these tables.

For most research articles in journals or books informative abstracts are preferable to descriptive abstracts (see ANSI Z39.14-1971[4]). Descriptive abstracts are the kind that say, for example, 'Experiments on reactions to nicotine are described and the results are discussed'; informative abstracts are defined as follows.

An informative abstract states the purpose of the article and of the investigation(s) on which it is based, indicates the methods used, and summarizes the results reported and the conclusions drawn. The editor should look at the article in as broad a context as possible, on behalf of readers. The abstract should say, for example, in what species of animal, or what part of the world, the work was done, as appropriate—authors often leave out essential information of this kind. Editors should, however, be flexible about the length and other details of abstracts. For example, even though it may be preferable for most abstracts to describe the purpose, methods, results and conclusions of an investigation in that order, editors should not automatically change the form of an abstract which starts with the conclusions, then fills in the background and provides the supporting facts. There is much to be said in favour of the second form, although, again, it would not be sensible to impose it on every abstract.

Landau & Weiss[5] have produced two useful sets of guidelines for preparing abstracts—a brief set which can be included in the guidelines for authors (see Appendix 4) and a back-up set giving more information. If an author's abstract fails to sum up the paper satisfactorily the editor should add facts and figures as necessary and tell the author what has been done.

Editors are often asked to print abstracts, or summaries, in three languages, one of them English, the most widely understood language in science. The nationality of the publication and the geographical distribution of readers determine which other languages will be used. For European publications the most popular combination is English, French (or Spanish) and German. Ideally, Russian, Chinese and Japanese might be included too but these all pose problems of translation and typesetting as well as cost.

Some of the few journals which print abstracts in more than one language arrange and pay for translations to be made; others ask authors to provide translations. Whoever is responsible, the translation should be done either by someone whose mother tongue is the language of the translation or by a translator who has lived for many years in the country of the language of translation. If the translator is not a scientist in the same discipline as the author, the translation must be checked by someone who knows both the language and the discipline. Linguists unfamiliar with a specialty rarely produce satisfactory translations of technical work.

The text of each abstract should begin with the 'article biblid' described in Chapter 7 (p 79), and end with the author's name and address, so that full information is available for abstracting services.

Keywords

Conventionally, keywords characterizing information elements in articles are added to the end of abstracts as an aid to indexing and retrieval systems. They often include words already in the title and abstract, which is wasteful. A richer way of using keywords is to add them below the title, in parentheses. This should help to prevent words in the title from being repeated, while telling readers that the paper includes methods or ideas subsidiary to the main theme. If a journal also prints keywords under the titles on its Contents page, readers who look first at titles only will see the terms as they scan either the journal itself or the title-listing publication, *Current Contents*.

Keywords may be supplied by either the authors or the editor. If authors are asked to supply them the editor can then edit each list of words to make them uniformly ·useful to readers and the current-awareness services. Professional indexers will make their own decisions about using or ignoring keywords.

A 'free vocabulary' is probably better for key phrases than a thesaurus of permitted terms, though if a short private thesaurus covers the field adequately it may be very useful. A lengthy thesaurus that is brought up to date only at long intervals, however, may oblige authors and editors in rapidly developing fields to use obsolete terminology. For example, the term 'micelle', which had been important in gastroenterology for over 15 years, did not appear in the Medical Subject Headings (MeSH) published by Index Medicus until 1975. Even now, only a well-informed editor would permit its use: it is still only a subheading listed under the main heading 'colloid', a term with a fine but antiquated flavour.

Presentation of statistics and accuracy of computation

For papers relying on statistics, a suitably qualified referee should comment on the statistical method but should not have to recalculate all the values given. Authors may be asked to supply their raw data if the referee doubts the methods or the conclusions based on the data. Editors should spot-check one or two computed values or ask a referee to do so. Where there appear to be mistakes, authors must be asked to re-check all values.

In papers where statistics form only a small part of the work, authors are not always careful about how they indicate variability in a sample or imprecision in a measurement, and many referees fail to notice this kind of fault. Values given simply as $x \pm y$ without explanation are examples of scientific illiteracy. Editors should familiarize themselves with the principles of correct presentation[6,7] and bring them to the attention of authors. Editing is not concerned with words alone.

Contents and design of tables, illustrations and legends

Authors often need guidance in designing tables (including titles and footnotes) and illustrations (including legends) that the readers can understand without reference to the text; this is discussed in Chapter 6.

It has been proposed that titles and footnotes for tables and the legends to illustrations should, like abstracts, be in three languages. This suggestion[8] may not be very practicable (though some Scandinavian journals insist on English captions for tables and illustrations) but it underlines the fact that many readers look at tables and figures before deciding whether a paper is worth reading. It is perhaps unfortunate that tables, figures and legends are usually placed after the text and references when manuscripts are assembled for the editor. This order is the one most convenient for the printer but it seems to discourage referees from criticizing tables and illustrations in detail. As an experiment, before manuscripts go to referees, the tables, legends and illustrations could be placed immediately after the abstract, to test whether they make sense on their own.

Lengthy protocols for experiments should not be placed in legends or in footnotes to tables, where they are often printed in type too small for comfortable reading. If authors ignore this requirement, the editor has to decide whether it is worth asking them to insert the material in the text, whether to do the job in the editorial office, or whether to accept the material as presented. If space permits, protocols can be printed in the legends in ordinary type, but many readers would still prefer the material to be included in the text under the heading of Methods.

Improvement of style

Most authors write not simply to be read but to be understood. Scientists in particular should always write comprehensibly for their readers. Though specialized technical terms are unavoidable (and are not classified as jargon), there is no need for the meaning of any chapter or article to remain hidden behind thickets of poor prose. Confused writing is indicative of confused thinking, not of superior knowledge of esoteric subjects. Yet editors are divided about how much they should do to improve the prose style of authors whose papers they have accepted for publication.

Some editors maintain that each author has a personal style and that editing destroys that style, generating a book or journal that is tedious to read because it lacks variety. These editors acknowledge that many scientific authors use language clumsily and express themselves in a pseudo-impersonal way that is soporific and obscures meaning; but they refuse to revise this kind of prose, saying that if they do so authors will never try to improve their writing, and that the authors will be made to sound like better scientists than they really are. This school of editors may educate authors by proxy—that is, by directing them to consult books on scientific writing—or by editing one or two paragraphs as a model.

The experience of 'interventionist' editors, on the other hand, is that most scientific authors have only mannerisms, not style. They conclude that the best medium for transmitting scientific information is a transparent style that draws no attention to itself but presents the facts and the argument simply, clearly and unambiguously. These editors tend to transform as much prose as possible into this simple style—though they try to leave untouched any writing that has a personal flavour but is neither verbose nor imprecise.

Scientific writing has suffered much from editors who mistakenly demanded impersonality in the name of objectivity, but many journals now encourage a more direct and personal style. The *Biochemical Journal* added this brave sentence to its Instructions to Authors in 1977: 'Authors are encouraged to employ their own style, although papers must be concise and should conform to normal English usage'.[9]

Some editors think that style is of no importance either way and should not concern them at all. But, if good scientific style is defined as being clear, logical and precise, it lies at the very centre of scientific thought and endeavour.[10–12]

One point of style that is of growing importance, especially in the USA, is the use of non-sexist language. Science is based on accurate observation but it is hardly accurate to use masculine nouns or pronouns when the sex of the person or animal is not specified or is not known. There are several ways round the problem, most of them more elegant than using 'his or her' instead of 'his' when pronouns are concerned. For example, the plural 'they' can often be used instead of the singular, sentences can be reworded so that the problem does not arise, or neutral words can be chosen instead of words that apparently refer only to the male sex. Authors should be encouraged to solve the problems for themselves but editors may have to make changes for them (see Ref. 13 for a useful set of guidelines on non-sexist language).

Whoever revises the style, revision should be done with the less knowledgeable reader in mind. Ambiguous or misleading passages, pompous circumlocution, unnecessary verbiage, passive constructions, heavy attempts at humour or irony, and the clichés of scientific writing (Ref. 3, p 93–98) should all be cleared away—not to economize on typesetting, ink and paper but to save readers' time and keep them awake. Most scientists, after reading poorly written papers for most of their working lives, reproduce certain patterns of writing without thinking what they are saying. Editors should sweep these patterns out of their own minds and translate authors' ritualistic phrases into simple language: 'Restrictions on ambulation are often favourable to inhibition of edema' is easier to understand if it becomes 'Rest prevents swelling', as the book reviewer who quoted this sentence in *The Lancet* pointed out.[14] However, if authors say what they apparently want to say clearly enough, editors must resist the temptation to go on polishing for ever.

It is useless for editors to advise authors to improve their style by reading Hoyle, Asimov, Julian Huxley or any other great scientific stylist: authors who follow this advice will simply submit mannered imitations of these writers. But editors should somehow find time to read the best modern writers, to remind themselves what good style can be like.[15]

On the whole a discreetly interventionist approach to editing an author's style is the best to aim at. But how is a personal style to be distinguished from a mannered one? Fortunately there are many books which provide editors and authors with good advice on style. In English, the classic text on the plain, unadorned style is Strunk's *The elements of style*.[16] Gowers' *Plain words*[17] preaches the same message. Trelease[18] has written a superb book specifically about scientific writing, while Barzun & Dunbar's *Simple and direct: a rhetoric for writers*[19] is highly recommended for experienced authors. Many other guides have been written for particular fields—for example, *Thorne's better medical writing*[20] and Booth's *Writing a scientific paper*,[21] the latter being a booklet written for biochemists but useful to many others. The essentials of scientific style are discussed at some length by Woodford[22] and Tichy[23] and are summarized by O'Connor & Woodford (Ref. 3, p 38–45). Authors can be directed to these books if they are doing their own revision. Alternatively, editors should make sure that at least one of these authorities supports any changes they suggest.

If individual authorities on style are not enough, there is a short and sensible section on principles of style in ANSI Z39.16-1972—the American National Standard for the preparation of scientific papers for written or oral presentation.[24] Far from imposing too much standardization in a field where individuality is to be encouraged rather than suppressed, this Standard is concerned with minimum basic requirements. Splendid advice on editing an author's style is also to be found in a study by Norman Howard-Jones[25] of editing in the World Health Organization. For general points of style Fowler's *A dictionary of modern English usage*[26] is the ultimate authority, though American editors may prefer Follett's *Modern American usage*.[27] A good general dictionary is needed too, as well as specialized dictionaries for particular fields. *The Random House College dictionary*[28] is excellent as a general dictionary for English-language publications since it gives both American and British spelling.

Papers from foreign-language authors

Whichever school of editing they belong to, editors should give special consideration to authors writing in a language not their own. These papers must be made fully comprehensible and acceptable to readers, but at the same time editors must beware of discouraging the authors from writing more papers in that language. Needless stylistic changes are even more disheartening for foreign authors than for those writing in their mother tongue.

Many foreign authors writing in English will have picked up the pomposities and circumlocutions common to British-American scientific publications, and proudly imitated them. These can be eliminated along with errors of grammar, spelling and punctuation. The editor or copy editor has to look out for English words that have counterparts in other languages but have been wrongly used in their English context. Examples are *remarkable* (better rendered *worthy of note* or *interesting,* or omitted altogether), *respectively* (English usage requires pairs or lists to be given in parallel when this word is used; one cannot write 'sensitive respectively insensitive'), ± (which means *approximately* in many European languages, but only *plus or minus* in English), *already* (often redundant, but sometimes meaning *previously*), and *to control* (meaning to check or monitor rather than to keep within bounds).

If a paper is in such fractured English that its meaning is obscure, someone who understands the content will have to spend a considerable amount of time revising it. This may be the editor, a member of the editorial board or other adviser, or the author, who should be advised to ask an English-speaking scientist for help (*not* a professional translator or interpreter), though in this case the editor must take into account which country an author works in and the likely availability of appropriate scientists there. Whichever alternative is adopted, authors should be given credit for their attempts to express difficult concepts in a foreign tongue.

Spelling

The differences between American and British spelling produce problems in these days of international journals largely in English. If the editor, publisher or printer cannot accept inconsistency between chapters or articles, the editor or copy editor should change the spelling, where necessary, to whichever version is more common in the country of publication.

References

Many articles and chapters are over-referenced, perhaps because authors imagine that a long list of references displays erudition.[29] If the list seems too long, authors should be asked to consider whether all the references are really necessary. They should also be asked to check the accuracy of references and to compare the details given in the final typescript directly with the original sources or photocopies of them. Whether the editorial office will check references independently is for the editor to decide. Editors who take their duties to readers seriously will have references verified if it is at all feasible to do so (Chapter 6): F. P. Woodford (personal communication) found that even in the 'best' journals among those that do not check references, at least 10% of entries were so full of errors that they could not be retrieved. But if references are verified in the editorial office, the work should not be allowed to hold up publication.

For books, the editor decides whether reference lists will follow each chapter or appear at the end of the book. If the chapters have little overlap, the first is the best choice, and is certainly the most common in multi-author scientific books. If there is much repetition of references in different chapters it is sometimes better to consolidate them in one list at the end of the book. This saves space and typesetting time but may take a lot of editorial time, and it poses a problem about reference lists for reprints of individual chapters. A third method is to place the references at the end of the book but list them separately for each chapter, as in this book. The deciding factor should be what is most convenient for readers.

The form of citations in the text and references in reference lists is discussed in Chapter 6.

ETHICS OF EXPERIMENTATION: THE EDITOR'S RESPONSIBILITIES

In biological or behavioural fields, editors have to decide how to han-

dle papers that are scientifically sound but apparently based on unethical or ethically dubious investigations. Journal editors sometimes
sidestep this problem by instructing referees to consider only scientific merit, leaving readers to judge whether the work was ethical.
Editors who adopt this solution argue that the investigations cannot
be undone and that the conclusions might as well be made public. But
publication of a paper of this kind without comment, especially in a
prestigious journal, encourages other investigators to do similar
experiments. Committees of the Council of Biology Editors (USA)
(Ref. 30, p 31) and of ELSE[31] have come to the same conclusion.

Both these committees recommend that the editor should first
determine from the author whether work that appears unethical was in
fact unethically conducted. If it has merely been inadequately
described the editor can ask the author to rewrite the manuscript more
clearly. The ELSE Working Group[31] recommends that if the editor is
not satisfied about the way the work was done, the paper should be
rejected, with a clear statement that it is being rejected purely on
ethical grounds. But the author can easily have the paper published by
a less high-minded editor and almost the same damage will be done as
if the paper had been accepted by the first publication. The editor's
and referees' doubts could instead be openly but tactfully expressed in
an editorial published simultaneously with the paper. Editors,
however, should neither launch outright attacks on the views
expressed in papers they accept for publication nor evade responsibility for publication of those views by failing to comment on them at all.
A reference to the editorial should appear on the first page of the
paper, so that people reading reprints or copies of the article are
alerted to the editor's reservations. Since there are often sincere
differences of opinion on the ethical nature of certain experiments or
investigations in animals or people, authors should always be shown
editorials of this kind and allowed to reply (see p 137). Open discussion of the matter is best in this as in other questions of editorial
policy.

Research in disciplines other than the life sciences also gives rise to
ethical problems of various kinds for journal editors and authors, but I
shall do no more here than draw attention to the existence of such
problems.

Authors of chapters in books or review papers at conferences can of
course record their ethical criticisms of other people's work, just as
they can express any other criticism, and editors may add their own
criticisms, in square brackets in the text or at the end of the text, if
authors have not done so.

MULTIPLE PUBLICATION

Editors are unanimous in condemning publication of the same article, or the same article slightly reworked, in two or more books or journals (Ref. 30, Ch. 8). The main arguments against duplicate or multiple submission and publication are that much time and money are spent on refereeing, editing, producing, circulating, abstracting and retrieving each piece of information, and that editors naturally do not like publishing stale news or infringing copyright. It is also very annoying for readers who have gone to some trouble to track down a reference only to find that they have already read the article elsewhere. Duplicate publication is acceptable only when articles are intended for two different language areas, especially if secondary services do not provide good coverage from one to the other, or when articles are intended for widely separated disciplines, e.g. geology and clinical science, where journals in one discipline would rarely be seen by workers in the other, and when even a large abstracting service would not include both journals in its coverage. Even then the editors of the two journals should agree beforehand to the dual publication and include cross-references for the reader's benefit.

At one time authors universally observed the code of good practice which requires them to submit their papers to one journal at a time, but in the last decade duplicate submission has become more frequent.[32] Most journals now protect themselves by explicitly forbidding duplicate submission in their guidelines for authors. An even better protection is for editors to make prompt decisions to accept or reject papers. The assumption that an editor will take a long time to make a decision is often what makes authors submit papers to several journals at once.

Editors of books face a more complex problem over duplicate publication than journal editors. Contributors to multi-author books may be justified in describing their published work again in some detail, but the descriptions should be completely rewritten for the book and each chapter ought to be related to other chapters in the book as well as to later work by the same author or by others. Similarly, a short paper for a conference may reasonably contain the same material as a journal article, provided that it is presented differently (see Chapter 10). This should ensure that the conference paper is worth reading as well as the corresponding journal article. A paper usefully presented at a conference may nevertheless be omitted from the published proceedings if a journal article has appeared and if the proceedings would not suffer from its absence. The editor should insert a reference to the journal article for the sake of conference participants who might look for the article in the published proceedings.

WRITING TO AUTHORS

Editors should write individually and sympathetically to authors, especially if a paper is being rejected or major revision is requested. The authors may feel that their life's blood was poured into the papers that are being returned to them. They will not be grateful for a few impersonal words in a form letter suggesting that their papers are useless or that they must tear them apart and put them together again before any editor could approve publication. Editors can contribute much to the harmony of the scientific community with their letters and comments on manuscripts, if their approach is right. One author's picture of how a great editor worked with his authors has already been quoted (Chapter 2); another author recalls his correspondence with Dr J. T. Edsall as follows:[33]

> One of the finest editors I've known was John Edsall of Harvard who edited the *Journal of Biological Chemistry* for years [1958–1967]. He spent untold hours writing lengthy and detailed comments to authors. His letters were of inestimable value in improving the quality of papers. If every editor were as diligent, scientific literature would improve greatly.

The preceding paragraph of the same article shows how disruptive some editing and refereeing can be:

> When I was younger and a manuscript was returned to me with rather strong criticism, I would be furious. It took me several days to settle down and give the reviewer's comments serious attention. Nearly every paper I've published has been improved by comments from reviewers and editors.

Editors should ask authors to return revised papers within a stated time. Delay may put the editor in a dilemma, as this case history shows (J. T. Edsall, personal communication):

> 'Author A submitted an interesting and quite original paper. It was sent back for suggested revisions; not very drastic. For some reason A held the paper for many months before submitting a revised version. In the meantime author B, clearly quite independently, discovered essentially the same phenomenon; and his paper was accepted by another member of the Editorial Board (who knew nothing of A's work; but presumably it would have made little difference if he had). When A

finally submitted his paper again, was the journal to decline it on the ground that it now duplicated work by another researcher that had been accepted and was in process of publication . . .?'

The best course in such a case is for the editor to telephone A as soon as B's paper is accepted, and explain what has happened. If A then submits the revised paper immediately, the two papers can be published in the same issue.

Editors sometimes receive excellent papers that are unsuitable for their particular journals. They should tell the authors that the wrong target has been chosen and encourage them to submit their work elsewhere. But when papers are really not worth publishing editors should not hide behind statements such as 'The work lies outside the scope of this journal' or 'The journal is very pressed for space'. Euphemisms of this sort raise authors' hopes that their work will be accepted if they restyle their manuscripts to match another journal's requirements. The authors' time and that of other editors is then wasted. Instead, editors should say as gently as possible that the findings are internally inconsistent, the methods unsatisfactory or the data incomplete, according to what they or the referees have found.

The theme running through this chapter could be taken as the editor's golden rule: work with authors, not against them. Be firm when editorial knowledge is clearly superior to an author's, but remember that the secret of good editing lies in the use of a velvet glove as well as—occasionally—an iron hand.

6 Manuscript editing: technical editing

Technical editing, the detailed preparation of manuscripts for the printer's information and for the reader's ultimate benefit, is often done at the same time as substantive editing and by the same person—usually a copy editor but sometimes an editor (see Chapter 5).

Technical editing includes checking that the form of each part of the manuscript matches the detailed requirements of the instructions to authors; that the nomenclature, abbreviations, units and symbols follow internationally accepted systems or are explained at first mention; and that small capital letters, Greek, Cyrillic or other alphabets, italics and bold type, rank of headings, and a host of other typographical details are marked clearly for the typesetter. It also includes seeing that all necessary parts of each manuscript and each book or journal issue are present, properly identified and assembled in the right order for the printer, as discussed in Chapter 7.

Substantive and technical editing together constitute copy-editing and if some authors question editing itself, they and the business managers of some journals cavil even more at copy-editing, which they regard, respectively, as an unnecessary and irritating exercise or an expensive luxury. It is true that if authors consistently supplied ideal typescripts completely ready for the typesetter, copy-editing might not be needed. And when printing has to be done from authors' camera-ready copy, certainly no copy-editing can be done on the final typescript; standards may then have to be sacrificed and the effect on the reader ignored. But whenever papers are typeset or retyped before printing, the copy editor's preparatory work saves an enormous amount of the typesetter's time[1] and the publisher's money, as well as improving the article for the reader—always provided that the copy editor or editor aims at clarification rather than at fussy tidying or an unrealistic level of consistency and perfection.

An indispensable book for copy editors is Judith Butcher's detailed account[2] of the copy-editing practices of Cambridge University Press. In the USA, Chicago University Press's *Manual of style*[3] is the most widely used reference book for general points but scientific copy-editing is more specifically dealt with in the *CBE Style manual*.[4] As only a general picture of copy-editing is given here, every editor/copy editor new to the job should consult one or more of those books (and see p 151).

Most editorial offices have a 'house style'—a collection of decisions on spellings, capitals, italics, hyphens, and so on, for use when a choice is permissible. The collected decisions can be card-indexed for easy reference. If this collection is kept within sensible limits it helps the copy editor to deal quickly with certain trivial but potentially time-wasting questions of form. For many minor points, however, it may be better to follow the author's usage, provided the author has been consistent. For consistency throughout a publication, copy editors should list the decisions they make, or that authors have made, and note where the words or terms first appear, in case a different style later becomes the preferred one. Sets of rules on nomenclature should be collected and filed alphabetically or in some other retrievable way. Instead of a simple card index or file, some large editorial offices, for example that of the American Psychological Association,[5] publish their own style manuals, providing useful guidance for both editors and authors.

One point that the editor or copy editor has to settle with the printer is whether manuscripts will be fully copy-edited or only partly copy-edited in the editorial office, or whether—when such a service is available—the printer's staff is to undertake copy-editing. If the printer is to make no changes at all but should follow the copy exactly, this must be stated; the copy editor/editor works accordingly.

Marking the type fount and size and giving other purely typographical instructions for the text, headings, tables, legends, etc., is usually known as 'printer's mark-up' and is indeed often done by the printer's staff; but practices vary in different countries. For an established journal, however, or in a book forming one of a series, many of these items conform to a standard pattern and little marking is needed. For other books and for new journals the editor or sponsoring body and the publisher or printer agree on these typographical points at an early stage (see Chapters 1 and 8).

Editors must know, or decide, exactly what their copy editors or other assistants will do and when they will do it, as mentioned in Chapter 5. As well as the work described in Chapter 5, the copy editor/editor deals with the items discussed below.

TABLES AND ILLUSTRATIONS

Although the editor or referees should already have examined the titles of tables, the copy editor checks whether the titles in each article are consistent in wording and terminology. The legends for the illustrations are examined from the same point of view. For the tables and illustrations themselves, the copy editor asks (Ref. 6, p 11–15): Are column headings, like titles, consistent in style and terminology? Would tables be easier to read (and typeset) if they were turned through 90°, so that lengthy column headings fit into the left-hand column (the 'stub') instead of being crowded across the top? Are all tables and illustrations numbered in the order they will appear in the text, and is their approximate position in the text marked in the margin? If any have been taken from previously published work, has the author obtained permission for them to be reproduced? Are all symbols and abbreviations explained? Are axes on graphs intelligibly and consistently labelled? Should photographs be cropped to remove irrelevant areas? Does the author's name and the title of the paper appear on the back of each illustration and is 'Top' marked where necessary? Are scale bars included or magnifications given where necessary?

HEADINGS AND SUBHEADINGS

A simple system for headings, subheadings and sub-subheadings helps readers to find their way quickly in a chapter or article. Headings can be designated A, B, C etc., and marked accordingly for the printer. Three levels of heading are enough in most cases; it is best to avoid having more as it is difficult to distinguish them typographically. The typeface, type size and placement of the different levels of heading are part of the agreed design for journals, or are decided at the specification stage for books (see Chapter 8). The editor or copy editor may have to decide on the author's behalf what is the logical ranking of the headings provided and, sometimes, insert headings when the author has changed the theme without warning.

The conventional first-order (A) headings for the main sections of a journal article are Introduction, Methods, Results, Discussion and References, but this order and these terms may be inappropriate for a given article (see p 132), and are almost certainly inappropriate for a chapter in a book. Within the main sections the B and C headings may need to be reordered. The copy editor/editor may find it useful to make a list of the headings, aligning the A headings at the left-hand margin and indenting the others appropriately, to see whether the listing looks logical. A list like this also shows whether there should be more or fewer headings to guide the reader to each topic.

NOMENCLATURE

Nomenclature begins to evolve rather haphazardly in each new field. After a while it becomes standardized and begins to evolve again, this time in a more orderly fashion, since certain principles are laid down and agreed during the standardization process. Journal editors and copy editors usually learn from their predecessors which standard authorities for nomenclature are used by the journal and where to look for new developments as they occur. Book editors can refer to the guidelines for authors in relevant journals, or consult the journal editors themselves about nomenclatural authorities and developments. A journal's guidelines ought to cite the main reference works but a letter to the journal editor usually elicits more up-to-date information, for example on nomenclature changes that are about to be in-troduced—since journal editors are often members of nomenclature committees. Editors should neither invent systems of nomenclature nor allow authors to do so; there is plenty of guidance available and editors should steer authors towards the most recent forms put forward in internationally agreed systems.

ABBREVIATIONS, UNITS AND SYMBOLS

Abbreviations are shortened versions of terms that are too cumber-some for easy intelligibility; deoxyribonucleic acid, for example, is more easily understood when abbreviated to DNA. Units of measure are nearly always abbreviated too. Symbols are usually single letters, or combinations of letters and digits, that succinctly convey a concept, e.g. V for volume or Q_{10} for a change of rate for every 10-degree rise in temperature (Kelvin scale).

Abbreviations, units and symbols obviously increase readability if they are deployed skilfully, but over-use has the opposite effect: 'Following an ECG and a BUN, the patient was found to have NSAP' is an incomprehensible code to most non-medical people. The names of units should always be abbreviated when they are preceded by a number but not when they appear in such phrases as 'concentration is expressed in milligrams per litre'. The Système International (SI) method of expressing measurements is obligatory in many journals and includes standard abbreviations for the recommended units. This method is used in all countries and all disciplines. Only members of a few professions now resist using certain SI units, on the grounds that during the period of transition there is dangerous confusion. The answer to this objection is to make the period of transition as short as possible. SI units will displace 'conventional' units as certainly as those units once displaced the dram, the scruple and the pennyweight in England, or their equivalents in other countries. Older units may still, if necessary, be given in parentheses after SI units, or even the other way round if the actual measurements were made in the older units.

Abbreviation of other words is less obviously desirable than abbreviation of cumbersome terms and units. Some editors forbid it entirely; others are so permissive that abbreviations flourish like weeds on the pages of their publications. The ideal lies somewhere in between. A good rule of thumb is that if an unwieldy word or phrase has to be used more than 10 times per 500 words a standard or sensible abbreviation (often three capital letters without stops) can be allowed if it is used consistently. It may, in fact, be unnecessary to repeat such phrases: if only one kind of treatment is being investigated, for example, it need not be specified by name each time. 'The monoamine-diarrhoeic (MAD) dogs' can be replaced by the 'experimental' or the 'treated' dogs; or 'the mineral' and 'the particle' can be used if only one of each is being discussed.

Abbreviations of words fall into three categories: internationally agreed by standards committees, arbitrary but preferred by leading journals, and newly coined for the occasion. Editors should make sure that authors have not invented new abbreviations where acceptable ones already exist. For recognized abbreviations in the life sciences the *European Journal of Biochemistry*,[7] the *CBE Style manual*[4] or O'Connor & Woodford (Ref. 6, p 82–88) can be consulted. The *CBE Style manual* draws a neat distinction between unequivocally acceptable, arbitrary but recommended (though obligatorily defined at first mention), and unacceptable abbreviations.

FOOTNOTES

Footnotes have become anathema to many editors and printers, though computer photocomposition can remove the objections to them. Traditionally footnotes have often been used on the opening page of an article or chapter to give information about an author's previous or present affiliation, if different from that in the by-line; to gather together all abbreviations used in the article or chapter, with their explanations or definitions; or to refer to any comments or criticisms by other authors elsewhere in the book or journal issue, especially if these concern ethical matters. They are also used to provide supporting evidence that would interrupt the argument if inserted in the text, or to make an editorial comment or cross-reference to a passage elsewhere in the publication which contradicts the author's argument. Whenever possible all these kinds of footnotes should be incorporated into the text or added at the end of the text as a 'Note Added in Proof' or an 'Editor's Note'.

'Footnotes' are sometimes used for bibliographical references. Useful though this may be for readers using microfiche or microfilm, reference details should normally be given in an alphabetic or numbered list at the end of the article, chapter or book, as described in the section on references below.

Footnotes to tables are considered part of the table, since they are often needed to supply information for which there is no room in the main body of the table. Authors should be asked to place them below the table or on a page immediately after it, not with any (unavoidable) footnotes to the text; and they should be asked to keep them short (see p 48).

The rare footnotes whose use can be justified are usually typed separately from the pages to which they refer, on a separate sheet in order of mention, and with identifying marks (superscript letters or symbols) to link them to the text. They may be printed separately from, and in a smaller type size than, the main text. Some printers prefer footnotes in typescripts to be placed immediately after the lines where they are referred to, set off from the text by lines ruled above and below the footnote. This point should be settled with the printer when style guides or guidelines for authors are drawn up.

ACKNOWLEDGEMENTS

The way acknowledgements are to be printed should also be agreed with the printer. To avoid a footnote on the opening page they can be printed with or without a heading, and perhaps in smaller type, at the end of the text.

Authors tend to be over-generous with acknowledgements. If

typists, technicians, illustrators and others have only been doing their normal work, their help does not necessarily have to be acknowledged. But authors should certainly be allowed to acknowledge any special help received if they wish to do so. Authors should be encouraged to show the proposed acknowledgement to the persons being thanked and to obtain their permission for the wording (see Appendix 4). Grants and other support for the work described should be acknowledged briefly.

APPENDIXES

Complex calculations, derivations of formulae, checklists and other items that would disrupt the text if inserted at the point where they are referred to can usefully be placed in appendixes. In journal articles, appendixes are refereed along with the rest of the manuscript; this distinguishes them from a Note Added in Proof, although both are often placed after the Acknowledgements and before the References. For mathematical work special typesetting may be necessary. The whole appendix may be set in smaller type than the main text and should be so marked for the printer if there are no standing instructions on this point.

REFERENCES

In journal articles references are usually confined strictly to publications cited in the text and listed at the end of the article under the heading 'References' or 'References Cited'. In review articles or chapters in multi-author books, 'Further' or 'Additional Reading' is sometimes added as a separate list. A 'Bibliography' refers to a full list of sources from which the authors have drawn ideas and inspiration but for which no specific citations are given in the text. If the term is used in this way, a Bibliography is obviously not appropriate for a journal article.

For chapters or articles with lists of references cited, the copy editor/editor checks that every citation in the text has a corresponding reference in the reference list, that every reference in the list is indeed cited, and that where names and dates are given in the text these match the names and dates given in the list. This cross-check is done separately from reading the text and in about 95 % of papers it shows up at least one or two discrepancies. Queries about the discrepancies in dates and spelling of names, and about incomplete, missing or redundant references, are listed for the author or copy editor to sort out before the paper is printed; minor points may be marked on the typescript for the author to deal with in proof. The copy editor then marks the author's reference list so that it is in the form required for the book or journal.

The form of references in reference lists has still not been standardized despite many years of discussion and many anguished pleas from authors that editors should agree on a single form for all scientific publications.[8] An international and multidisciplinary Workshop on references has now put forward a simple and uniform system designed to benefit authors, editors, readers, typists and typesetters. Those suggestions are given in full in Appendix 6. The main suggestions from the Workshop are that the same sequence and form of elements should be used for references in reference lists in all scientific publications, no matter which system (names/dates or numbers) is used for citations in the text, and that any extra punctuation and typographical instructions that the editor or publisher feels are essential for asserting a publication's individual style should be added as required.

The standard layout recommended for a reference to a journal article is as follows (see Appendix 6 for examples of references to books):

> Smith A B, Schmidt Y Z 1978 Iron bars are getting tougher. International Metals Journal 12:28–38

Once one of the key recommendations—that the date should be placed immediately after the authors' names—has been accepted, the chances that authors and authors' typists will prepare references correctly increase, because the sequence and form of other reference elements can then be kept the same for every publication for which the authors prepare papers. This utopian state of affairs depends, of course, on editors either agreeing to have references printed in the form suggested by the Workshop or accepting that if their publications insist on special forms for references, they themselves, or their copy editors, will have to mark authors' reference lists accordingly. The rationale for this is that it is many times easier for copy editors or editors to mark reference lists to conform to one particular style with which they are familiar than it is for authors and their typists to cope with the myriad 'systems' now in use.

Another key suggestion put forward by the Workshop is that a 'master typescript' or 'final draft' system should be used in which names and dates, not numbers, are typed for citations *in the text*. If a paper originally prepared for a publication that uses names/dates is rejected and then submitted to a publication using numbers, the author simply deletes the names and dates neatly and inserts numbers instead of having to have the whole text retyped. Conversely, if authors submitting papers to 'numeric journals' make a copy of the name/date text before deleting the names and dates, they can then submit the copy to a 'name/date journal' if the paper is rejected by the numeric journal. Reference *lists*, however—unless the second journal follows the same system as the first—have to be typed according to each journal's requirements, though this is much easier with the recommended standard layout than where every element may be in a different sequence and form.

Many editors already ask for titles of journal articles to be included in reference lists, as in the example shown. In most disciplines the advantages to readers of the titles of journal articles being included in the list of references outweigh any extra trouble caused to the author, editor and publisher—except, perhaps, the extra typesetting costs (Ref. 9, p 85–86). The title gives readers a great deal of information and often tells them whether they need to spend time finding and reading the article; it may help them to track down the article if there are errors elsewhere in the reference; and it shows them in what language the article was published. Until authors make a practice of noting titles with the rest of the bibliographical information about their sources, they may protest at having to consult the cited article again to obtain the title; but this chore may also benefit them, because they may discover that memory has played them false about what the article contained; or they may find that it was not the article they meant to cite at all.

Another recommendation already widely observed is that first and last page numbers of articles should be given in references. Inclusive pagination indicates to readers whether the article cited is on a grand scale or is merely a short note. Knowing the length is helpful, too, when photocopies are ordered from a distant library and the cost has to be calculated. Again, the information may assist readers or librarians in identifying an article if other elements in the reference are wrong.

The only other Workshop suggestion that needs to be discussed here is the one stating that journal titles may be *either* unabbreviated, *or* abbreviated according to the 'International List' system (Appendix 7, para. 3.5). Provided that each reference list follows one style only, there is no good reason why these two ways of treating journal titles should not be allowed in the same book or journal issue. As this would lead to savings in time and money, and as both methods give readers and librarians sufficient information for retrieving articles, it seems reasonable to suggest that on this point inconsistency between chapters or articles—but not within them—might be allowed to creep in. (The International List system, incidentally, is very simple and much quicker to use than the 'World List' system still used by many journals.)

The Workshop made no recommendation on whether names and dates or numbers should be preferred in the text, or on whether numbers should be sequential (with a non-alphabetic reference list) or non-sequential (with an alphabetic list). Again, one solution would be to allow inconsistency between chapters or articles but not within them. Many editors, and some publishers, however, have very strong feelings on how references should be cited in the text and it is highly unlikely that a single system will ever be universally acceptable in scientific publications.

Numbers in the text take less space, are less distracting in mid-sentence, and—if they are sequential numbers—ease the chore of finding a citation which the reader identifies in the reference list as being of special interest. The arguments against numbers are that they supply no immediate information to the reader, that in long reference lists it is difficult to find whether a particular author has been cited, that the numbers can be confused with other numbers in highly numerical texts, and that it is difficult to add or delete citations during revision without making mistakes. With the name/date system the author and editor can identify citations which are added or deleted during revision and readers know just what work is being cited as they read the text. Against the name/date system are the extra space taken, the disruption to sentences, and the fact that it is not easy for readers who see an interesting reference in the reference list to find where that reference appears in the text (but the Workshop describes a solution to this problem).

Most editors find that the number versus name/date question has already been settled for them by the traditions of their journals or the house style of the publisher. Editors who are free to choose a system must decide what their authors can cope with and what their readers will find most useful. Most readers seem to want alphabetical lists, and many find they adapt easily to seeing names/dates in the text. If alphabetical lists are preferred but if numbers are needed for economy, the non-sequential numbering system can be used—but this is perhaps the most difficult system for authors. With both the name/date and the non-sequential numbering systems, if the editor wants readers to know where in a lengthy text a reference seen in the reference list can be found, it is possible—though laborious—to add to the reference list the pages on which each reference is cited.[10]

Verification of references

Authors are asked to supply accurate references but the responsibility is one that many take lightly. Editors rarely have time to verify references and the same is true of copy editors. If an editor decides that references ought to be verified (Chapter 5), a technician or secretary may be happy to do the work for pocket-money. A six-month or 1000-reference experiment will show whether the cost of checking is justified (it is not usually very great).

The reference verifier should be given a copy of the reference list either when copy-editing begins or earlier, so that verification is complete before the copy-edited manuscript is ready for printing. Primary sources, if available, should be used for verifying references; otherwise, secondary (abstracting) services may be consulted.

DATES RECEIVED AND ACCEPTED

Depending on the policy of the journal concerning printing the dates of receipt and/or acceptance (Chapters 4 and 12), the copy editor inserts these dates on the manuscripts in the preferred position—usually after, or immediately before, the references.

When editorial work on individual chapters or articles is complete, the copy editor may send photocopies to the authors for checking (see Chapter 5). The material for a book or journal issue is then assembled and prepared for the printer as described in the next chapter.

7 Completing books and journal issues

When material for a book has been copy-edited and is ready for the printer, the editor or copy editor arranges the typescripts in their running order in the book and checks that the sections are numbered and complete (see items 1–7 of checklist, Appendix 5). Several more parts of the book and pieces of information remain to be prepared for the printer, as described here. Journals, in addition to their regular contents, need various extra items for each issue and for the completed volume. Books and journals are discussed separately in this chapter.

COMPLETING BOOKS

Front matter or preliminary pages ('prelims')

The preliminary pages of a book include the half-title page and its reverse side or verso, the title-page and its verso (the copyright page), possibly a preface or foreword, and a contents list and list of contributors. Most of the material (the 'copy') for the prelims is prepared for the printer by the copy editor, who follows the design specifications agreed at an earlier stage (see also Chapter 8).

On the *half-title page* with which books conventionally begin, the title of the book—and nothing more—is printed towards the top of the page. The back of the half-title page is often left blank. If this page carries a *frontispiece* the copy editor obtains copyright permission if it is needed, and provides a legend, as for any other illustration. Instead of a frontispiece, information about the sponsoring organization may be included, or a list of related books in the same series.

Title pages must be carefully designed. They carry the title, the subtitle if there is one, the editor's name (with affiliations if appropriate), the year of publication, the publisher's name and colophon (an identification symbol), and the place(s) of publication. Since they show librarians how to catalogue books and authors how to cite them, title pages must not be cluttered up with bibliographically superfluous information. Editors of conference proceedings, in particular, must condense unwieldy titles into easily cited forms and banish the details of where meetings were held to another part of the prelims (see p 71). 'Proceedings of the 8th conference of the International Association of Fisheries held at the Duke of Wellington Hotel, Oban, Argyll, June 4 to 7, 1978, on the occurrence and development of larval stages of commercially valuable fish species', for example, would be better transformed into 'Fish larva: proceedings of the 8th conference of the International Association of Fisheries, 4–7 June 1978'.

The back of the title page is often called the *copyright page*. The copyright sign, ©, the date (year) and the name of the copyright-holder form the copyright notice. The copyright notice must appear on this or on another agreed page in all books published in countries that support the Universal Copyright Convention (most developed and many developing nations). In these countries copyright in any written work, published or unpublished, automatically belongs to the author until it is formally assigned to a publisher, an editor or anyone else (see Chapter 3 and p 76). Copyright protection in published work lasts, usually, for 50 years from the end of the year in which the author dies. In some countries, even though copyright protection is automatic, registration is required on publication. In the USA, for example, two copies of the book (or one copy of a work first published outside the USA), application form TX and a fee (at present $10) must be sent to the Register of Copyrights (Copyright Office, Library of Congress, Washington, DC 20559) within three months of publication. In the UK registration is not necessary and no fee is payable. Instead, one copy of each new publication must be deposited within a month of publication with the Copyright Receipt Office of the British Library (Store Street, London WC1E 7DG). This requirement also applies to works first published elsewhere and then imported for sale in the UK. Up to five more copies of each work may have to be supplied for specified British and Irish libraries.

The publisher arranges registration and deposit of copies, when necessary. If multi-author books or conference proceedings are being privately published in countries other than the USA or UK, the editor or sponsoring organization should consult a librarian or the national publishers' association about local copyright requirements. (See Cavendish's book[1] for a readable account of English copyright law; the 1976 copyright law in the USA has been usefully summarized by Wagner[2,3] and briefly mentioned in *Science*.[4])

A notice about the restrictions imposed on copying the whole or parts of the book is printed below the copyright notice, usually in the following form:

The notice can be made less restrictive, or may even be omitted, if the sponsors want to allow passages to be copied for study or teaching purposes, but this is for the publisher and the copyright-holder (if they are different) to discuss. (See also Appendix 2 and p 76.)

The copyright page includes the International Standard Book Number, a 10-digit identifier unique to each title. The ISBN system, which is the subject of an International Standard,[5] was developed to provide a machine-readable system of identification for publishers, distributors and data-handling services; it is also used for ordering and billing by publishers, librarians and booksellers. The ISBN may be used, too, as part of the 'article-fee code' required for the collection of photocopying fees, as discussed for journals later in this chapter (p 79). The ISBN is the publisher's responsibility. An organization publishing its own books for the first time should arrange to have an ISBN identifier assigned by the national ISBN Agency (the international system is administered by the International ISBN-Agentur, Postfach 1407, D-1000 Berlin 30, West Germany; in the UK apply to Standard Book Numbering Agency Ltd., 12 Dyott Street, London WC1A 1DF; in the US apply to R.R. Bowker Co.; for address see p 76).

Another item usually obtained by the publisher for the copyright page is the Library of Congress Catalog Card Number, which is useful to librarians everywhere and essential for books sold in the USA. Even more useful is the full cataloguing information that the Library of Congress or other national libraries or agencies supply to publishers who support the Cataloging in Publication Programs which operate in the USA and several other countries. The publisher sends a Cataloging Data Sheet to the CIP office of the British Library or the Library of Congress, Washington, DC, or the equivalent form to the appropriate national office, with a complete set of prelims and/or a set of first proofs. A card or slip of data ready for reproduction on the copyright page is sent in return. The CIP Program may not sell many extra copies of a book but it is a valuable bibliographic tool, making books easier and cheaper to catalogue and retrieve.

Sometimes the month and year of publication are printed separately from the copyright notice on the copyright page, and the number of tables and illustrations may be included. This is also a convenient place to provide a sample citation to the book, especially for conference proceedings or for a volume in a series. The full postal address of the publisher should be given. The printer's name and address, which is mandatory in many countries, often appears here too.

After the copyright page there is sometimes a *preface* or *foreword*. Although the words are really synonymous, a preface is usually written by the editor and a foreword by an external sponsor. The object of a foreword is to recommend the book or indicate its significance to the public. The preface often explains how the book, or the conference on which it is based, came into being and why it is being published. This gives potential readers and book reviewers valuable information about the intended readership for the book. The preface and foreword may be included in the list of contents even if they precede the list. Any *Introduction* dealing with the subject and arrangement of the book is usually better placed after the contents pages, since it is an integral part of the text.

To reduce the possibility of inconsistency, the *Contents list* is drawn up directly from the final versions of the title pages of the chapters. Except on camera-ready copy, no page numbers can be typed at this stage.

After (or just before) the Contents pages, the *contributors* to the book or the participants in the symposium or conference may be listed, with their affiliations and full mailing addresses. The top of this list is a good place to note where and when a conference was held, and its original title, if the title of the published proceedings is different.

Running heads

Many books have headlines ('running heads') above the text on every page; occasionally footlines are used instead. The running head in multi-author books often consists of the authors' names on even-numbered (left-hand) pages and the chapter title or short title on right-hand pages. The printer needs a list of running heads and if authors have not supplied short titles these have to be invented. Short titles of consecutive chapters should not, of course, be identical.

Pagination

Although half-title pages carry no numbers they count as either page 1 (arabic) or page i (roman, lower case). British and other printers often use roman lower-case to number the prelims separately from the text; this complicates the bibliographic description and should perhaps be discouraged; on the other hand, prefaces and forewords are often written last, and using roman numbers for the prelims allows the text to be paged before the number of prelims is certain. When roman lower-case is used for the prelims, the first right-hand page of the first chapter or item after the lists of contents and contributors becomes page 1 (arabic).

If the book is divided into parts, the editor may want to insert *'dividing' pages* with 'Part I', 'Part II', etc., and the title of the part, printed on them. These dividing pages are counted in the pagination but they do not carry numbers: like the half-title pages and their reverse sides these pages are 'blind folios'.

Common Reference List

If it has been decided to print all the references at the end of the book (p 52), the reference lists for each chapter are now assembled or a consolidated alphabetical list is typed. The editor may also want to include a list of additional reading.

Indexes

Every scientific book needs an index or indexes, which may be compiled by the editor, the copy editor or a specialist indexer.

It is better to separate the *index of authors* or *contributors* from the subject index, although the practice of making one author–subject index is not unknown. In an index of contributors all authors of every chapter, and all contributors to any discussions printed in conference proceedings, are listed alphabetically by surname. Problems over alphabetizing compound names can be resolved either by asking the author or by asking a librarian what system should be used. The index of contributors is prepared on cards or slips of paper either when the manuscripts have been arranged in running order or when paged proofs are ready, the second method being more usual. Cards prepared from manuscripts must be kept in the order of appearance of entries until page numbers have been inserted, after which they can be sorted into alphabetical order and numbered. Some printers accept the sequenced cards to work from but others want typed lists prepared from the cards.

An *index of cited authors* is sometimes included. This is straightforward but takes time to prepare. Again, if the indexer works from manuscript pages in order to save time at proof stage, the entries on cards are kept in order of appearance until page numbers are known.

Constructing a useful *subject index* is hard work. The person best qualified to do it is the person who knows the book best—for a multi-author book usually the editor or copy editor. A hard-pressed editor might persuade one of the contributors to take on the work of indexing the whole book but getting individual contributors to underline indexable items on their proofs is not particularly helpful: the index will be more consistent if one person decides what is to be included. If neither editors nor contributors can find the time, a professional indexer with some experience of the relevant scientific disciplines will be needed, but indexers with the right qualifications are rare. The publishers may help the editor to find an indexer. Indexing fees, if paid by the publisher, are deducted from the royalties.

The indexer is given any keywords or indexing suggestions supplied by contributors, and the printer sends paged proofs, which may be either first or second proofs, as soon as they are ready. If indexing is begun from manuscript pages or galley proofs, the entries are kept in order of appearance until page numbers can be inserted.

The indexer should be asked to over-index rather than under-index if in doubt, as the editor can delete superfluous entries later. The editor may also specify how many levels of indexing are wanted: entries, subentries and sub-subentries should be sufficient. The indexer may begin by reading the whole book quickly to get a general picture of what it is about—though there is rarely time for this, and re-reading the book after the index has been made may be more valuable. The indexer then goes through the material page by page, underlining selected items for indexing or making entries immediately on cards or slips of paper for every indexable topic on each page. Later, when page numbers have been written in, the cards or slips are sorted into alphabetical order, redundant entries are eliminated, synonyms are rationalized, cross-references are inserted, and the cards are numbered. Editors making their own indexes should proceed similarly. (For useful advice on indexing see the *CBE Style manual*[6] and Anderson.[7])

Time and funds permitting, the entries made on cards or slips may be retyped in list form, double-spaced, with subentries and sub-subentries appropriately indented, before the index is edited. It is easier to edit an index when it has been retyped in list form but if the editor expects to eliminate or alter many entries the extra time spent on typing before the index is edited may be an extravagance.

Editing the index, an extremely important task, depends on the editor's special knowledge of the subject. It has to be done carefully even when the index has been compiled by the person editing it. Over-indexing is as unhelpful to the reader as under-indexing and editors should eliminate or combine entries wherever possible, inserting cross-references liberally—'see X' or 'see also Y'. The editor must try to predict which of two or more synonymous or related terms the reader or information-retriever is likely to look for first, and eliminate as many confusing prepositions ('in', 'of', 'from') as possible without obscuring the connection between each entry and its subentries. In a professionally compiled and typed index there should be no need to verify all the page numbers, but it is wise to spot-check every tenth entry or so for correctness.

Cover, dustjacket and promotional information

The cover and any dustjacket are usually designed by the publisher's designer, in consultation with the editor (see p 8 and p 84). The copy editor supplies the wording and other information that is to be printed on the cover or jacket or on both.

A *hard cover* usually carries the title of the book, and the editor's name or the name of the sponsoring organization, as well as the publisher's name or colophon, on the spine. The title and editor's name are usually repeated on the front cover, although the front may remain unlettered if there is a dustjacket. A simple design sometimes appears on the front cover. The ISBN should appear on the back of the cover or in whatever position may yet be internationally agreed as most convenient for machine reading.

On a *dustjacket* or on a paper or other soft cover, the title of the book and the names of the editor or sponsor and the publisher usually appear on both the spine and the front cover. The jacket or cover may carry an illustration, either commissioned by the publisher or borrowed from elsewhere (in which case permission will have to be obtained from the copyright-holder). If the illustration is taken from one of the chapters in the book, copyright will already have been assigned to the copyright-holder of the book, but a polite editor will probably write to tell the author what is being done. A credit line for the design or illustration may need to be supplied for the front flap or elsewhere on the jacket or cover. On the front and back flaps of the jacket a description of the book (the 'blurb') and a list of contributors can be printed. Sometimes the blurb goes on the back of the jacket or paper cover, where it can be read even if the book is in a transparent wrapper; or the back may be used for advertising the publisher's or a sponsoring organization's other books on similar subjects. The ISBN must also be printed on the back of the jacket or paper cover.

Blurbs

Blurbs for multi-author scientific and technical books are usually written by their editors or copy editors, who understand best what the books are about, who they are for, and what distinguishes them from other books on similar subjects. The publisher often asks for two blurbs of different lengths: one for use in catalogues, leaflets or advertisements and one to be printed on the jacket.

If the blurbs are to be, say, 60 words and 200 words long, every word must count. In a typical 200-word blurb, the first couple of sentences set the scene, explaining the need for the book or the conference on which it is based.

'Water and solute exchanges in the lung are important at birth and under various circumstances later in life (e.g. lung oedema and drowning). Hitherto they have been discussed much less than gas exchange.'

The next two sentences make the theme or purpose of the book clear:

'This symposium adjusts the balance by focusing attention on the formation, distribution and absorption of liquids in the lung of the fetus and adult. It also indicates how research on epithelial membranes can contribute to an understanding of the factors that control liquid movements.'

Four or five sentences then summarize the contents:

'The symposium opens with a section on some aspects of lung structure. The water and solute permeability of lung capillaries and epithelium in fetal postnatal life and their function in controlling bulk water movements are then considered. Some comparative aspects of epithelial function and, more specifically, ion transport across the fish gill, the amphibian lung and the mammalian lung are dealt with. Special attention is directed to the fetus. Finally the pathogenesis and pathophysiology of lung oedema are discussed.'

A final sentence might name the likely readership:

'The book will interest physiologists, physicians, paediatricians, pathologists and zoologists working on the lung or gill.'

In a 60-word blurb the summarizing sentences are left out and the other are modified as necessary.

The prelims, manuscripts, jacket and index copy are the printer's raw material for making the book, but the publisher needs more help in promoting and selling the book. The editor is usually asked to name the main fields of interest covered in the book; to list its most important features, including the features that distinguish it from other publications in the same field; and to name some of those other publications. The publisher also asks for the names and addresses of individuals likely to be interested in the book and for details of societies, institutions and congresses whose members might be sent information about the book. The editor is consulted, too, about journals (at least 20) that should be sent review copies, journals in which advertisements might be placed, and congresses etc. where the book might be put on display. *Science, Nature* and other journals that list 'books received' should be included in the review list even when the book is unlikely to be reviewed, as this is another way of announcing that the book has been published.

A personal letter from the editor of the book to the more influential journals when the book goes out for review is often effective in bringing the book to the attention of the journal editors. Sponsorship by scientific organizations, especially international ones, can also be valuable in promoting a book, but manuscripts may have to be submitted for their approval well before publication.

What is done to promote privately published conference proceedings depends on the resources of the sponsoring society and on the expertise of the organizing committee. Members of a society can easily be told when the proceedings are published, especially if the society publishes its own journal or journals, but wider publicity is essential if the book's existence is to be made known to librarians and potential readers (see Chapter 10). As well as sending out review copies and advertising the book's existence in suitable journals, the editor should arrange for it to be listed, when published, in *Books in print* (R. R. Bowker Co., 1180 Avenue of the Americas, New York, NY 10036) or in the weekly lists in *The bookseller* and the annual *British books in print* (notify Whitaker's Books Listing Service Ltd., 12 Dyott Street, London WC1A 1DF).

Copyright assignment forms and permission to reproduce copyright material

For most multi-author books and journals authors are now asked to complete forms of assignment of copyright (Appendix 2) when they accept the invitation to contribute to a book or when their papers are accepted for a journal (Chapter 3). The copy editor makes sure that these forms have been received from authors and either sends them to the publisher or files them in the editorial office.

Authors must themselves obtain written permission to reproduce any previously published tables or illustrations or to quote more than a small part of someone else's text in their papers (see Appendix 4); the total quoted from any one piece of work should be less than a 'substantial part' (Ref. 1, p 40) of the whole. The copy editor sends the permission letters (releases, to the publisher with the manuscripts, or assures the publisher in writing that the necessary releases have been obtained or are being sought.

The copyright-holder has the related chore of giving permission for work published in a book or journal to be reproduced in other publications written by either the original author or other workers. Many permission requests are sent to editors instead of to the publishers but book editors, in particular, can usually send them on for the publisher to handle. Permission-seekers other than the original author should be reminded that they must include a full reference to the original work and that it is both practical and polite of them to obtain the author's permission too (Ref. 8, p 16).

COMPLETING JOURNAL ISSUES

For each issue of a journal, copy must be supplied for the cover and Contents pages, and possibly for the Guidelines for authors (see Appendix 6) and for an author index. As the last issue of a volume nears completion, such items as a volume title page, volume Contents list and volume indexes have to be considered.

Cover

It is easier for readers and librarians to find a particular unbound issue among a stack on a library shelf if the journal's *spine* carries the title, volume number, issue number, date of issue and inclusive pagination. Any issue containing a volume index should, if possible, carry the words 'Index Issue' on the spine too.

The minimum information needed on the *front cover* is the title of the journal, the date of issue and the ISSN (see below), although the other details printed on the spine are often repeated on the front. This information should be repeated in, or included with, the cover 'biblid' (see section on Page and article identification, p 79), which also gives the page run of the issue. The Contents list is best printed on the front or back cover, as mentioned in Chapter 1.

The journal cover should carry a numeric or alphabetic code (or both) that uniquely identifies each serial publication for the data-handling services. The International Standard Serial Number, for example, is the counterpart for periodicals of the ISBN for books (and books published in series may qualify for ISSNs as well as ISBNs). The ISSN is an eight-digit code which should be printed at the top right corner of the front cover, though it may appear in any other prominent place and is often included with the masthead.

The ISSN is particularly useful as part of the 'article-fee code' required for collection of fees for photocopying, as discussed below (p 79). ISSNs are assigned either by a national centre of the International Serials Data System (ISDS) (see Ref. 9; UK address is ISDS

National Centre, UK Serials Data Centre, British Library, Store Street, London WC1E 7DG; US address is Library of Congress, National Serials Data Program, Washington, DC 20540; for countries without an ISDS centre, requests are handled by the ISDS International Centre, CIEPS, 20 rue Bachaumont, 75002 Paris, France).

The other machine-readable system used for identifying journals is the CODEN: five or six upper-case letters based on the journal's title. Codens are assigned by the American Society for Testing and Materials through the International CODEN Service of Chemical Abstracts Service (Ohio State University, Columbus, Ohio 43210, USA), which requires to see a copy of the title page and masthead of the journal. Some information services may prefer Codens to the longer and unmemorable ISSNs for some time to come, though ISSNs seem destined eventually to overtake Codens for most purposes. The information services are more likely to record the correct Coden if it is printed on the outside front cover.

If a journal changes its name (not recommended—see p 17—but if a change is essential it should be made with the first issue of a new volume), or if a journal is about to stop or suspend publication (preferably after the last issue of a volume has appeared), this should be announced on the cover as well as inside the journal.

List of contents

In the Contents list, elegant design should give way to legibility if the two requirements clash. Most readers find that Contents lists in which authors' names, article titles and page numbers are arranged in columns are the easiest to scan for items of interest.[10] If the list is not printed on the cover it should start on the first page of the journal so that readers are not forced to hunt through an unpredictable number of advertisement pages to find what each issue contains. Everything published in each issue should appear in the list, with names and initials of all authors, title of articles or other features, and amplifying keywords if possible (see Chapter 5). When items are left out of a Contents list it is almost impossible for readers to find them again later. For example, 12 short articles on medical writing by Clement A. Smith, published in the *American Journal of Diseases of Children* in 1975,[11] have become almost invisible because they were inserted as 'fillers' and did not appear in the journal's Contents list. Short items such as 'notes' may not interest the secondary services but this is no reason for allowing them to be left out of the Contents list. Corrections should be listed prominently too (see Chapters 1 and 12), as should the guidelines for authors if these appear in the issue.

Masthead

The masthead printed at or near the beginning of every journal issue names the owner, publisher, sponsoring body (if any), editor, editorial board and editorial staff. It gives the frequency of issue; the cost of subscriptions; the address(es) to be used for correspondence relating to subscriptions, manuscripts and advertisements; and similar pieces of information. It may state the purpose and scope of the journal. If a postal notice stating the journal's mailing category is required, as in the USA, this may form part of the masthead if it is printed within the first five pages. The copyright notice may also be included in the masthead. If fees are to be collected for photocopying by a system like the one described below, a statement about this is needed. If guidelines for authors are not printed in each issue, a statement below the masthead should give the whereabouts of the most recent set.

Running heads

In journals that use running heads, a list is prepared for the printer, as described earlier for books (p 71).

Page and article identification

Readers often photocopy a single page from an article and later discover they have forgotten to note the source. The journal's full name, or its name abbreviated according to the 'International List' system (see Appendix 6, para. 3.5), and the volume number and year should appear as a headline or footline on every page, as well as the page number. This bibliographical identification, or 'biblid'—recommended by an American National Standard[12] and by a draft International Standard[13]—is of more value to the user of a journal than the conventional running head containing first author's name and short title; if there is space for only one of them, the biblid is to be preferred.

Each article should also have an 'article biblid' printed on the first page of the article, preferably at the head of the abstract, and giving the author's name, the year of publication, the article title, the title and volume number of the journal, and inclusive pagination of the article. The ISSN may also be given.

Article-fee code

The US Copyright Law enacted in 1976 has given rise to a scheme by which fees can be collected by the copyright-holders for articles or chapters photocopied from journals or books. The scheme applies particularly to US-based publications but publishers in other countries may join it or they may join other national schemes where these exist—for example, in West Germany. Theoretically, for the US scheme a publisher simply prints the necessary codes and includes an appropriate statement in the journal's masthead, but the Copyright Clearance Center (310 Madison Avenue, New York, NY 10017) recommends that a serial registration form should be completed for each journal.

The coding system and other procedures are detailed in a handbook[9] prepared for the Center. Briefly, if a journal publisher wants to receive fees for authorized photocopying of chapters or articles, the first page of each must carry an 'article-fee code'. The Center recommends that for this purpose the first page of articles published on or after 1 January 1978 should carry a 23-digit code. The code consists of the ISSN (or the ISBN for books), the last two digits of the year, an item number—which could be the volume number and the first page number of the article—assigned by the journal or publisher, the fee per copy, and an author-royalty indicator. The code should preferably be accompanied by a copyright notice (©, the year and the copyright-holder's name).

Contents of the issue

The progress-chasing systems described in Chapter 3 show the editor what manuscripts are available as press day for an issue approaches. The number of articles and other items that the editor sends to the printer for an issue depends, obviously, on the length of each item and the number of pages to be filled. The length of an article is estimated when it is logged in (Chapter 3), while the average length of issues is a matter agreed between the editor and publisher or other sponsor well in advance of the first issue of a new volume. For journals that are not weeklies, it is probably better not to have a rigidly fixed length for each issue but—within certain limits—to publish every article that is ready by the deadline date for the issue. If this practice is followed, and if the number of pages per volume is limited by financial or other considerations, pressure on space may become considerable as the end of a volume comes in sight; alternatively, the editor may have to scour the highways and byways for enough articles to fill the last issue.

Advertisements

If a journal publishes advertisements, these are often handled by the publisher's business manager or a managing editor. The scientific editor merely has to ensure that the advertisements are suitable for the journal to print, as discussed in Chapter 11. Pages of advertising matter are usually numbered in roman lower-case numerals, which allows these pages to be prepared separately from the text and to be torn out before issues are bound in volume form (but see Chapter 8, Binding).

Issue indexes

If issues contain 20 or more articles, an alphabetical list of every author of every paper can be extremely useful for users of the journal who wish to retrieve an article which they remember appeared in a certain issue and had a particular scientist as one of the authors (not necessarily the first). All that is needed is a simple list of names and accompanying page numbers, without titles of articles or cross-references to co-authors. An index of advertisers is sometimes useful in journals that carry advertisements.

Completing journal volumes

The volume title page and any volume Contents lists or indexes needed to complete the volume before binding are either printed at the end of the last issue of the volume or prepared for insertion in the first or another early issue of the next volume. These pages may usefully be numbered in roman lower-case numerals, as they are always printed out of their eventual sequence in the bound volume.

The *volume title page* is often similar to an issue front cover, unless the issue Contents list is customarily printed on that cover. It carries the 'title-page' biblid[13] (the same as the cover biblid, p 77, the journal's title, the volume number and year, the ISSN and sometimes the Coden. On the reverse should appear the masthead and accompanying information (see earlier, under Masthead). On the same page or on a separate *acknowledgements page* the referees consulted during the period covered by the volume may be listed and thanked for their work.

In the USA, a *statement of ownership, management and circulation* has to be filed with the Postal Service for each periodical and the statement has to be published in a prescribed form once in each volume.

Journals with a small number of articles in each volume often print a *Volume Contents list* after the volume title page. The type or printing plate for the Contents list in each issue is sometimes stored so that it can be re-used, with the insertion of appropriate headings corresponding to each issue. The value of this practice is debatable; it is not useful for journals containing more than 20 entries per issue.

Most journals provide a *volume author index* and *subject index,* or a combined author-subject index. Sometimes there are separate indexes for abstracts, biological taxonomy, book reviews, editorials, corrections, correspondence, obituaries, news columns that report research data, sponsors or advertisers, and the date on which each issue was published (so that publication priority can be established[14]). All these, however, can usually be included under appropriate headings in the subject index, but separate indexes for corrections and for book reviews are well worth considering, since these items are difficult to retrieve if handled in the traditional sketchy manner.

Making author and subject indexes for journals is in principle the same as making them for books, although journals are more likely than books to have 'subject indexes' that are little more than title indexes—which is another reason for publishing titles enriched with additional keywords in the first place. If cards are prepared for items in the indexes when each issue is printed, these can be quickly combined when the volume is complete, and the volume indexes can be printed in the last issue. Computer indexing, in which words to be indexed can be flagged at the keyboarding stage of composition, is particularly useful when prompt indexing is required. Some journal sponsors argue that because abstracting journals are indexed, the primary journals need not go to the expense of issuing their own subject indexes. This is not very convenient for readers. Instead, the editor of a primary journal might arrange to buy the appropriate printout from the abstracting service at a small charge and print it in the journal.

When all the material for a book or journal issue has been assembled and prepared for the printer, the two steps left before publication takes place are proofreading and printing (Chapters 8 and 9).

8 Printing

Most journal editors inherit a printer, unless the journal is a new one. Book editors looking for a publisher are influenced to some extent by the quality of printing and production of the publisher's other books; that is, by the typeface, quality of illustrations, layout—whether the pages looked cramped or spacious, easy or difficult to read—and strength and quality of the binding. Most publishers use several printers and can influence many of these variables according to an editor's requirements, though only within the limits of the printer's capabilities and the publisher's own financial constraints.

Finding or changing printers is not a step to take in a hurry. Any editor faced with this task should visit several printers and ask them to set some material to show the range and quality of their work. It is important to know what facilities the printer can offer (copy-marking, proofreading, binding in-house, distribution to subscribers, invoicing), what form quality control takes, and how large the printing team is. Other points to note are the error rate in proofs (ask to see some proofs) and whether the agreement includes penalty clauses for errors or for late delivery. Most publishers of any size will employ experts to deal with these matters but will expect editors to take an interest and become involved in the production processes.

This chapter deals first with the general question of design, mainly as it applies to journals, and then with the specification and style sheet that the editor and copy editor should agree with the printer, either directly or via the publisher. And since editors need at least a theoretical knowledge of the main procedures, ancient or modern, that go towards the making of books and journals, the rest of the chapter discusses typesetting, printing, artwork, proofing, paper and binding, with a final note on offprints and reprints.

DESIGN

New editors often feel they should change the design and format of the journals or book series they have taken on, and scientist-editors sometimes think they know more about the design of scientific publications than any professional book designer. As consumers they are sometimes right: but major changes in design raise complicated issues and the arguments for and against a new look should be carefully weighed. A distinctly obsolete appearance, for example, may seem to be a disadvantage, yet it may turn out to be a selling-point for a journal—because it emphasizes that the journal is long-established.[1] The important issue is whether the format or design impedes legibility or comprehension. If necessary, the editor or publisher should call in a designer, whether freelance or employed by the publisher or printer, and explain what problems need to be solved.

The cover design of a journal is one candidate for change. Here the designer must take into account both the essential and the desirable items for the cover discussed in Chapter 7. The editor should provide at the outset as much information as possible about what is wanted, so that the designer does not have to produce innumerable mock-ups of possible covers.

A change in a journal's page size is rarely popular with librarians and should never be made in the middle of a volume. An increased page size may, however, allow tables or figures to be printed where readers most want to see them—on or opposite the pages where they are discussed. If the increase in size entails a change from single to double-column layout, the editor should make sure that the new layout is appropriate for the journal: where there are many complex equations or large tables a single column is preferable.

The designer and the printer can advise the editor which standard page size (economically available in the type of paper required) would best suit the needs of the journal. The printer should at the same time advise the editor whether a new mailing wrapper or envelope can be provided easily and economically.

In the text itself, the editor will want headings and abstracts to stand out boldly. Typefaces should be chosen to marry happily (and economically) with the type used in the text, and here a typographer's help is particularly valuable. In principle many typefaces are available but not every printer carries every fount. Some founts are more suitable than others for particular kinds of work, for example mathematics. The typographer can suggest which typefaces should be used, after making sure what the printer has to offer.

If type size is reduced, more words can be printed on a page, saving paper and mailing costs. The 10-point type still used in some scientific publications can with advantage be reduced to 9-point, but any further reduction in type size would be bad for readers' eyesight. (A 'point' as used by British and American printers is about 1/72 of an inch, or 0.3515 mm; a point in the Didot system, widely used in Europe, measures 0.376 mm.) The 10/12 setting (i.e. 10-point characters on a 12-point body, giving a 2-point space between the lines), formerly widely used, is now often replaced by 9/11 or 9/10. Subsidiary matter such as acknowledgements, footnotes, appendixes and references can be reduced to 8/10. To save space, some journals reduce the type size for references to 6/8; this is the lowest permissible limit, even for material that is not read continuously but only referred to. Computer typesetting can provide many gradations in point size, giving 9.2 on 10.5 and so on. This flexibility is useful if there are short or long pages.

In spite of the general need to save space, wide inner margins, i.e. those forming the 'gutter' of a double-page spread, should be specified so that the reader can make satisfactory photocopies from the bound book or journal volume. Publishers may resist this (because they wish to discourage photocopying); so may designers (because they will say that the double-page spread falls apart visually); and so may printers (who will think it is untraditional). They should all be overruled: photocopying of single items for individual users is legitimate and desirable for the progress of science, and this is what counts.

A well-designed book or journal has a unified appearance throughout, with all the chapters or articles styled in the same way, and with the cover, prelims and indexes fitting in with that style. If, for example, all chapter or article titles, legends, headings and sub-headings in the text are printed flush with the left-hand margin (which saves typing and typesetting time and is therefore more economical than having them all centred), the jacket or cover looks best if it matches this style. The tables and illustrations should then in theory also be set to the left instead of being centred, although to many eyes this looks peculiar. In this style, if there are more than three levels of subheading—which should not often be necessary—a variety of type sizes and typefaces will be called for if the reader is to understand the structure immediately. The flush-left style then presents its own impediments to the achievement of a unified appearance. One solution is to centre all main headings as well as all tables and illustrations but otherwise keep to the flush-left style, making sure that third-order headings are clearly subordinated to second-order headings. The important principle is that aesthetic considerations, important though they are, must be secondary to the reader's rapid grasp of structure.

Layout is in the printer's domain (and see the section on Paste-up in this chapter), but some printers are over-fond of the notion that each page or double-page spread should look balanced, with (for example) two illustrations always placed at diagonally opposite corners of a page or spread. This idea should be forgotten: illustrations must be printed as close to the relevant text as possible, and if the balanced look conflicts with this principle it will have to be abandoned—it is not a work of art that is being created but a carrier for a piece of scientific information.

Manuscripts with a high ratio of illustrations to text present other layout problems. Editors can help to minimize these problems by asking authors to supply clear and simple illustrations that can be reduced as far as is consistent with legibility; or pairs or triplets of illustrations can be combined; or photographs can be cropped so that only the strictly relevant parts are shown—at full magnification but taking up only as much room as is strictly necessary.

PRINTER'S SPECIFICATION, STYLE SHEETS AND COPY-MARKING

The designer and the printer's typographer will be concerned not only with over-all design but also with the detailed printing specification. This should be agreed between the editor, copy editor and publisher or printer at an early stage. A well-thought-out specification is a powerful timesaver for the editorial office. It may take weeks or months to get it right but the effort is worth it. The editor (or publisher) should be guided, but not bullied, by the printer in discussions of the specification. The printer knows what is routine in the printing plant, what is easily arranged, and what will lead to difficulties and mistakes. On the other hand, if the publication has special requirements that the printer cannot meet, another printer will have to be found.

The specification will include some or all of the following:

(a) size of page and size, quality and weight of paper
(b) type of binding
(c) approximate number of pages in the book or in each issue of a journal
(d) type founts for all parts of the publication, including prelims, indexes, running heads, headings, references, legends, tables and footnotes (if any) for the text
(e) type size and body for the different parts
(f) type area or imposition size; that is, the length of the lines and the number of lines on each page—or, put the other way round, the size of margins
(g) style or arrangements of legends, table titles and column headings

(h) use of horizontal lines and their relative weights in tables, and use of vertical lines, if allowed (these should be used rarely, if at all: they are expensive to set)

(i) symbols for linking footnotes to tables (superscript letters, superscript numbers, or other symbols, such as *, †, ‡, §, ||, ¶)

(j) typeface, size and placement of acknowledgements

(k) style for reference lists

(l) method of identifying mathematical symbols or Cyrillic or Greek letters in the margins of typescripts (either spelt out, e.g. 'Gk mu' or by means of a code referring to the type fount, e.g. 'Gk no. 34')

(m) spacing above and below illustrations and on the title page of chapters and articles

(n) placement of page numbers

(o) typeface, size and number of indexes

Once the specification has been agreed, specimen pages showing chapter openings, subheadings and so on are usually prepared and shown to the editor. When the details have been approved, a style sheet can be prepared for printer's copy-marker, showing what has to be done in marking up typescripts. The editor and printer (or publisher) also discuss whether typescripts will be fully copy-edited, partially copy-edited, or perhaps not copy-edited at all (Ref. 2, p 20; and see Chapter 6). It is important for both the editorial office and the printer to know how much marking should be done, and by whom: there is, for example, no point in copy editors marking every Greek mu in a paper full of measurements in micrometres. With a well-prepared style sheet which lists the relevant points from the specification, copy-marking becomes almost automatic; with modern typesetting methods it can even be partly computerized.

This brings us to the basic process of 'printing', which in fact consists of several processes, the two main ones being composition (typesetting or keyboarding), and the actual printing (presswork, machining) during which recognizable patterns appear on the paper. For information about these two processes I have relied heavily on Jennett,[3] Varley,[4] Dessauer[5] and Seybold.[6] Plate-making, which takes place between the main two processes, is not described here.

METHODS OF COMPOSITION

There are four main methods of composition:

(1) 'hot-metal' or 'hot-lead' composition on Linotype, Monotype or similar machines;

(2) handsetting, which is used as little as possible;

(3) typewriter ('strike-on') composition, including IBM Composer composition; and

(4) filmsetting and photocomposition, usually computer-assisted.

Typewriter composition and photocomposition are also known as 'cold composition'. Editors who want to mark and arrange typescripts intelligently, with the smallest probability of causing misunderstanding and costly mistakes, should visit their printers and see the processes in action.

Hot-metal composition

With Linotype composition whole lines of type are cast from a reservoir of molten metal after the compositor has keyboarded the copy. Monotype casters produce single characters from a similar hot-metal alloy. The keyboards on Linotype and Monotype composing machines look like large typewriter keyboards, except that on the Linotype machine the characters are arranged in a different order.

The Monotype compositor has seven alphabets, plus numbers and extra characters, to choose from. For book work (including journals) the alphabets might be upper- and lower-case roman, italics and bold face, and small capitals. The Monotype machine produces a punched paper tape which is used to drive a separate casting machine. Some Linotype machines are tape-driven too, but they have a built-in caster.

Compositors using either Monotype or Linotype machines must judge, when they get near the end of a line, how many more characters can be fitted in, since books and journals are conventionally justified (aligned) on the right as well as on the left. The compositor may decide that a word should be split at the end of a line, according to well-defined hyphenating rules, or that the spacing between words already on the line should be increased in order to extend the line to the full measure. On the Monotype machine a measuring device shows how much space is left and the compositor presses justifying keys which punch spacing instructions in the tape at the end of each line. Since the tape is fed into the casting machine backwards, from the end of the last line of the piece of copy being set, the spacing instructions reach the machine first and spaces of the correct width are set in each line.

The Monotype casting machine holds an exchangeable matrix case containing 255 characters in one type fount and size. The punched tape instructs the casting machine to centre the required character in the matrix case over a mould. Molten metal is pumped into the mould, the character is stamped out and the resulting piece of rectangular type is quickly cooled and ejected. The character on the piece of type is reversed left-to-right so that it comes out the right way round when printed on the page. The size, or body, of the rectangular piece of metal in relation to the size of the character determines the width between lines of text (e.g. a 9-point letter on an 11-point body).

As the type comes out of a Linotype machine or Monotype caster, the metal slugs (Linotype) or separate pieces of type (Monotype) slide into long metal trays called galleys. When enough galleys are full, the type is inked and proofs are 'pulled' for checking by the printer's reader, who marks obvious errors on these pages. Corrections are made almost immediately. With Monotype setting, incorrect letters can be picked out with a pair of tweezers; the correct letter is then substituted from a tray of ready-cast spares and the line re-justified. With Linotype machines, the whole slug has to be reset on the machine if a line contains a single mistake. With either Linotype or Monotype setting, a damaged or dirty matrix will produce a defective letter every time that matrix is used. This is why sections of proof are sometimes found in which almost every 't', for example, seems to be broken. The printer's proofreader usually sees this and replaces the 'broken' letters.

The speed of the Monotype caster is limited to about 11 000 characters an hour by the stop-start mechanism and the time the metal takes to cool. Another limitation is that a matrix case contains only one typeface in one size of type, so the matrix has to be replaced each time a different typeface or size is needed; alternatively, sections of the copy may be set separately on different machines. Linotype composition can be a little faster than Monotype and it was, for a long time, the machine used for setting newspapers. However, its slugs of type make it less flexible for book or journal work than Monotype and it has not been used so often for these purposes in Europe as it has in the USA.

Both Monotype and Linotype are labour-intensive—and they are both rapidly being superseded by cold composition. But where hot-metal composition is still available, it may for various reasons cost less than photocomposition, and some printers may be using it for many years to come. The vocabulary of printing is largely based on this method.

Handsetting

Handsetting may still be used for display work in which unusual type sizes are needed, for lettering that runs diagonally or vertically, and for complex tables, mathematical equations or chemical formulae. With this method ready-cast Monotype characters are inserted by hand between blanks (for spaces) in a pattern as close as possible to the author's or designer's requirements. The process is, of course, expensive. This is why editors should instruct authors to translate terms such as $\frac{a}{b}$, which usually has to be handset, into a/b, which can be set mechanically. Authors (or editors) should also transform exponential functions with superscripts and super-superscripts into logarithmic functions, and simplify the construction of tables as much as possible—for example so that column headings can be set straight, not sideways, and so that vertical lines are not necessary.

Typewriter, or 'strike-on' composition

The cost of conventional printing can be cut drastically if perfectly typed material is provided which is suitable either for photographing and printing by offset lithography or for feeding though a scanner which produces a drive tape for a photocomposer (see next section). Typescripts ready to be photographed ('camera-ready copy') may be supplied by the author or prepared by the editorial office, the publisher's staff, specialist outside firms or the printing firm itself. (Printing unions often object to the first three of these, and editors thinking of changing to this system should enquire first about the local attitude.) The copy must fit within stated limits and special typing paper with limiting rectangles and lines printed in blue is sometimes provided by publishers or required by printers who use this method. The luxury of justified typing is usually abandoned in favour of the more economical (and possibly more legible) ragged right-hand edge. Although justifying typewriters exist, most people consider that the slightly improved appearance does not warrant the expense.

Typewriter composition may be done on anything from an ordinary typewriter with a fresh ribbon, or an electric typewriter with a one-time carbon or plastic ribbon, to an IBM Composer or a word processor (see Chapter 13). The IBM and other typewriters that offer a choice of typefaces and sets of symbols on exchangeable 'golfball' heads can produce results which on the printed page compare well with the appearance obtained with hot-metal systems.

With typewriter setting, authors know exactly how the finished pages will look and can insert diagrams and figures just where they want them. They see their work in print quickly too, since the production process is fast and proofreading for typesetting errors is not necessary. The editor will, however, have to do some checking of proofs for other kinds of mechanical faults. Publishers may agree to publish material produced in this way even when they expect sales to be small, because their production costs are much lower than usual (although marketing costs are unchanged).

The disadvantages of the method are that typed characters take up more space than typeset characters, so that more pages are needed for the same amount of material, and that some readers (and authors) dislike the look of the product, although this prejudice is disappearing as typewriter setting becomes more widespread and techniques improve.

Filmsetting and computer-assisted photocomposition

Mechanical filmsetting led composition out of the age of hot metal towards the era of electronics. The Monophoto filmsetter, for example, is based on the Monotype caster but uses a case of photographic images instead of a metal matrix case. The filmsetter contains a lamp, lenses, prisms, mirrors and a drum of film and is driven by punched paper tape produced on a slightly modified Monotype keyboard. The punched tape causes the required characters to be projected in turn by the lamp through the system of lenses, prisms and angled mirrors onto the film. The mirrors move as each line is being set, reflecting the characters to their place on the film. At the end of each line the film moves on, ready for the next line. A major advance over hot-metal systems is that different sizes of 'type' can be produced from one matrix by adjusting the lenses and prisms. Mechanized filmsetters are still in use but they work at only about the same speed as the hot-metal caster—around 11 000 characters an hour.

Electromechanical photocomposing machines work 20 to 30 times faster than filmsetters, although they operate on a similar principle. Photo-matrix (transparent) characters are held on a spinning disc, a drum or a grid, and the machine operates with a light source and a system of lenses and mirrors or prisms. The light source, often a xenon flash, projects each character onto a photosensitive medium (film or paper) in response to instructions from a punched paper or magnetic tape, or direct from a keyboard operator. Many type sizes and founts are available on these machines, and changes from one size or fount to another can be made automatically.

Cathode-ray tube (CRT) photocomposers operate even faster than the 'second-generation' electromechanical machines, producing up to a million characters an hour. In CRT photocomposers, characters stored either on a photographic master or in digital form are generated on the CRT by an electron beam and then photographed. Photocomposers are highly flexible devices which can be instructed not only to change the type size and fount but to expand or condense letters horizontally, change them from roman to italic or bold, and compose complete pages, dealing with line-end hyphenation and justification and all the other problems of page make-up.

The paper or magnetic tapes, cassettes or floppy disks that drive second- and third-generation photocomposers are usually produced by computer-linked keyboards. Some keyboards produce a paper copy ('hard copy') as well as computer-input tape; others are linked to a video display which shows the operator what has just been keyed, and the tape can be corrected immediately, if necessary; a third kind of keyboard produces only tape or disks, though many machines of this kind now display the last 16 or 32 characters keyed by the operator. The keyboarding step may be eliminated if the original manuscript was typed, with or without coded printed instructions, in an optical character recognition (OCR)-readable typeface. Perry, Courier-12, OCR-A and OCR-B typefaces can be 'read' by a scanning machine such as the Compusan Alpha. Scanners produce paper or magnetic tape for driving a photocomposer or they may be linked directly to a photocomposer.

Direct-entry photocomposers are now available which are technologically somewhere between the first- and second-generation machines and are much cheaper than the more advanced photocomposers. They have small memories and set one line at a time. They produce good quality work and are easy to use—as the name implies, the copy is entered directly from a typewriter-like keyboard that has extra typesetting commands to control founts held on film or on a glass disk.[7]

With all kinds of photocomposition, the images captured on film or photosensitive paper are transferred to metal, plastic or rubber plates for the printing process described in the next section. Once the film has been made corrections are often expensive, as pieces of corrected film may have to be stripped in carefully by hand. Authors should therefore be encouraged more strongly than ever to avoid making trivial changes in proof.

The main advantages of photocomposition over other methods are speed, flexibility of type size and form, and the degree of automation which can be achieved with the help of computers. Not all photocomposers now in use are linked to computers, but future developments will undoubtedly depend on such links.

In spite of the great speeding-up of this part of book or journal production, photocomposed text is at present still being printed by the mainly mechanical processes described next.

PRESSWORK

The three printing processes in widest use until now have been letter-press, offset lithography and photogravure. Printing is done either direct from metal type (letterpress) or from plates (all three methods). Only letterpress and lithography are mentioned here, as photogravure is rarely used for scientific books or journals.

Letterpress, used mainly in conjunction with hot-metal composition, is the long-established method in which sheets of paper are pressed directly against the inked surface of type held on a flatbed press, or in which sheets or rolls (webs) of paper are pressed against inked plates. The printing plates are moulded from the metal type and they may be flat or curved, and made of metal, plastic or rubber. Curved plates are made for rotary presses, which work much faster than flatbed presses. 'Perfecter' presses are rotary presses which print both sides of the paper in one pass through the machine. Another development is the Belt Press, in which the printing plates for one or more books fit on a continuous belt, which prints in sequence on a web of paper. The machine also slits, folds and collates the pages ready for binding, and may bind them too, which greatly speeds up the production processes.

In *offset lithography* the film produced by the composition process is photographically reproduced on printing plates. Each plate is wrapped round a cylinder on the printing press and then moistened and inked. A chemical process allows image areas to accept ink but not water, while the non-image areas accept water but not ink. When the cylinder rotates, the image is transferred—that is, offset—onto a rubber blanket on another cylinder, and from that blanket onto the paper.

The only difference in quality between good offset printing and letterpress is that letterpress may give a slightly sharper effect. Illustrations (see the section on Artwork below) are easier and cheaper to print by lithography, and cheaper paper can often be used than for letterpress. Offset lithography is therefore likely to be the method of choice until new methods are discovered and developed.

ARTWORK

For printing by letterpress, line drawings are first photographed and then transferred to a plate from which the non-printing areas are etched or hand-tooled away, leaving a raised surface to be inked.

For offset plates the image is transferred to the plate surface photographically, as for the text.

For half-tone illustrations, the original prints are photographed through a screen of two sets of fine lines crossing each other at right angles, each set being regularly spaced at (usually) 100, 133, 150 or even 200 lines to the inch. The finer the detail required, the more lines to the inch are needed, i.e. the finer the screen. For a photograph of a piece of equipment, the printer might use a 100-mesh screen; for a light micrograph, 150-mesh with offset printing; and for an electron micrograph, possibly 200-mesh will be used. The finer the screen, the more care has to be used to prevent the ink from smudging, and the better the quality of paper needed. In letterpress printing, 200-mesh is about the finest screen that can satisfactorily be used, even on coated paper and with careful engraving; when screens finer than 200-mesh are used there is a loss of contrast. With offset lithography, screens of 133 or 150 lines to the inch are quite common.

The principle of the half-tone process is that light reflected from the photograph through each square in the mesh impinges on the photosensitive plate, and the greater the degree of blackness in the original print, the smaller the area within that minute square that is affected. A white area on the original print will produce a series of discrete exposed ('black') squares on the plate. For letterpress printing the plate is then dipped in an etching fluid which dissolves away the 'black' areas, leaving the unexposed areas—corresponding to black in the original—raised above the exposed ones. When the plate is inked these areas will print black. Grey areas in the original give rise to exposed squares of varying size according to the depth of grey. The purpose of these hundreds of tiny squares is to break the picture into dots, with areas of white between the inked areas. The printed picture then looks as if it had various shades of grey.

In letterpress printing the half-tone process, with its metal plates mounted on wooden or metal blocks, is expensive and authors are usually asked to keep the number of illustrations to a minimum. The original photographs must be of the best possible quality, since some quality is lost in even the best reproductions. If the high quality paper needed for 200-mesh reproductions is too expensive for a journal, the editor should warn authors and settle for medium quality semi-gloss paper and 100-mesh screens.

To reduce costs without sacrificing the scientific evidence, the editor may select portions of photographs supplied by the author and reproduce them at full magnification rather than reduce whole photographs. Authors' photographs should never be cut; instead they should be cropped or masked. That is, the margins of the photograph are marked to show which part is to be reproduced; or a rectangle of the appropriate size is marked on an overlay fixed to one edge of the print.

In letterpress printing the process known as 'routing out' can be used to remove any small blemishes from a plate, and this is cheaper than having a new photo-engraving made. Nothing can be added to, or altered in, the engraving at this stage, which explains why photographs must be sent to the printer in the best possible condition, having been well protected throughout the editorial process. Paperclips must never be used on photographs and only the softest pencil should be used to identify them on the back. A completely flat surface, to be pressed against the screen, is essential, though slight bending or rolling is not harmful. Several small photographs may be mounted together on white card if this is carefully done (Ref. 8, p 36–37) but, in general, authors should be asked not to mount individual photographs: some glues produce a bumpy surface; and if each photograph is mounted, mailing costs soar. A piece of thin cardboard on either side of each set of photographs protects them adequately during mailing and the editorial processes.

The editor, or printer, may choose to reduce costs by grouping several photographs together to make a large plate, which is later cut up as necessary. It is not a good idea to combine photographs and line drawings if an engraving is being made, first because it is twice as expensive as an ordinary block, and secondly because the screen needed for the half-tones will make the line drawing look grey.

Most illustrations are reduced in size during printing. The editor may have to decide which illustrations can be reduced to one-column width and which should run right across the page or occupy a full page, turned sideways if necessary. The larger the page size, the greater the choice in this regard. The degree of reduction can be stated simply as 'Reduce width to 50 mm', or expressed as a percentage: (desired width of the illustration) divided by (actual width of the original) × 100 %.

Colour

Colour reproduction costs too much for most scientific journals and books. If colour is wanted, the editor will either have to persuade the publisher that colour is essential for scientific or commercial reasons or ask the author to cover the extra costs—which are amazingly high.

The principles of 'process' colour printing are the same as for black and white, except that four different plates are usually made for each photograph. Three plates are made by photographing the original through coloured filters (red, blue and green, for printing in blue, yellow and red respectively); the fourth plate is made for printing in black, to give richer shading and contrast. The final reproduction is made by printing from each of the four plates in turn. The skill and expense lie in getting the four plates exactly aligned, or 'in register'.

Two-colour printing (for line drawings, diagrams, etc.) is less expensive than four-colour process printing. It can be done by prior separation of the colours, that is by getting an artist to prepare two separate versions of the picture, each showing where one of the colours is to go.

An inexpensive alternative to two-colour printing for book jackets or journal covers is the use of screens of different mesh sizes to produce shades of colour with a single ink.

GALLEYS OR FIRST PROOFS

Strictly speaking, galley proofs are produced only in letterpress printing, where metal type is collected in long trays (galleys) as described earlier. But the term is widely used for the first set of proofs, which usually go to authors as well as to the editor for correction. The first proofs may be 'page on galley', already measured into numbered or unnumbered pages on the long galley sheets, or they may be actual page proofs, which are easier to handle than galleys. Proof correction is described in the next chapter.

PASTE-UP AND FINAL PROOF

The paste-up process varies with each printer's practice. In the most orderly, and leisurely, procedure it goes as follows for hot-metal composition. Galley proofs are pulled by hand from the type standing in galleys. When corrected galley proofs are received, corrections are made in the type accordingly. Another proof is made, and this is cut up and pasted onto pages ruled to the size of the book or journal. Illustrations are placed appropriately, and the paste-up artist deals with problems like headings that land at the very bottom of a page, or single-word lines ('widows') that land at the top of one. The paste-up person does this usually by instructing the printer to adjust the amount of space between lines or around headings, sometimes by directing that the type on several lines should be squeezed closer together or that a tightly-set line should be opened up to make an extra line. This sort of planning may have to take several pages into consideration.

When the paste-up is satisfactory the type is moved from the galleys and arranged, together with the blocks for the illustrations, in page 'formes' (metal frames) in accordance with the paste-up. Page numbers and running heads are added before the formes are locked up ready for carrying to the press. These formes hold 16, 32 or other multiples of four pages, and the pages are so arranged that they will come out in the right order (and the right way up) when the printed press sheet is eventually folded into 'signatures' (a portion of a publication containing however many pages are printed on each sheet).

To speed up publication, the total process has been streamlined by modern printers. Paste-up may be done while the authors are correcting proofs. Then, when authors' corrections result in an increase or decrease in the number of lines of text, the paste-up has to be adjusted before the type is placed in formes. Some printers do not only the paste-up but also the page make-up before sending out the first proofs. For either of these procedures it is evidently highly disruptive if the author makes changes in proof which alter the number of lines, or the number or sequence of illustrations, and this is why such changes are so strongly discouraged. Sometimes the editor or other proofreader can make a judicious further change that shortens or lengthens a sentence slightly and brings it back to its original length without changing its meaning (see p 103).

Direct photography of typescript and photocomposition are easier for the printer to work with than hot metal, as there is no heavy type to be moved around in the late stages, with the attendant risks of small pieces of type being lost or getting out of alignment. On the other hand, adjustment of vertical or horizontal spacing by cutting and stripping in small pieces of film is difficult to do well. Re-setting a whole page by computer may be done in a moment, but it can be an expensive moment. Alterations in any system are troublesome; that is why it is important first to find a printer who makes few typesetting errors and then to provide well-prepared, thoroughly edited copy.

Final page proofs usually go to the editor only, unless an author insists on receiving a set too. Corrections (see Chapter 9) must be kept to the absolute minimum at this stage. When final adjustments—for example inserting page numbers in the contents list or index—have been made, the book or journal is ready for printing by one of the methods already described.

PAPER

The editor should ask the printer's or publisher's advice before specifying a particular quality of paper for a book or journal (see section on printer's specification, p 86). Printers can work more economically with some papers than others, depending on the machines they use and other factors. Economy usually has to be balanced against the quality desired. For textual material, near-opaqueness, lightness of weight and a matt surface giving good contrast without glare are the desirable properties. If the book or journal has many illustrations calling for first-rate reproduction (e.g. electron micrographs), a glossy paper may have to be used throughout. Where there are only a few photographs in one or two places, the heavier paper can be inserted in four-page sections but this makes printing and binding much more expensive than usual. Articles with electron micrographs, or the electron micrographs alone, are sometimes grouped on glossy paper at the end of a journal so that cheaper paper can be used for the rest of the issue. Another method is to have single sheets of glossy paper 'tipped in' or 'hooked in'—glued to the following page—or 'wrapped round'—wrapped round the first and last page of a section. With all these methods machinery has to be stopped for manual processes, at exorbitant expense, so that if superb reproduction is essential it is sometimes cheaper to use glossy paper throughout. Because of the manual work involved, fold-out pages are expensive too.

Paper may be either 'free sheet' (wood free) or groundwork stock. 'Free' means that the wood pulp has been chemically treated to remove the impurities and reduce the acidity of ground wood. Wood-free paper is the kind mainly used for scientific books and journals, though coated groundwood stocks with a reasonably long life are now available.

The weight of a paper is quoted in grams per square metre (g/m^2, sometimes written as 'gsm') or as pounds per ream (500 sheets). Papers weighing 75–100 g/m^2 are commonly used for books and journals. Papers of the same weight may differ in bulk (measured in pages per centimetre or inch), depending on how much air has been whipped into the pulp during milling, on how much fibre content there is, and on the method of milling. Except in North America (for the present), paper is usually supplied in 'A' sizes or the book sizes (Demy, Royal, Crown) and a press sheet may hold 16, 24, 32, 48, 64 or more printed pages, depending on the size of the press and the size of the book being printed.

The opacity and finish of a paper are important. It is distracting to read a page if the text from the next page shows through clearly. Substances such as titanium oxide are added to increase opacity. The 'finish' refers to the final treatment in the manufacturing process, when a paper may be coated with china clay, to give it a glossy appearance, or 'supercalendered'—pressed between metal rollers to make it very smooth. 'Machine-finished' papers are the kind most commonly used when a glossy finish is not needed.

The colour of the paper ('white' is not a precise term), and whether it has a high or a low glare, are other important qualities to take into consideration. Some coated papers now have a low glare, which makes for easier reading.

BINDING

Binding may be done either in the printing plant or in a separate bindery. Journals and paperback books are usually bound in the printing plant, and binding may follow printing without any interruption. The processes involved are folding, gathering, sewing and/or glueing, trimming and attaching a cover. A book may be given a dustjacket, and books and journals may also be protectively wrapped for mailing, all in one series of mechanized processes.

The printed sheets that come off the press are folded into signatures, each signature representing one press sheet. The uncut signatures are gathered or collated to make up complete books or journal issues, and they are then saddle-wired (stapled at the back, for publications of up to 64 pages), side-wired (stronger than saddle-wiring and taking more pages), sewn (with the pages in each signature sewn together and sewn to the next signature), or glued direct to the spine without any stitching (so-called 'perfect' binding). Perfect binding is probably the most widely used method for binding both journals and paperback books.

For books that are to have hard covers, 'endpapers' are attached at the beginning and end before the paper is trimmed, and the backs (spines) are then rounded. Reinforced gauze ('crash') and 'headbands' and 'footbands' are attached to the spines and these are glued to accept the covers ('cases'). Cases usually consist of 'boards' of various materials to which cloth, plastic or certain kinds of treated papers have been glued. Covers are usually prepared in advance, with wording and design as agreed in the specification. The title and other lettering are stamped on the front cover or spine, or both, with ink or through coloured foil. The books are then either pressed between heavy boards until the glue has dried and the characteristic crease along the spine has taken shape, or they are seasoned to this stage in a few seconds in 'building-in' machines. Dustjackets, if used, go on last of all.

Finally, binding practices for journal volumes should be mentioned. In the USA, UK and some other countries—though not in Scandinavia, it seems—binders customarily remove advertisements and other 'extraneous matter', as well as covers and contents pages, from journal issues before volumes are bound. Where pages are removed in this way the editor should arrange to have at least one copy of each volume bound exactly as the issues were published, complete with covers, and stored in the editorial office. Queries of various kinds, including legal problems, may arise in later years and a reference copy is essential.

OFFPRINTS AND REPRINTS

Selling copies of articles to produce income for a journal is considered in Chapter 11. Here I need only mention the methods the printer uses to produce extra copies of chapters or journal articles. Authors are often given 25, 50, or sometimes more, free copies of their chapters in a book, and sometimes of articles in journals, in partial recompense for writing the chapter or article. They can usually order further copies at a price slightly higher than the cost of producing them. The printer makes the extra copies either by printing more sheets than are needed for the print run of the book or journal issue, or by reprinting copies by photo-offset from the finished book or journal issue in accordance with the numbers of copies ordered. The offprint or run-on method provides authors with their copies as soon as, if not before, the book or journal is published (which authors like); however, orders can be accepted only until the time that the relevant signatures go on the press. The second, or reprint, method is more flexible in that reprints can be made at any time, however late the order is received; and no paper is wasted since only the required pages (and not unwanted ones in the same signature) are printed.

The relative costs of the two methods depend on many factors, including the variability in size of reprint orders for different articles, the size of the printing plant, and the way it is organized. The editor's main object when negotiating reprint or offprint arrangements with the printer should be to ensure that the copies, especially of journal articles, are reliably available within a few weeks of publication.

9 Reading proofs

FIRST PROOFS

The first-proof stage can be shortened if the editor arranges for authors' proofs to be sent not to the editorial office but direct from the printer to the principal author of each chapter or article, together with the edited manuscript itself or a photocopy of it. The editor should supply a letter or form for the printer to enclose with the proofs. This letter or form asks authors to send corrected proofs to the editor within a specified period and should include the reminder that corrections are expensive and must be kept to a minimum. The letter should be short but should emphasize the importance of prompt action on the proofs and point out that reprint orders requiring official approval or payment can be forwarded later; these orders should not be a cause of, or an excuse for, delay in sending corrected proofs to the editorial office.

The printer usually keeps two sets of proofs and sends two sets to the editor, one of which—the master set—carries the marks made by the printer's proofreader. The date of receipt of proofs is recorded in the editorial office. Depending on the demands of the schedule agreed with the publisher or printer, the editor may then either wait for corrected proofs to arrive from the authors or, to avoid delay, arrange for the master set to be checked immediately against the edited manuscripts or photocopies of them.

For books or for small journals the best proofreaders are likely to be the copy editors. Apart from the extra satisfaction they get from seeing papers through the final stages of publication, they probably pick up more errors and inconsistencies than a new reader would. Even if a specialist proofreader is employed for cross-checking manuscripts and proofs, the copy editor should read the proofs for sense and general errors. But in large organizations where several copy editors handle manuscripts, it may be impracticable or uneconomic for each proof to be read by the copy editor who handled the manuscript.

Ideally, two people are needed for proofreading: one to read aloud from the edited manuscript and the second to mark corrections on the proof, using the marks discussed later in this chapter. This kind of proofreading is a luxury for any journal with a small staff and a tight budget, but for an authoritative monograph it is important to find the time and staff to do it. An alternative is to have the edited manuscript read aloud into a tape recorder. The tape or cassette can be played back whenever the proof-marker wants, which does away with the difficulty of finding a reader who is free at the right time.[1]

The more common procedure of silent proofreading is best done in two stages: a complete reading first for sense and general errors, followed by a detailed check, possibly by a specialist proofreader, against the manuscript; or the other way round. In some disciplines a separate check of certain items, e.g. references, names of species, or chemical or mathematical formulae or equations, may be needed at this stage as well as during copy-editing.

Checking the proof against the manuscript calls for care, patience and good eyesight—it is easy to overlook the omission of small but important words such as 'not', or the omission of whole lines of typescript when a word or phrase is repeated in two successive lines. The lone proofreader looks from the typescript to the printed sentences and back, and checks the printed version character by character, holding a ruler or some other guide under the typescript line with one hand while moving a pen along under the characters in the proof with the other. Particular attention has to be paid to titles, by-lines, other preliminary matter for articles or chapters (and front matter for the whole book or journal issue), as well as to abstracts, running heads, page numbers (in paged proofs), footnotes (if any), appendixes, tables, legends and references. Authors tend to take these parts of their papers for granted and forget to examine them critically.

The proofreader has to bear in mind the style specifications for the particular book or journal and watch for inconsistencies in the placement of headings and the arrangement of tables. The styling of references in journals or book series is also important. Correcting minor errors such as the omission of a comma or full stop in references may seem fussy, but it is good for both the printer and for future authors if the editor/proofreader always demands a high standard of consistency even at this level. The printer is likely to make fewer mistakes in the long run, since the correction of printer's errors costs the printer money; and conscientious authors of new articles who use published reference lists as a guide will not perpetuate earlier errors. Against this must be weighed the possibility that any correction may produce another and possibly more serious error.

Changes are always expensive, not simply in charges made by the printer but also in time spent by the editor or other proofreader in checking the revised proof to see whether changes have been made correctly, without the introduction of new errors. Proofreaders can help to reduce the cost of resetting after correction by substituting (preferably with the author's approval) words or phrases with the same number of characters as the original version. Again, if a change has to be made early in a paragraph, the next line or two can sometimes be modified in such a way that there is no need to reset the whole paragraph (though with computer-controlled photocomposition this may be much less important than with hot metal). Naturally, these cost-cutting devices must not be used if they conflict with scientific sense or the normal rules of grammar.

Many printers ask for printer's errors to be distinguished from the author's or editor's changes of mind. The editorial proofreader makes the distinction by using red ink for printer's errors and blue or black for the author's and editor's changes. The recommended colour for corrections made by the printer is green (BS 5261: Part 2[2]). Charges can then be correctly assigned either to the publisher or to the author. Usually 5 or 10 % of the total cost of alterations is allowed without charge; after that the publisher or author may have to pay for corrections, according to the agreements drawn up.

With typesetting in hot metal, some lines may look very uneven in the first proof, as type has not been locked into formes at this stage. The waviness should disappear when the type is finally locked in before printing, but the sections may nevertheless be marked for the printer's attention. Letters that look faulty or faint may also be marked, even if a second set of hand-pulled proofs shows them to be apparently in order. It is wiser to have a possible fault checked than to let it go through to final publication unchallenged.

With photocomposition, minor corrections are sometimes even more expensive than with hot-metal composition, though this depends on which particular system the printer uses. Proofs of photocomposed material are usually photocopies of a single master and are not as good as proofs pulled from metal type. Photocopied proofs are corrected in the normal way—that is, with marks in the margins as well as in the text, as discussed later in this chapter. If the 'proof' provided is typescript with an overlay, corrections are made on the overlay above the appropriate pieces of text.

If authors are late in returning their proofs, book editors may write, cable or telephone in an effort to get corrected proofs back in time to meet the printing schedule. Journal editors usually have such tight schedules that they either proceed to publication without waiting for an author's corrections or hold the paper over until the next issue.

Some editors have experimented with eliminating the time-consuming stage of authors' proofs by sending the authors photocopies of fully edited and copy-marked manuscripts for comment and correction either before the manuscripts go to the printer, or while typesetting is already under way. The authors are told that they will see no proofs at all and must insert any corrections on the photocopy. The burden of proofreading then lies wholly on the editorial office and the printer, but with correction costs rising ever higher this system seems eminently sensible. Authors (and editors) may have to adapt more and more to making changes before composition instead of afterwards, whether for this method of typescript 'proofing' or when camera-ready copy is used.

Authors' alterations may have to be translated into standard proofing marks (see below) before being transferred to the master set of proofs. The editor or copy editor also has to decide whether all the alterations are allowable. Authors are rarely fully familiar with a journal's style for abbreviations, references and so on, and they may be unaware of the most recent rules of specialist nomenclature. Some of their other changes may seem whimsical or inessential. Where these changes may nevertheless be important, the editor usually accepts them on the first proof and sorts out any doubtful points with the authors while revised proofs are being prepared.

Authors often complain about the quality of proofs of half-tone illustrations, even when the printer has noted on the proof that they have been printed on paper of poorer quality than will eventually be used. On the other hand, if the paper used for proofs is too good, the complaints arrive after publication. It is really best if the printer can be persuaded to use paper similar to, if not the same as, the paper that will be used in the actual publication. The editor has to look after the author's interests in this regard and make sure that every half-tone will be reproduced to a satisfactory standard in the printed book or journal.

Before the master set of first proofs goes back to the printer, all the corrections should be copied onto a second set, which is kept for reference in the editorial office together with the original edited manuscript, which usually need not be sent to the printer again.

PROOFING MARKS

Signs for proof correction have not yet been standardized internationally, although printers in most countries recognize most kinds of correction marks. There is, however, universal agreement that every change has to be marked twice on the proof: once in the text where the change is needed, and once in the margin, where the instruction for change is given. In the USA, marginal instructions are given with the least possible punctuation; if an 'a' is to be substituted for an 'e' in the text, the marginal instruction is simply a (and the text e is struck through diagonally). In the British system the marginal instruction is a/, the diagonal stroke indicating that the end of the correction has been reached. Other corrections further along in the same line of text can be added immediately afterwards, since they are separated from the first correction by the diagonal line. In both these systems the marginal instruction is written as near as possible to the piece of text that is to be corrected. In the system used in continental Europe, text errors are marked with signs bearing flags or rings at the top or bottom of the diagonal strokes; this unequivocally connects the text mark with the marginal instruction, which begins with the same symbol, and the proof-marker is therefore free to write marginal instructions anywhere on the same page of proof if there is no space close to the error.

Any long passages that have to be inserted or substituted may be typed and taped, not stapled, to the top or (less desirable) to the bottom of the proof, *never* sideways up the margin. Inserts are linked by arrows or, in the new British system,[2] by an identifying letter inside a diamond, to their position in the text.

Sets of proof-correction marks are to be found in large dictionaries, style manuals, and the British[2] and American[3] Standards. The examples in large dictionaries and style manuals often do not give enough detailed guidance; the British and American Standards are much more useful in that they give textual *and* marginal marks, together with examples and notes. The recent British Standard[2] has succeeded in eliminating English (and indeed all languages) from the proofing marks, and the way is now open for an internationally accepted system. Authors should be asked to mark changes in proof in straightforward language rather than attempt to use marks with which they are not really familiar (Ref. 4, p 78–79). The editor or copy editor can then mark the master proof unambiguously for the printer.

FINAL (PAGE) PROOFS

When final proofs arrive, the editor or other proofreader first makes sure that all the changes marked on the master copy of the first proof have been made correctly. Where even a single-letter change has been made the whole line is checked, as well as the lines above and below it, as these may have been displaced or disturbed by the change. The proof is marked according to the changes needed, with 'see first proof' being added if an earlier instruction for change seems to have been ignored.

If illustrations were proofed separately for the first proof, their position in relation to the point where they are referred to in the text is checked at this stage. But even if the reader will have to turn over a couple of pages before finding an illustration, the proofreader should think carefully before suggesting that the illustration be moved closer to where it is mentioned: the problems the paste-up artist at the printers had to contend with may become evident after the alternatives have been considered. The editor should measure up the possibilities before insisting on a different layout (see Chapter 8).

All the 'corners' of the text, i.e. the first and last letters on the first and last lines of each page, are checked, as are any passages interrupted by a table or illustration. With hot-metal composition, when type is moved during make-up or correction, a slug or piece of type may slip out of alignment or fall out and be replaced either upside down or not at all. Wherever there are breaks in the text (from page to page or on either side of illustrations), there is a danger that whole lines may be omitted, and the proofreader must check for this.

Illustrations must, of course, be the right way up and legends must correspond to the illustrations under which they are placed. To check this, the proofreader may have to consult the edited manuscript that was kept in the editorial office when first proofs were returned to the printer. Although this procedure seems troublesome, it is well worth while even if only one glaring error is caught per year or volume. At this stage the quality and alignment of the illustrations are checked too.

Next comes an examination of the accuracy and placement of running heads, running footlines (if any), and page numbers. This examination is best done as a separate task from checking the text and illustrations, as mistakes are otherwise easily overlooked. For journal issues after the first in a volume, page numbers must also be checked to see that they run on correctly from the previous issue.

Page numbers for the Contents list are inserted directly from the first pages of articles or chapters. Cross-referencing page numbers —which editors should try to keep to the minimum needed by readers—also have to be inserted in the text whenever they occur. The printer usually brings cross-references to the proofreader's attention by inserting conspicuous black squares or—less strikingly—by inserting zeros.

For a book, if first proofs are paged proofs from which the index can be prepared, the index is printed with, and checked against, the second proofs. Otherwise, the index(es) should arrive from the indexer, or be compiled by the editor (see Chapter 7), before second proofs are returned to the printer. In either case the editor notes any changes in pagination necessitated by shifts of text and corrects the page numbers in the index accordingly. The author index is checked completely from the opening pages of chapters. Ideally, the subject index should also be thoroughly checked, but a spot-check every tenth entry or so that reveals no errors in the first hundred or two hundred entries probably indicates that the subject index is reliable throughout. For a journal, the index of Corrections (see Chapter 7), whether printed as part of the subject index or separately, should be checked particularly carefully.

The accuracy and layout of the front matter of a book should also be checked with particular care, since readers gain their first impressions of a book from these pages. The cover material of a journal, and especially the Guidelines for Authors, must be checked too. Lastly, if there is time, the proofreader may read the whole corrected set of page proofs through for general sense and correctness before returning the proofs to the printer.

Throughout the reading of second proofs the editor/proofreader has to remember that changes in them are far more costly than in first proof, and that alterations must therefore be kept to the minimum consistent with high scientific standards.

Proofreading, the last step before publication, is also the last of the editorial processes common to books and journals. The next chapter, which deals specifically with conference proceedings, is followed by two chapters on two different aspects of editing journals.

10 Editing conference proceedings: a closer look

Conferences have a special part to play in the transfer of scientific information. The organization of conferences and ways of selecting speakers for them have been described elsewhere.[1-7] Organizers and editors new to the work may also benefit from the advice of their predecessors on the organizing committees of conference series. This chapter deals with the questions: which conferences are worth publishing and how should they be published and edited?

The publication of conference proceedings is criticized on many grounds. The commonest objections are that 'routine publication . . . clutters up the literature and overburdens library budgets', that published proceedings 'are not profitable to scientific endeavour', and that by the time they are published, many of the papers have already been 'printed with essentially identical data in academic journals as proper publications. Those that have not may have been disapproved by reviewers and editors. The symposia proceedings are not subject to review and there is no distinction between invited and proffered papers'.[8] Other objections are that proceedings volumes often sink into obscurity, are carelessly edited, and are published far too long after the conferences they record.

Decisions about whether to publish conferences are influenced by pressures on and from the many conference-goers who are apparently obliged to present papers to earn their travel grants, by the overt or covert aims of organizers and sponsors, and by the opportunism of certain publishers who view conference-goers and libraries as captive markets. The first kind of pressure often results in many mediocre papers being offered at conferences. To counteract this, in their circulars and invitations the organizers should point out to intending participants and to grant-giving bodies that all kinds of communication at the meeting—contributions to discussion as well as formal papers—are important in their own right.[9] The other two kinds of influence—the ambitions of organizers and of publishers—tend to encourage the publication of mediocre volumes of proceedings. Obviously, some conferences can be transformed into admirable books, and many publishers serve science excellently (and with little profit) when they produce these books. Equally obviously, other proceedings should never have reached the printing presses, and there are publishers who are seduced by guaranteed sales rather than the prospect of a worthwhile product. But while good sales figures are a legitimate goal for publishers, the organizers, sponsors and potential editors must remember their wider responsibilities to science when they assess whether proceedings are worth publishing. It is not a good idea for editors to lend their names to publishing projects over which they may not have, or do not wish to take, full editorial control.

WHICH CONFERENCES SHOULD BE PUBLISHED?

Some clues about the content of conferences that succeed as books are provided by book reviewers. In a typical review the writer points out that although the material in the proceedings volume is available elsewhere, 'the juxtaposition of diverse, loosely connected topics is useful, particularly for someone trying to survey several fields of current interest quickly. I found the volume introduced me to interesting lines of work relevant to my own interests, and I suspect it will serve the same purpose for others. That, after all, is one of the things a good symposium should do.'[10]

Another reviewer praises the clarity of the discussion sections and then says: 'At many meetings such discussion is more valuable than the formal presentations, for it brings out the points which the speaker may have passed over but which other participants do not follow; much of the disparity of research results between different centres can be resolved during such an interchange.'[11] As this review implies, the most important contribution from many smaller meetings is indeed publication of the discussions (see p 115–118).

Organizers and editors can help to dispose of some of the objections to the publication of proceedings either by designing their conferences specifically for a well-defined readership or by considering carefully whether all or any of the work presented is worth publishing in collected form. If there is no editor on the organizing committee when (and if) publication is decided on, an experienced editor should be appointed as soon as possible after this decision is taken.

The criteria for publication of conference proceedings are, or should be, the same as for any other book, namely that the work described is original, authoritative, up to date and readable, and that a need exists for the information offered. Not surprisingly, it is no easier to decide whether a genuine need exists for conference proceedings than it is for any other kind of book. The pressures mentioned earlier (p 108) do nothing to smooth the decision-making path. One signpost may be found in the distinction between 'collegial' and 'positional' conferences.[12] Collegial conferences are those at which research findings are exchanged and their relation to other work is discussed. They are worth publishing if the subject and the size of the meeting are right. Even congresses with 1000 or more participants may be worth publishing in full when a field needs strengthening because it lacks funds or journals, or both. For large meetings of this kind, poor papers should be weeded out by a selection committee and/or refereed before publication. It is easier to convert medium-size conferences with 100–1000 participants into good books than it is to make successful books out of vast congresses, but in both cases there should be some selection and plenty of guidance for contributors on what is expected of them.

The small specialist symposium of up to 100 people is perhaps the most promising source of a worth-while book. At meetings of this size there is usually plenty of time for discussion and criticism of the work presented, and poor papers cannot easily slip into print unnoticed. Contributors' comments on each other's papers are in fact a good substitute for refereeing—though if there are no referees the speakers should be carefully selected.

On the other hand, small workshops held to resolve differences in methods or results between different research centres are probably unsuitable for full publication, especially as speakers at this type of meeting may not be keen to express their doubts freely or strongly if they are to be recorded in print. Similarly, positional conferences[12] at which people try to reach a consensus on a particular issue are not suitable candidates for full publication. The appropriate product of a positional conference, if a consensus is reached, is an announcement in a journal, not a blow-by-blow account of how that consensus was won.

WHAT KIND OF PAPERS SHOULD BE PUBLISHED?

As duplicate publication does so much to give conferences a bad name, editors of proceedings must guard against it even more carefully than journal editors do (see Chapter 5). Ideally, papers destined for a proceedings volume should either (a) report completely new work that has not been and will not be published elsewhere by the same author(s), or (b) be designed specifically as conference papers related to the themes of other speakers at the meeting and differing from journal articles that describe the same work. For the second kind of paper authors might, for example, be encouraged to include new hypotheses or preliminary findings and to speculate on the significance of their own or other people's results. The two kinds of paper correspond to two different categories of meeting. The first kind of paper is more suitable for the larger meetings at which people expect to hear the leaders in their fields describe new work. The second kind of paper is better for smaller meetings, especially meetings where discussions as well as papers will be published, and where the papers are intended to form a provocative basis for discussion.

The guidelines for authors (see Appendix 3) should tell contributors to both categories of meeting which kind of paper to prepare. Contributors should be assured that their contributions will be published quickly and distributed widely, and that the proceedings will be easy to retrieve—that is, the papers will be published either in a journal or in a book that is adequately listed in catalogues and by the secondary services.

WHAT FORM SHOULD PUBLICATION TAKE?

The organizers, sponsors and potential editor must first ask themselves seriously whether the subject of the meeting would be better dealt with in a multi-author monograph, where the structure, coverage and standards of presentation can be controlled much more closely than is possible for most conferences. If the answer is that it would, they should abandon the thought of publishing the proceedings, or should perhaps replan the meeting with publication in mind (which may make for a less successful meeting).

Another point to consider is that publication of proceedings as journal supplements or in regular issues of journals is often preferable to publication in book form: distribution is better, retrieval is simpler, production may be faster, and papers usually receive the refereeing that so many proceedings lack. Many proceedings are successfully published in journals, especially in well-defined fields where suitable journals exist and where editors are willing to donate enough space and then either hand over editorial control to the conference editors or undertake the work themselves. Alternatively the conference organizers may advise contributors to submit their papers in the usual way to one or two selected journals, in which case there will be no need for a conference editor.

For multidisciplinary conferences it may be difficult to find appropriate journals to take a collection of the papers. The large-circulation general journals rarely have space for more than a few papers from any one meeting, and other journals may be too specialized to reach the readership envisaged for the proceedings. If a multidisciplinary symposium is worth publishing, it is therefore probably best published in book form.

When conference proceedings are published together in a journal issue or supplement for which the organizers appoint their own editor, problems may arise when editorial policy for the proceedings differs from policy for the journal, for instance over the type of article required. The conference editor should discuss policy with the journal editor and resolve major differences before telling contributors what kind of papers to prepare. If contributors are asked to follow the journal's guidelines for authors, minor problems over presentation of the typescripts should not arise.

For most large congresses, abstracts or synopses may be the best and only type of publication needed. If these are circulated before the meeting participants can use them to select the speakers they want to hear or try to meet. The collection of abstracts remains useful to participants long after the meeting, especially if the speakers' addresses are included, as they ought to be. Participants should, however, be asked not to cite these abstracts as if they were published papers: abstracts are often difficult or impossible to obtain after the meeting, and presentation of a paper at a meeting does not constitute publication of the full paper.

WHO SHOULD THE PUBLISHER BE?

Some conferences are published privately by their organizing committees or sponsors. Unless these bodies already have a publishing programme and an editorial department, the editor of a one-off conference will have to find and deal directly with the printer. Editors faced with finding a printer should look at the work of several printing houses before asking one to produce detailed specifications (see Chapter 8). The organizing committee and the editor also need to agree on several questions to which the printer will want answers. How long is the volume (or volumes) likely to be? How many copies are to be printed (just enough for participants; or are other sales likely?)? Is the material highly technical (mathematical, chemical, etc.) or likely to be heavily illustrated? What date will the copy be ready for typesetting or printing? What kind of cover is wanted (hardback, paperback or flexible)? Are there any special binding requirements (e.g. ring or spiral binding)? Can the material be supplied in camera-ready form?

Camera-ready copy can be a good way of reducing costs and publication time but it is not always the best solution to production problems. If the conference secretariat (the editor's secretary?) has to retype all the papers this takes a lot of time and money; in extreme cases it can be more expensive than paying for professional composition, unless the cost is hidden in institutional overheads. On the other hand, if authors are expected to provide perfect typescripts, the editor is either unable to do any editing or has to persuade authors to have their papers retyped after editing and copy-editing are finished. The guidelines for authors must make these points clear as well as giving detailed information on how the desired appearance of the typescript is to be achieved and on the layout of titles, headings, references, tables, legends and illustrations.

Promotion and distribution also present problems when proceedings are published by a sponsoring organization which has little or no previous publishing experience. The retrievability of proceedings published in this way is often low,[13] as it can be difficult for librarians or anyone else to find the address, or even the name, of the publisher. Some journal editors go so far as to ban these semi-mythical volumes from reference lists. To counteract this kind of objection, editors of privately published proceedings should arrange for review copies to be sent out and for the book to be advertised and listed in appropriate journals and other publications (see p 75–76). If the sponsoring society publishes a journal, free exchange advertisements might be arranged with other journals.

The main advantage of private publication is that the proceedings can cost much less than with commercial publication. 'The price is often fixed by ... dividing the sum of the paper, printing and binding costs by the number of copies printed; all other costs, such as salaries of copy editor, administrator and typist, being inconspicuously absorbed by the learned institution which employs them.'[4] If a small mark-up is added and all the copies printed are sold, the sponsoring organization may make a useful small profit. More often it will make a loss, unless the 'administrator' happens to be a hard-headed business manager who can deal successfully with costs and costing, and with promotion, sales and so on.

Much of the work of instructing authors, making arrangements with printers and promoting and selling retrievable information is lightened for editors and organizing committees by good commercial publishers. How to go about finding a publisher for a multi-author book is described in Chapter 1, and the same general advice applies to conference proceedings. The financial arrangements that the organizing committee makes with the publisher will vary, depending on the requirements of the sponsoring society, the market for the volume(s), and the publisher's usual method of handling conference proceedings. The organizers may, for example, arrange to pay the publisher an agreed share of the registration fees in return for n copies of the proceedings being supplied to the participants, with the rest of the print run being sold by the publisher in the usual way; or the publisher may put all the copies on the open market, knowing from past experience what percentage of participants and how many libraries will buy copies.

TIMETABLE FOR MANUSCRIPTS AND SYNOPSES

Apart from the editing of participants' discussion remarks (see next section), most editorial procedures for conferences are as described in Chapters 1–7 (and see p 118). It is worth repeating that the editor must draw up a firm timetable for receipt of synopses and manuscripts. The dates depend on what has to be circulated before the meeting, what has to be ready (and in what form) at the time of the meeting, and what is to be published after the meeting.

Circulating reprographed copies of the complete papers beforehand, or printing them by the time of the meeting, may seem to free participants from having to make detailed oral presentations that cut into or do away with discussion time; but both methods have drawbacks. Even for small meetings, copying and circulating all manuscripts is expensive; it is also wasteful, since not all the participants will bother to read the papers.[14] Circulating the printed papers in proof form, however, may produce good discussions at the meeting, since more people read printed papers than would read reprographed copies. But if the discussions are to be included in the proceedings, special arrangements then have to be made with the printer.

The best solution seems to be to circulate synopses of informative abstracts about three to four weeks before the meeting (see p 13) and ask authors to supply manuscripts either shortly before the meeting or during it, to allow the manuscripts to be as up to date as possible. The deadline for submission of synopses or abstracts may have to be about 12 weeks before the meeting.

If there is a set date for publication of the proceedings, manuscripts will be needed some 5–12 months beforehand (see p 8)—unless there is to be no editing and papers are to be supplied as camera-ready copy. Except when papers have to be printed for circulation before the meeting, the deadline for their receipt should be not later than the last day of the meeting (or earlier if papers are to appear in a journal with an earlier deadline): even the best-intentioned authors lose much of their incentive to work on manuscripts as soon as they leave one conference venue for the next, or for home. If the discussions at the meeting are not being published, editors must be particularly strict with authors over the deadline for receipt of manuscripts: if there is no buffer period of essential editorial work on the discussions, the date of receipt of the last manuscript is what determines the date of publication.

For a small symposium where informal discussions as well as formal papers are to be published, the deadline for receipt of papers might be set at, for example, three weeks before the meeting. This allows the editor to deal with at least some papers beforehand. During the meeting the editor can discuss queries with authors and persuade any who haven't submitted their papers to part with them before the meeting ends. For this kind of conference, authors should be told that they may modify their manuscripts during the meeting, if they wish, to take account of what is said by other participants or to allow last-minute results to be included.

EDITING MATERIAL FOR CONFERENCE PROCEEDINGS

Discussions at conferences are often more illuminating than the papers that provoke them. Formal papers nearly always report work that members of an invisible college already know through preprints and personal communication. During discussion, on the other hand, most people talk openly about their most recent work and lines of thinking; they are stimulated to discuss work in progress and to report negative results; and in the right atmosphere they speculate freely, in ways that can open up new areas of study. The best discussions take place at small informal meetings designed to include plenty of time for discussion and attended by some 15 to 25 people. The edited record can make stimulating reading. With good organization and thorough editing larger meetings of up to 100 or 200 people may also produce worth-while discussion; large congresses never do.

However good the discussions may be, they are never worth printing verbatim. When discussions are included the editor therefore has a heavier task, though a more creative one, than when papers alone are published. The guiding principle in editing discussions should be that whenever comments are attributed to individuals, the speakers should see a copy of what they said (or what the editor thinks they said), preferably in context. They should then be allowed or persuaded to correct their comments, clear up obscure points, and provide references as necessary.

If a conference includes a session towards the end of the meeting at which the topic as a whole is discussed, it can be exciting for participants if this is transcribed, edited and presented for comment before everyone disperses. The mechanics are that the editor and assistants work extremely hard through most of the day or night (or both) after the general session, while the conference participants enjoy themselves sightseeing, shopping, or relaxing in other ways. A final session is then held to correct misapprehensions, sharpen some conclusions and provide participants with tangible evidence that the conference has been worth-while. In published form, this kind of discussion section serves as a useful summary for the reader and nicely rounds off the book.

There are several other ways of handling discussions at large or medium-size meetings. At some conferences, speakers write down their comments and hand them in immediately. At others, tape-recorded discussions are transcribed quickly and unedited transcripts are given to participants to correct before they escape from the conference room; at these meetings, if there is no stenographer present, the editor or an assistant should list the speakers' names and take down enough words for the transcriber to be able to attribute the right statements to the right speakers. Another method is for each discussion session to be summarized by the editor or by a rapporteur appointed for the purpose—though summaries of this kind tend to lack the cut-and-thrust of the original debate.

For meetings of 15–25 people, if discussion is intended to play an important part in both the meeting and the eventual publication, the following procedure for dealing with tape-recorded discussions is recommended. The editor, who attends all the sessions and must quickly get to know each of the participants by sight, lists each person's name as he or she speaks in discussion. This allows contributors to join in the discussions informally without giving their names each time they speak. As well as writing down the names, the editor makes long-hand notes of what each person says, giving either the gist of the comment or a few verbatim phrases—especially any difficult technical words and comments obscured by coughing or other noises. Rough drawings or notes of anything drawn on the blackboard or shown on the screen are made, to help with editing the transcript later. The tape-recordings are transcribed (typed in *treble* spacing) by audio-typists who use the editor's notes to identify the speakers.

Later the editor, after re-reading the manuscripts under discussion, listens to the tape-recording and edits the transcripts fairly strictly, improving the grammar, structure and style but leaving in as many of the speakers' own words as possible. Irrelevant references to the temperature of the room and empty compliments on papers that are then verbally torn to shreds are deleted, as are any inessential introductory phrases addressed to or made by the chairman, and all comments that are recognizably repetitious. When 'audio-editing' is finished, the editor polishes each transcript into what sounds like an intelligent conversation amongst the participants, writes queries and requests for references or further information in the margins, and rearranges the comments in a more logical order whenever necessary. A list of the points made or topics covered sometimes helps to show which comments should go where—and the list may convince the editor that the order of some papers needs to be changed too, if the discussions show that they are closely related. It is more important to obtain a smooth progression of ideas in the published discussion than to present the comments in their original order in the supposed interests of historical accuracy.

The edited transcripts are next retyped, again in treble spacing, to give speakers enough room to make changes, and the queries and requests for documentation that were noted on the original transcript are transferred to the retyped version. Participants are sent copies of every page of edited transcript on which their own comments appear, plus the pages immediately before and after each of their comments, to remind them of the context. They are asked to correct and return the edited transcripts within two to three weeks, and are warned that they will not see any proofs of the discussions. When corrected transcripts come back, the editor makes sure that comments still flow logically and that editorial queries have been answered. Other points to check are whether participants' questions to one another have all been answered, deleted or reworded as statements instead of questions and whether all the necessary references have been supplied. A final version of the discussions can then be typed for the printer.

This method may sound laborious, but it works. Sending speakers either unedited transcripts of their own remarks in isolation or transcripts of the whole meeting is a recipe for disaster, or at least for unrewarding reading.

A final point about discussions is that they should be indexed as carefully as the papers, and speakers' names should be included in the index of contributors, with page numbers for each discussion comment.

Both discussions and papers at conferences are, like material for any other book, edited with the expected readership in mind. That is, the editor or copy editor expands specialist shorthand into more generally recognizable language, condenses rambling comments, spells out abbreviations or explains them at first mention, inserts cross-references, introductory passages or linking statements between papers as needed, reconciles contradictions, monitors the level of writing, arranges papers in the most logical order, and does all the other editorial work described in Chapters 5–7, with proofreading later on (Chapter 9).

If commissioned or invited papers turn out to be unsuitable for publication, it is probably best to reject them at once (see p 39–40). This course, however, can hardly be followed unless authors have been told, when invited to contribute, that their papers would be refereed. If no warning of this kind was given, the editor has to exercise much tact in persuading authors to rewrite their papers or revise them drastically in time to meet the printing schedule. Alternatively the editor has to do the work and then ask the authors to approve what has been done.

Summary

(1) A conference that is worth holding is not necessarily worth publishing.

(2) A conference worth publishing is not necessarily worth publishing in full. Further, the papers need not always be collected in a book but might appear in a journal issue or supplement, or even be submitted separately to journals in the usual way.

(3) Published proceedings should consist either of original papers, preferably refereed, and similar to journal articles, or of papers written specifically for the conference, especially for the kind of meeting that allows plenty of time for discussion; both kinds of proceedings should be published as quickly as possible, and in a retrievable form.

(4) A firm timetable for receipt of synopses and manuscripts must be drawn up.

(5) Discussions should be carefully edited to make them useful, readable and retrievable.

11 Starting a new journal: financial aspects

Journals are conceived and born in much the same way as multi-author books (p 3), except that for journals the active role is even more likely to be taken by publishers or learned societies than by individual scientists. The first question obviously is: does a real need exist for a new journal in the proposed field?[1] The numbers of potential subscribers and contributors, the extent of the competition, the editorial and production costs and so on must be calculated before any decision can be made (see Langley[2] for a detailed questionnaire; Russak[3] and Grossmann[4] cover editorial, marketing and financial aspects succinctly). Russak[3] says that a quarterly journal that wins at least 1000 subscribers (the minimum needed) out of a potential market of at least 4000 could reach 'operational breakeven' within three to five years, but the real break-even—that is, allowing for start-up expenses—may not be reached for seven or eight years. Some journals may do better: Grossmann[4] gives actual figures for a successful biomedical journal that reached these points at two years and four years, respectively.

If the calculations show a reasonable chance of success for a journal, the sponsor's next steps are to choose an editor, or—since journals are sometimes built around editors—confirm one already chosen; and then select an interested and supportive editorial board or committee (p 14–15), define the journal's policies and scope (Chapter 12), and assign, or allow the editor to assign, responsibilities among the journal's staff.

The limit of the editor's responsibility for journal management is usually to select the best possible contents and make sure that the budget allocated to the journal is applied to the best possible effect. The brief account of financial management that follows is included because some editors have more detailed responsibilities for their journals. In any case it is a mistake for scientific editors to ignore administrative and financial matters affecting the journal: managing editors or administrative officers who are unaware of the scientific policy and aims of the editorial office can easily undermine the editor's good work, for example by adopting an unpopular pricing policy or by operating a distribution system that is inexpensive but does not succeed in getting the journal to the readers.

Balancing the journal's budget can be tackled in two ways: by increasing income or by reducing expenditure. One useful principle is that increasing income is always preferable to reducing expenditure—and ways of increasing income should always be examined thoroughly before economies in production or in editing procedures are considered. Extravagances should be eliminated, of course, but steps to increase income should be taken first.

SOURCES OF INCOME

The main sources of income for a journal are subscriptions, page charges, direct subsidies or grants, reprint sales and advertising sales. In monitoring a journal's profitability it is particularly important to see whether the number of subscribers is high enough for the journal's break-even point to be achieved.[5] Some journals have found, however, that acquiring extra subscribers is unprofitable, because of the high costs of order fulfilment and mailing. Subscription prices should then be increased, if necessary. 'If you can't raise the subscriber level, raise the price.'[5]

Subscriptions

Subscriptions are the largest source of income for journals. The cost of a subscription should be competitive with subscriptions to other journals in the field, i.e. about the same as, or not much more than, the price of the other journals, calculated per 1000 words or per volume containing the same number of pages as a comparable society-sponsored or commercially published journal.

Some societies allocate a portion of members' dues to the journal budget. The calculation of income is then done by adding the total amount allowed for 'subscriptions' from members to the amount expected from non-members. If there is no other source of income, the resulting figure shows how much can be spent per page or how many pages can be printed in each volume. The calculation, however, is usually more complex. Subscription income has to be offset by the cost of subscription fulfilment, i.e. the clerical work involved in keeping the mailing list up to date, sending renewal notices, banking the cheques, correcting errors and arranging for the mailing of back issues, all of which are surprisingly costly in time and salaries.

Some journals operate a two-tier subscription system, in which society members pay less for the journal than non-members. Or there may be a three-tier system, with libraries paying more for their subscriptions than individual non-member subscribers. This is justifiable on the grounds that without the lower rates those subscribers would be lost to the journal. Provided that the individual pays slightly more than the run-on cost to the publisher of producing the extra copies, no one is worse off. Librarians, however, object to paying as much as 10 times the rate paid by individuals, although this may seem reasonable in terms of numbers of readers per copy. Societies that expect the income from libraries to balance their journal budgets are being unrealistic if members get free copies. If the proportion of free copies is high, these copies reach the libraries either direct from the society's members or via the secondhand market. It is probably best to assume that nobody has a personal subscription to more than one or two weekly journals nowadays, and to settle on one price for all non-member subscribers.

The way to attract a large number of subscribers is to cater for a wide readership in active fields of research (which may be impossible in certain specialties) by including enough articles in every issue to interest the various groups of readers, and by publishing plenty of critical review articles. Editors will, of course, probably also want to try to produce journals of such high quality and up-to-dateness that no library can afford to be without them, but it may take several years for a journal to build up the reputation of offering top quality to readers and first-class service to authors and readers. In the long run financial success will depend on the ability of the editor to achieve or maintain the necessary scientific quality for the journal (see Chapter 12).

Promoting a journal becomes less necessary on the journal's home ground after the first five years, when it is either well established, or dead or dying. After that, growth in the number of subscribers will depend on how often the journal is cited by authors in other publications, especially monographs and annual reviews. Sales abroad, however, may continue to benefit from publicity efforts. Promotion of a new journal is best left to the publisher, though the editor can help by getting editors of established journals to mention the new journal in their editorials or in book review sections.

Page charges

Making authors, or rather their institutions or governments, pay the costs of publishing their articles is common practice for society-sponsored journals in the USA but it has never been popular in other countries. The rationale for the charge is that the publication of results deserves subsidy just as much as the research that goes into obtaining them, and that journal subscribers should not have to pay the costs of getting articles into publishable form any more than they have to pay to equip laboratories. US funding agencies therefore accept page charges as a necessary part of research costs, and money for these charges is included in research grants. The conditions are that the journal publishing the results is a not-for-profit undertaking, does not make publication contingent on payment of the charges and does not discriminate among authors according to whether they are supported by government funds or not.[6] These conditions are unfavourable to commercial journals; on the other hand, the commercial journals receive articles from authors who are unable, or who refuse on principle, to pay page charges. Some journals operate a (reprehensible) 'two-track' system whereby authors who pay page charges have their accepted articles published more quickly than those who do not pay.

Those who benefit most from the page-charge system are subscribers. When the *Journal of Biological Chemistry* abandoned page charges temporarily in 1973, its subscription price leapt from $75 to $120.[6] The reason for this journal's change of policy in 1973 was that more and more authors had begun to plead poverty and the inability to pay the charges (which had never been compulsory). Charges were nevertheless reinstated in 1975.

The US Postal Service complicated the page charge question in 1976 when it ruled that certain journals which receive money from compulsory page charges must label the papers as advertising matter; if there is more than a certain amount of 'advertising' the journals may therefore lose their second-class mailing status and have to pay first-class postage.

In the UK the Royal Society rejected the principle of page charges when they were first suggested in the early 1960s, pointing out that they discriminated against investigators working on their own, or supported by private funds, or in countries which did not allow government grants to be used for this purpose. The charges were therefore never introduced in British journals. At least one European journal, however, imposes charges when authors submit papers of more than a permitted length. This has been an extremely effective tool for obtaining papers of exactly the permitted length or just under. Another journal prints pages over and above its usual allocation if authors pay for the extra pages.[7] These seem legitimate and constructive ways of using page charges.

Another argument against page charges is that they encourage editors to accept too many papers of less than the highest quality and to ignore efficient and economical methods of managing their journals.

Similarly page charges may also allow editors to turn a blind eye to the harsh fact that not enough subscribers buy their journals. If a journal is worth publishing it is usually worth publishing commercially, according to the experience of the many societies in the UK that turn their journals over to commercial publishers.[8] If commercial publishers can make journals with 1000 subscribers viable in the USA, as it seems they can,[3] this principle is apparently valid there too. Many journals already expect authors to prepare perfect typescripts and illustrations for use as camera-ready copy, and a few ask authors to provide papers typed in an optical character recognition (OCR) typeface ready for scanning. If page charges are added to these demands, authors or their institutions face very heavy burdens.

Clearly, journals that already make page charges are unlikely to abandon them suddenly. New journals, however, or journals that have so far survived without imposing charges, should be very wary indeed of instituting either page charges or submission charges (non-returnable fees for every article submitted): few journals seem able to wean themselves off income of this kind once they acquire a taste for it.

Direct subsidy

Instead of page charges the Royal Society proposed that high quality but financially unviable journals might be rescued by subsidies. Income of this kind is often essential for journals serving specialties with a limited number of potential readers. Which journals should receive subsidies and who will provide the money are difficult questions. Direct grants, and the consequent possibility of direct control, from governments should be avoided. But grants channelled through organizations such as the Royal Society or other bodies run by scientists ought to be acceptable, and grant-giving bodies, unlike individual authors, can ensure that the money they provide is used as effectively as possible. Similarly, more subsidies could be given to libraries to enable them to buy the journals they want.

There is of course a serious question about whether journals with very small circulations should be allowed to survive. Should they instead amalgamate with other journals to cover a wider total field—one less likely to be blown out of existence with the next change in direction of the scientific wind? Or should the editor strive to retain the journal's autonomy but reduce its overheads by sharing the editorial workload and overhead costs with other journals in an Editorial Processing Centre or a Cooperative Publishing Office, as discussed in Chapter 13? If the circulation is miniscule, the subscribers might prefer their journal to continue in the simplest possible form—perhaps as reprographed or offset litho copies of letters or articles—rather than see it disappear altogether. Or the subscribers might form themselves into an Information Exchange Group, with a newsletter containing unrefereed communications—but this kind of information exchange is not regarded as formal publication. (Usually the development is the other way round, from informal exchange to conventional journal.)

Sale of reprints

The sale of reprints can be a considerable (5–10 %) source of revenue. Authors deserve some free reprints or offprints to send to other workers in their particular fields. The number of free copies varies with the wealth of the journal or sponsor but authors are not obliged to buy extra reprints: if they wish, they can tell readers that no reprints will be distributed, for the system is certainly widely abused.[9,10] On the other hand, authors who believe that widespread distribution of their reprints will further their careers or the research-grant prospects of their departments must be prepared to pay for extra copies. Reprints can therefore be priced according to purely commercial principles: a mark-up of 100 % or 200 % on printing costs is quite legitimate, especially as overheads have to be covered too, but the price should remain competitive with the cost of reprographed copies. Administration is simplified if reprints are sold in multiples of 100, and without covers. Title-pages for articles should be designed in such a way that a cover with citation details is unnecessary—that is, the title-pages should carry an article biblid (p 79).

Advertisements

In the USA, the sale of advertising space is not usually worth considering unless a journal has more than 5000 subscribers in the medical field, or 20 000 in other fields. (The figures differ in other countries, but are of the same order of magnitude.) Without circulations of these kinds, the rates that can be charged may be less than the cost of soliciting and printing the advertisements—something that many editors forget.[11] The use of identifiable reply cards or forms giving the name of the journal can help in soliciting further advertising.[12]

A strong editorial policy on the permitted content of advertisements must be laid down, with guidelines or a code for advertisers (Appendix 8). Advertising copy should be examined carefully when it is submitted, perhaps by an advisory committee. Even then, the editor must be prepared for brickbats:[13] there are sure to be errors of judgement which will produce irate comments from readers or from the journal's sponsoring society.[14] But cooperating with advertisers in providing accurate and unbiased information on books, equipment and materials needed by scientists[15] is an appropriate activity for scientific editors who want to serve their readers.

The practice of printing advertising copy on the same pages as text material, or inserted between text pages, may annoy readers, but advertisers pay more for such advertisements.

Since opportunities for free exchange advertising are usually welcome, it is worth approaching commercial or learned society publishers of journals in similar fields to see whether mutually beneficial arrangements can be made.

Other sources of income

Minor sources of income to which attention should be paid are sales of back issues, rights, lists of subscribers, and microform publications.[16,17]

EXPENDITURE

The main items on which journals spend money are production, mailing, storage, editing, copy-editing, order fulfilment and promotion. Other items include office, subscription and advertising overheads.[17] Another small item that must not be forgotten, especially for large-circulation journals in the medical field, is libel insurance or indemnity. Some of these items are discussed here briefly.

Production costs

Production costs are the largest single expense for most journals and are the obvious target for economies—always provided that quality does not fall below a certain minimum standard. 'Areas for possible production economies include change in format, standardization of style and paper, keeping the use of special types to a minimum, providing a single set of proofs, and careful watching of correction costs'.[18] Composition costs may also be reduced if the editor gives the printer very clean copy, eliminates footnotes, limits changes from one type size or typeface to another (a simplified layout for references, for example, can save a lot of typesetting time), and (if the printer has a scanner) provides text typed in an OCR typeface.[19] Type size and the spacing between lines can sometimes be reduced slightly and the width and depth of columns increased to get more material on a page (see Chapter 8). A cheaper paper might be used, provided that it is a standard quality stocked by the printer, that it is opaque enough for comfortable reading, and that it is lighter in weight rather than heavier than the previous quality (otherwise extra postage may reduce the saving on paper). Printing by web offset may also be worth investigating, even for journals with short runs.[11]

Where they are not already being used, photocomposition and other new methods of composing and assembling text and the rest of the copy (see Chapter 13) should be explored for possible economies, though newer is not always better: it is not unknown for journal editors to revert thankfully to hot-metal typesetting after disastrous experiences with cold composition.[20] The one sure way to economize is to adopt photo-offset reproduction of camera-ready typewritten copy, largely because it throws the burden of the expense back from the journal onto the author—except where all the retyping is done in standard form in the editorial office (and see p 113). But reduced composition costs with camera-ready copy are partially offset by increased expenditure on paper and postage, because with ordinary typewriter typefaces there are fewer words to a page than with typeset material. The process known as miniprint, which reduces the size of the typewritten characters, overcomes this objection to some extent (see p 145); and so do certain typewriters such as the IBM Executive.

Binding can be a needlessly expensive operation. If the printer is stitching 16-page signatures, it is worth investigating whether 'perfect' binding (p 99) with modern adhesives would not be just as effective, and cheaper.

Mailing costs

Mailing costs can sometimes be reduced, or a better delivery time obtained for little extra cost, by finding out what the postal services have to offer. All countries have different regulations but in the UK, for instance, adding the words 'Reduced Rate' to the words 'Printed Matter' on the envelope brings down the cost of mailing to other countries. In the USA, journals usually register for second-class mail. Bulk shipment by air freight to a distribution point can reduce airmail costs by two-thirds and still get the journal to its subscribers six to eight weeks earlier than by surface mail.

Editorial costs

Even if editors are paid a nominal salary or none at all, some or all of the copy-editing, secretarial help, postage and paper will have to be paid for. Costs have to be kept to a reasonable proportion of total income, depending on the size and wealth of the journal. Expenditure should never be cut too drastically. If authors become disgruntled and readers dissatisfied because editing and copy-editing standards have fallen, the eventual result will be reduced criculation, loss of income and collapse of the journal.

Libel insurance

In some disciplines, especially medicine, over-critical references to other people's work can lead to libel actions. As well as taking legal advice on the wording of risky-looking articles, editors should make sure that they and their journals are well covered against the possibly very high cost of any such action, whether won or lost.

More detailed discussion of financial matters affecting scientific publications will be found in the CBE booklet edited by Day et al.[15] and in the seminar on Economics of journal publishing referred to several times here.[3-5,16,17]

Above all, to ensure that their journals survive financially, editors must of course transform them into, maintain them as, or create superlative products that will attract the best authors as well as large numbers of readers. Some ways of achieving this aim are discussed in detail in the next chapter.

12 Editing a successful journal

In scientific journals sections of the scientific community are talking to themselves, much as a nation talks to itself in its newspapers. But the relationship between journal editors and their readers is a more intimate affair than national newspaper editors could ever achieve with their readers. Journal editors need their readers in a unique way, because those readers are also authors who supply all, or nearly all, the material published in the journals. Journal editors should therefore conduct the relationship with their reader-authors as carefully as they would conduct any personal relationship that they hope will continue and grow into something valuable, enjoyable and of lasting significance to both parties.

A new journal, in particular, depends enormously on how skilful its editor proves to be in shaping, balancing and developing the contents so that people not only read the journal but also subscribe to it (p 121). Eventually the journal will gather its own momentum and will be able to maintain its individuality when a new editor takes over. But however well established the journal may be, the editor should at all times exercise firm but flexible control over what goes into it and how the material is processed and presented to readers.

Many questions specific to these aspects of journal editing have so far been touched on only lightly, if at all. This chapter therefore considers editorial responsibilities in general; the mix of contents; archival information; and the journal as a forum. Under these main headings the points covered include rapid publication, the structure of research articles and priority dates for them. Letters to the editor, editorials and book reviews, anonymity (or otherwise) for the writers of these items, and the time lag in the appearance of book reviews are also discussed, together with society business/professional news, and corrections.

EDITORIAL RESPONSIBILITIES

Most sponsors endow editors of their journals with considerable

128

autonomy and the responsibility for observing scholarly traditions as they apply to publication. Autonomy allows or stimulates editors to produce successful journals; it also leaves room for the occasional failure. With an eye on success rather than failure the wise editor takes an active interest in helping to define or redefine the journal's aims, policies and editorial coverage, and in recruiting members for the editorial board (Chapter 1) or for the regular panel of referees (Chapter 4). Associate editors and board members should be chosen for their ability to provide support and seasoned advice. For society-sponsored journals the editorial committee should meet regularly and have clear responsibilities in decision-making on general policy matters. This also makes it easier to find a natural successor when an editor resigns or retires.

For any journal to succeed, the editor must aim to publish research articles of exceptional quality (for the criteria of quality see p 2). The publisher of a new journal will probably press the editor to accept papers that are rather less than excellent at first, in order to fill the pages of the early issues. Nondescript or third-rate papers should nevertheless be rejected: better a slim journal of reasonable quality than a substandard, fat one.

Of course, the more successful a journal is in attracting papers, the higher its rejection rate will be: 80 % is typical for weekly medical periodicals, falling to 45–60 % for specialist biomedical periodicals, though rates differ in different disciplines.[1] Some well-regarded journals in fact accept only those articles rated as outstanding by referees—a policy well worth considering.

To attract large numbers of papers from which the best can be selected for publication, a journal needs a wide scope. On the other hand, if the scope is too wide, it will be difficult to identify the readers and promote the journal to them; and readers will not subscribe to a journal for the sake of one or two articles in each issue that might interest them. The right balance has to be found for this as well as for other aspects of editorial work.

Rapid publication

One of the editor's main responsibilities to authors and readers is to arrange for papers to be published as promptly as possible. Many journals build up a backlog of accepted articles to give the editor and publisher some leeway in filling issues of a standard size and to allow the editor to balance topics in each issue if it is journal policy to do this. Although extra articles that are ready for publication can usefully go to proof stage, forming an emergency reservoir for each issue, the manuscript backlog should not be allowed to grow to an unhealthy size. Most authors would prefer immediate rejection to acceptance if there is to be a year-long lag while papers work their way through the pipeline.

For the editor, a giant backlog produces the risk that authors whose work and ideas have progressed during the waiting period will make numerous changes in proof. To avoid this, editors can offer authors the choice of acceptance with publication within a specified period, or the opportunity to submit their work elsewhere. A better method is for the editor to accept only the most exceptional papers as they arrive, publish them quickly—in issues of uneven size if practicable—and return the other papers to their authors immediately (with a suitably worded letter—see p 55).

Some journals have experimented with accelerated refereeing (or no refereeing) and fast production for certain papers only. The editor may have a hard time deciding which articles deserve such treatment and coping with the consequent disruption of printing schedules, but the results for the journal are often worth the extra trouble. Better still is to publish all the accepted papers very quickly, omitting one or more proof stages but maintaining the overall quality of the journal.

Faster publication can also be achieved by reorganizing procedures in the editorial office and—if it seems necessary and if funds are available—by obtaining extra editorial assistance.[2] It is worth discussing the production timetable with the printer to see whether and where any of the printing and proofing procedures could be speeded up (or omitted). Camera-ready copy can of course save time as well as money if authors can be persuaded to prepare it to the editor's and printer's satisfaction (and see p 90 and p 113).

THE MIX OF CONTENTS

Most journals include both archival and current-awareness elements in their make-up. It is in mixing these elements to match readers' needs and wants, while fulfilling the journal's aims, that editors give their publications a distinctive character. The list of items that may be included in journals is a long one (see p 15 and p 134). In a new journal the mix will depend on the journal's scope, on the interests of the editor and editorial board or committee, and on the publisher's assessment of the market.

Editors of weekly journals tend to place more weight on newsworthiness when they consider publishability than do editors of monthly or quarterly archival journals. In the medical field, for example, Sir Theodore Fox[3] argued that in a weekly journal such as *The Lancet,* which he edited for many years, the research articles might well be dropped, as they were read by only a small number of subscribers. Ingelfinger[4] disagreed with this view, arguing that part of the function of a weekly medical journal is educational, and that doctors ought to be informed of current research activity even if it is not of immediate practical value to them. In fact, *The Lancet* continues the mixed tradition with much success.

The sequence of the various sections in each issue of a journal is an indication of editorial priorities. In medicine, for example, the *New England Journal of Medicine* (a society-sponsored journal) publishes original scientific articles first in each issue and has the editorials in the middle, after the case records of the Massachusetts General Hospital (i.e. 'local society' activity) and before the letters to the editor. The *British Medical Journal,* on the other hand, with editorials that are often on medicopolitical as well as scientific issues, puts these first, followed by the original scientific articles and, towards the end of the issue, official reports of the British Medical Association. *The Lancet* (independent) begins with major original articles, hypotheses, review articles and the like, then launches what may be called the 'commentary' side of the journal with the editorials (leaders and annotations), followed by the letters to the editor. The society-sponsored *New England Journal of Medicine* is, therefore, closer in arrangement to the independent *Lancet* than to the society-sponsored *British Medical Journal,* and it seems likely that the editors rather than the sponsors or publishers chose the sequence of sections.

It is also interesting to look at *Science* (society-sponsored) and *Nature* (commercially published), which both begin with editorial pages. *Science* confines itself to a one-page editorial before printing major scientific articles and reviews, followed by lengthy news features and commentary. In both journals the short scientific contributions are relegated to the second half of each issue. These arrangements are subtle announcements of editorial purpose, not dictated by pressures from the sponsoring organization, and new editors may learn something from them.

ARCHIVAL INFORMATION

The description 'archival', applied here to research articles, brief communications and review articles, means that the information is expected to have lasting value, not that it is expected to be dull. But unless journals can afford to pay editors or copy editors to rewrite papers skilfully, in cooperation with authors, there is not much that editors can do to make papers more lively, apart from exhorting authors to take courses in scientific writing, if any are available, and to study the style manuals recommended in the journal's guidelines for authors. The conventional IMRAD structure (Introduction, Methods, Results and Discussion) of articles in the life sciences is often blamed for the dullness of the average scientific paper. The real reason is more likely to be that many scientists, however much they want to see their work in print, regard writing up completed studies as a chore for which they have little patience and which gets in the way of the next piece of work.

The IMRAD structure is in fact suitable for many articles and provides novice authors, in particular, with a comforting and familiar framework for their papers. But editors should be flexible and encourage variations on or departures from the conventional structure. The historical-survey type of Introduction, in which 'the problem' too often remains undefined, could well be replaced by an outline of the hypothesis tested, followed by the reasons for examining the hypothesis. Methods and Results can usefully form a single section, and many Discussions would benefit from less rigorous editing, as ideas thrown out casually may spark off new trains of thought in readers' minds.

Experiments with journal conventions could inject much-needed life into scientific writing[5] and show that scientific work, like much else, has exciting moments that compensate for the daily slog.

Another tradition worth breaking is the one decreeing that negative results are not worth publishing. Publication of these results would often prevent the work from being repeated needlessly. This is especially true of work showing that statistically significant correlations were not found when these were a reasonable expectation. Editorial policy on publication of negative results was changed in two journals in the early 1970s (*Journal of Experimental Education* and *Journal of Education Research*) after Walster & Cleary[6] published an article in defence of negative results.

A good way of creating interest in a new journal, or any journal, is to include a few solicited review articles on subjects of topical interest or in a new field or a neglected one. Review articles are often what readers want most. Solicited reviews, of course, bring with them the problems common to all solicited articles (see Chapter 4). Unsolicited review articles in a new field or presenting an unusual synthesis of ideas, perhaps covering several disciplines, should be considered sympathetically. Established review series tend to be conservative in their choice of topics and authors, and journals can provide a useful service by occasionally publishing more unorthodox reviews. An example of a journal whose editor took on the role of scientific critic and interpreter, a role too often forgotten or neglected, is provided by the *Journal of the Royal College of Physicians (London),* launched in 1966. This journal aims to publish review articles which synthesize information gleaned from many scattered articles, and to present that information in a form helpful to physicians who are too busy to find and correlate all the primary research articles.[7]

An experimental method of generating review articles, or surveys, in an interdisciplinary field has been described by Jesse.[8] An extensive bibliography was compiled and copies were given to a number of scientists in disciplines related to quantitative microscopy. These workers modified the bibliography and prepared papers which were first presented at meetings and then published in *The Microscope,* together with the revised bibliography which was basically common to all of the papers. The method seems especially promising when information retrieval services can be used in compiling the bibliography.

Priority dates

A final point about research articles is that *priority dates* are important to authors and can be vital in some fields if a claim for priority has to be established inside or outside the law courts. Editors have a responsibility for protecting authors' claims to priority by assigning dates to articles. Several dates can be used (Ref. 9, p 42): the date the typescript is complete; the date of submission, taken from either the covering letter or the postmark; the date of receipt in the editorial office; the date a manuscript is provisionally accepted; the date a revised version is received; and the date a final version is accepted. Martinsson has suggested that authors should give the date of completion at (for example) the end of the abstracts submitted for publication with their articles.[10] This is a useful idea but may not be acceptable in some cut-throat fields of science. The most practical dates to print for published articles are the dates of receipt in the editorial office and of acceptance in the form in which the paper is printed (ignoring copy-editing changes). (Editors who run their offices single-handed could, however, base the date of receipt on the date of the covering letter for articles that arrive in their absence.) If a paper is heavily revised the date of receipt should be the date of receipt of the revised version. If the author makes substantial changes in proof, or adds new material after the final manuscript has been accepted, the additions should be called a 'Note added in proof' or should be distinguished in some other way so that readers realize that the material is newer than the main part of the paper (Ref. 9, p 46).

The year in which an article is published is the date used when an author's work is cited, but if questions of priority arise the published dates of receipt (year, month and day) of the manuscripts make it clear who has absolute priority. Editors or publishers should also record the dates on which journal issues are delivered to the post office or other agencies for distribution to subscribers, as these dates can be important in patent disputes and for establishing priority for taxonomic descriptions (Ref. 9, p 47). The date on the journal cover may be quite different from the date on which the journal actually appears, as well as from the date on which it reaches subscribers—though editors should make every effort to match the printed date with the actual date of issue.

THE JOURNAL AS A FORUM

A conventional archival journal which never publishes anything but original research lacks an important dimension. Many journals therefore publish one or more sections providing for comment, criticism, feedback from readers, discussion and controversy. Editors of new journals have a wide range of items to choose from, including Letters to the editor, Editorials (or 'leaders'), Book Reviews, Hypotheses, Speculative articles, Controversies, Current concepts, Personal views, Seminars, Case conferences, Open letters to public bodies and so on. Editors of established journals may add to, or change, the mix of ingredients from time to time. For example, in 1976 the *British Medical Journal* introduced five new features: Condensed reports, Side effects of drugs, Where should John go? (for would-be emigrant doctors), Views, and Briefing—a balanced mixture of science with practical professional matters.[11]

It is sometimes argued that self-criticism by scientists in their journals may encourage the general public and lay press to criticize scientists unnecessarily. Some editors have therefore discouraged discussion of professional ethics, the environmental dangers of some kinds of experimentation, potential cruelty to animals in experiments, and even standards of scientific writing. But the answer to this is fairly obvious: the public will criticize science and scientists from time to time anyway, and if there is something to criticize it is better for scientists to put their own house in order first.

The recent rash of new journals on the philosophical, cultural and ethical implications of science, which Ingelfinger[12] has commented on, perhaps reflects the failure of established journals to accept enough articles on these implications. The segregation of subjects like this into a subspecialty may mean that fewer scientists than before will reflect on the *raison d'être* of their profession and its contribution to civilization. The blame for this will be laid at the door of shortsighted editors.

Among the many possible discussion and opinion-forming sections of journals, Letters to the editor, Editorials and Book reviews are the ones that appear most often.

Letters to the editor

Many letters to editors are badly presented, in spite of being written with an eye to publication. Even if an assistant deals with the Letters section, the editor should read all the letters, either before or after the assistant has worked on the selection to be published. Most journals that publish correspondence point out that the editor reserves the right to reject, shorten, excerpt or edit the letters for publication. Editing should, however, be restricted to removing intemperate statements or examples of bad taste. Spelling mistakes should be corrected but the grammar should not be changed unless the writer's point is unclear. Letters should be published as soon as possible after receipt and, except in rare cases, they should be signed. Readers' attacks on an editor's own editorials or on editorial policy should be printed whenever possible—either with a reply if a reasonable one can be given or an apology if one is needed.

The time to announce 'This correspondence is now closed' is when letters on a given topic begin to repeat points made earlier, or when the letters are from the same two or three correspondents. At this stage the writers who disagree can be left to carry on their correspondence privately.

Letters to the editor rarely need to be refereed. Any letters criticizing a previously published article should be shown to the author of the article, whose reply should preferably be published in the same issue as the critical letter.

Editorials (leaders) and anonymity

Editorials, often called 'leaders' in British journals, are statements of points of view. They deal with one of three types of subject: a new research advance (perhaps underlining the importance of an article in the same issue or putting it into a broader context); a statement of position on some aspect of one of the scientific disciplines represented in the journal or on the interaction between science and society at large; or a discussion of the journal itself—its objectives and editorial policy.

Some journals never publish editorials or any kind, but even archival journals ought to explain their editorial policy at least occasionally, so that contributors, potential or actual, know where they stand. The guidelines for authors, if well constructed, state the purpose and scope of the journal and describe refereeing procedures and the criteria for selection of papers, but the purpose and scope should not be static and any change in editorial policy should be brought to readers' notice in an editorial.

Editors who want to know whether readers think the purpose of their journals is being achieved can most easily find this out by writing appropriate editorials. Readers will certainly react and if their letters are published they will feel that they are influencing the direction a journal takes. Even the unpublished letters can give editors food for thought. The days of authoritarian journals with the attitude 'The editor and the editorial board know best' are surely over.

Not all editorials are written by editors and not all editorials are signed. Is this anonymity justifiable? Shouldn't the authors be named, to make it clear that they are real people whose judgements may be fallible rather than superior beings making *ex cathedra* pronouncements? The standard answer to this question is that the editor takes responsibility for all editorials, whoever writes them, and takes the blame for any that seem unacceptable or inaccurate to readers. But this is carrying editorial responsibility too far. If the argument were extended to its logical conclusion, no papers in the journal would bear any authors' names, since the editor ultimately assumes responsibility for the papers too.

There are several better arguments in favour of anonymity, as pointed out in a recent anonymous editorial.[13] One is that editorials are sometimes the work of several of the editorial staff, who could not sign *en masse*. Other editorials may be based on the advice of one or more experts who would not necessarily agree wholeheartedly with the interpretation—perhaps a political one—expressed in the final version. A third kind of editorial may have been provided by a well-informed expert but may need to be heavily rewritten before it can be printed. Or a prominent scientist may be unwilling to sign an editorial because the position it takes either compromises or pre-empts the stand of the writer's professional organization on that issue. Anonymity also gives younger or less well-known scientists an opportunity to speak freely without fear of being harmed in their careers or having their views discounted because readers have not heard of the writer before.

Although signed editorials are to be preferred, anonymity can therefore sometimes be tolerated. In addition, it might improve the situation if a new distinction were to be drawn between leading articles and editorials in scientific journals: leading articles by experts who are asked to comment on the scientific content and significance of work by other people should be signed, while editorials that are the work of editors and/or their editorial staffs need not be signed. If the distinction proved difficult to make, editors could allow the outside consultants to decide whether they would sign their work.

Statements of opinion about or on behalf of the profession should usually be signed, whether written by the editor or by an outside consultant, since the opinion may be against what most people in the profession believe, and an unsigned editorial may carry too much weight with the lay press, the public and the government. Similarly, in a society-sponsored journal an anonymous editorial might be taken as reflecting the society's collective opinion or policy. Either a disclaimer should be included or the editorial should be signed.

Editorial comment on research articles in the same issue is particularly valuable in a journal of wide scope, whose readers may not immediately recognize the importance of every piece of work described or its potential application to their own or another field. To obtain expert comments which can be published at the same time as the article commented on, the editor should first telephone the potential writer to ask whether the leading article (or editorial) could be completed within, say, two weeks. A copy of the final manuscript of the research article can then be sent to the commentator, who may well have been one of the referees. Since it is usually considered an honour to be invited to contribute a leading article, most people will produce it in time. The leading article could even be accelerated through the printing process to avoid any delay, or the authors of the research papers may accept a short delay if it means that their article receives greater prominence.

An interesting use of an editorial is to comment unfavourably on an article that the editor has nevertheless decided to publish. *The Lancet* of 17 September 1977 published an editorial[14] on 'Bladder cancer and saccharin' which listed what the editor considered to be faults in the research design of an epidemiological study reported in the same issue. The editorial made clear the editor's reasons for accepting the article for publication despite its faults: rumours about the study's results were already circulating and were influencing public policy on whether saccharin should be banned, but since the design of the investigation was open to criticism the study, with its detailed description of the design, had not been accepted for publication elsewhere and could not be judged objectively. The authors agreed to this procedure and their reply to the editorial criticisms was published in a later issue. It would not be good policy to print many editorials of this kind but the example shows how effective it can be to throw away the editorial rulebook. Editors should assess their work often, asking not 'Will this set an awkward precedent?' but 'What, in this particular instance, will be most conducive to the public good?'

Book reviews

Anonymous book reviews provoke the same objections as anonymous editorials. The answer is much the same, too: signed reviews are preferable from many points of view but anonymity allows people to write freely when they might not otherwise do so in reviewing books by their friends, enemies or colleagues. Editors who want to be flexible on this point could state that reviews will normally be signed but that the writers may remain anonymous if they insist.

Book reviews can be either descriptive or evaluative. Descriptive reviews, which merely recast the blurb and the list of contents, help to make a book's existence known but do not help anyone to decide whether to buy it. A list of Books Received is more useful than a collection of descriptive reviews, since many more books can be listed than can be reviewed.

Evaluative reviews are helpful to both readers and authors provided that the reviewers in fact discuss the books named: some reviewers take advantage of their platform in the journal to publicize their own thoughts on the subjects covered, with hardly a mention of the books themselves. This essay type of review is encouraged in journals devoted to book reviews, such as the *American Sociological Review*, but is inappropriate in journals with short book review sections.

Guidelines (Appendix 9) and/or review forms can be used to set the tone of the book review section and to discourage reviewers from writing essays instead of evaluating the books under review. The guidelines should state the word limit or range, the time allowed for writing the review, whether it will be signed (as discussed above), whether the reviewer will receive a fee, and what the review should ideally include. 'Good reviews state the contents of the book, convey its flavor, evaluate it critically, then stop' (Ref. 15, p 12)—though 'depth and extent of coverage' might be substituted for 'flavor'.

Book reviewers should be as carefully selected as referees are—but good reviewers are hard to find. 'The qualities that make for a good critical reviewer are to a large extent the same qualities that make for a good editor, or a valuable member of an editorial board, or a helpful dissertation adviser' (Ref. 16, p 68). Editors should impress on reviewers the necessity for speed, and should telephone beforehand to make sure that the reviewer can take on the work and write the review by the date required (see Appendix 9). The book review section might also be given preferential treatment, with accelerated production for all or most reviews.

Although reviewers are not usually responsible for the whole of the lag between publication of a book and publication of a review, delay by reviewers is a major headache for editors as well as exasperating for authors and publishers. It is unfair to authors if reviews do not appear for months after publication, especially if the book is about a fast-moving subject. Editors can compensate for this by listing 'Books received' as soon as they arrive, whether or not they are going to be sent out for review. Some editors print lists of 'delinquent reviews';[17] this shows that the editor considered the books worth reviewing but was let down by reviewers.

In newspapers and magazines the apparent zero lag between publication date and review date is achieved for books of general interest by review copies being sent out before the official publication date. Even though publication dates are not usually set in the same way for most scientific books, and though their reviewers are rarely paid, the review lag for scientific books is disproportionately long: Chen found that among 3347 reviews published in 54 biomedical journals in 1970 the review lag ranged from 0–2 months to nine *years*, but the mean lag was about 10.4 months.[18] In the two journals (*The Lancet* and the *British Medical Journal*) with the shortest review lags the average lag was 5.8 and 6.6 months, while in the two journals with the longest lags (*Acta Radiologica* and *Therapy, Physics, Biology*) the average lag was 42 months.

Editors who can find a way of shortening the lag for evaluative reviews to weeks instead of months and years will be rendering a great service to librarians and potential readers as well as to authors and publishers. Many publishers would be happy to help editors by supplying advance information about books in press, or even by providing sets of proofs if reviewers agree to read material in this form. It is worth writing to the major publishers to enquire about this and to establish a convenient mechanism for receiving review copies immediately after publication.[19]

Editors can exercise flexibility and flair over book reviews as well as over other features. One interesting 'review' published not long ago[20] took the form of a long letter to the editor declining the invitation to write the review and stating the writer's lack of qualifications for doing so. But in his letter the writer threw such interesting light on the book in question that many readers must have rushed out to buy or borrow it.

Unsolicited book reviews should be considered on their merits. Editors who don't want to receive such reviews should say so in their guidelines for authors.

Book reviews, like letters to the editor, should be edited lightly, if at all. Errors of fact, spelling and grammar should be corrected. Vituperative attacks on authors or publisher should be softened into something more civilized and not open to a libel action. Negative reviews, however, need not be avoided: readers want to know what not to read as well as what to read or buy. Comments on the price are superfluous in a review: readers should be able to judge from a well-written evaluative review whether a book is worth the money. Suggestions to the publisher that the reviewer would prefer a paper-back, or that the book might have been cheaper if glossy paper had not been used, are also redundant: a paperback is only cheap if there is a large market for the book (see p 7) and coated paper, which for a short-run book may not be significantly more expensive than matt paper, may be essential for good reproduction of the illustrations.

Journals with Book review sections should always have a Letters to the editor section, and the author (or others) should be allowed to set the record straight on facts about the book or to point out cases where the reviewer has misunderstood the purpose of the book or its intended audience. Attacks on the reviewer's evaluations are not, however, in order.

In the journal, each review should be headed with the full title of the book, the name(s) of the author(s) or editor(s), date of publication, publisher's name and place of publication, name of series, number of pages, number of tables and illustrations, price, and sometimes other information such as the size of the pages or the name of a translator (see Manten[19]).

Book reviews are often badly indexed in the Contents lists of journal issues as well as in volume indexes. If there is space for all the books reviewed to be included in the Contents lists, the books and their authors should be given priority over the reviewers' names; if the reviewers' names can be included as well, so much the better. In the volume index, a list of book reviews is invaluable, whether as a separate index or included in the subject index under 'Book reviews'.

Reviews are then listed alphabetically under the name of the first author of each book. The title and the date of publication should be given, and preferably the reviewer's name too, though this will appear in the author index.

Editors should send two copies of every review printed in their journals to the *publishers* of the books reviewed. The copies should include the volume number, page number and date of the issues in which the reviews appeared, as well as the journal's name.

Society business and professional news

Editors of society-sponsored journals may have to publish some or all of the following items of society business: presidential addresses (usually no editing allowed); abstracts or synopses of meetings (which should be edited, if only to show how abstracts of papers in the body of the journal should be presented); reports and resolutions from the society's general meetings; conference papers; and news and notes. If conferences have separate editors who suggest editorial procedures different from those usually applied to papers in the journal, the editor has to decide what the policy will be (see p 112). If the conference papers are published in a separate issue with a guest editor, there may be delays and disagreement over copy-editing standards (see Ref. 9, p 61–63). For news and notes, editors must usually accept what their societies provide, editing only for grammar and technical points of style, but ensuring that the amount of material does not outweigh the scientific content of the journal.

A problem facing editors of some society-sponsored journals is that members may expect to have their papers published without any refereeing and even without review by the editor. This privilege is becoming less common but older members of a few societies or national academies may still expect to benefit from out-dated rules. Editors should try to see that, when rules are revised, a procedure is provided by which the editor can appeal to an editorial committee if there is a dispute.

In both society-sponsored and commercial journals, especially weekly or monthly publications, a section on forthcoming meetings is useful to readers. This section usually needs accelerated production. It should include a note of the publication deadline for such announcements.

Corrections

From time to time authors point out errors or omissions that they have noticed since their papers were typed or printed. It is more important to correct these mistakes for readers than to establish who was responsible for them. Corrections should be printed in type of normal size, with a heading clearly advertising their existence, and they should be listed as *Corrections* on the Contents page, preferably always in the same position and giving the full title of the article that is being corrected; corrections should also be listed in at least two places in the subject index of the volume (see p 82). They should not be buried in an obscure place in the journal in the hope that nobody will notice that a mistake has been made; this practice goes against good scientific principles, though it is common in many leading journals (see Ref. 8, p 82–84).

CONCLUSION

This chapter has mentioned a few ways of handling some features in journals, but the best mix of articles and other items will always depend on the personality and ability of the editor and on the particular circumstances of the journal—the field(s) it covers, its readership, its state of financial health, the quality of its editorial board and referees. There are no blueprints for producing successful journals, and even if there were, editors would be right to ignore them and create journals out of their own imagination, intuition, good sense and knowledge of the field.

Some questions on a quite different level still remain about editing. Will new technology, for example, help editors to cope with the more mundane problems of keeping their journals going in times of steeply rising costs? Or will that new technology instead destroy journals and books as we now know them? These and similar questions are discussed in the final chapter.

13 Editing in the future: innovation and education

It is over 30 years since Vannevar Bush (1945)[1] described his vision of the communication system of the future. Only in the last five to ten years, as computers and video display terminals have flooded into scientific laboratories and percolated more slowly into printing-houses, has the dream moved much nearer to reality, at least in scientific communication. Traditional methods of scientific publication still flourish and more journals are born than die every year (see *Ulrich's International periodicals directory* from one edition to the next), but now every conference of editors or publishers pays much uneasy attention to the changes looming ahead and those already on us.

With one computer terminal available for every 15 professionals, 'computer pervasion of the research process is virtually complete' in the USA, as Baker et al[2] have pointed out. In Europe and other parts of the world the computer explosion is perhaps 10 or 20 years behind the point it has reached in the USA. Nevertheless on both sides of the Atlantic the age of electronics is already affecting the scientific information system in certain ways, and other possibilities are being investigated now or are forecast for the future. These technological innovations may soon drastically alter the way scientists work and communicate with each other. One confident prediction, for example, is that in 15 years' time electronic journals will be cheaper than the conventional kind printed on paper.[3]

The present uses of computers in scholarly publishing include making printing faster, and sometimes cheaper, through the processes described in Chapter 8; easing distribution, by maintaining and updating subscription lists and printing addresses; keeping records and organizing the refereeing system; and possibly helping with the copy-editing of manuscripts and preparing them for publication. Other technical advances have led or will soon lead to new forms of publication. I shall mention these developments first (for fuller details see Refs. 4 and 5), then refer to the computer-based processes already in use or under investigation, and end with some comments on professionalism in editing and on the outlook for editing and editors.

MICROFORM

The term microform (or micrographics) covers both microfiche and microfilm. Microfiches are sets of reduced transparencies of typescript or printed pages, with 80 to 100 pages mounted together. Ordinary microfiches are reduced by a ratio of 24. There are also ultrafiches, reduced by a ratio of 150, allowing 3000 or more pages to be concentrated on a fiche the size of a postcard. A microfiche reader is used to project an enlarged copy of one page at a time onto a screen. Paper copies can be made from the microfiche on reader-printers or separate printers. Microfiche versions of journals or books are ideal for libraries that are short of space, provided that the publication which they have condensed is likely to be needed only occasionally, for reference: it is no pleasure to browse through microfiche or scan many articles in succession on a microfiche reader.

Microfilm, which is less convenient for the user than microfiche, is useful for archival purposes, and many journals now provide microfilm versions when each volume is complete. Users apparently do not like microform journals much yet, but societies whose journals have a very small circulation may find microform the best (or only) way to keep their journals going, especially if authors cooperate in providing good clean typescripts and illustrations, since production and mailing costs are much lower than for paper journals. A few journals are in fact successfully published in microfiche or microfilm alone (e.g. the *American Journal of Computational Linguistics*).[5] Microforms and journal publishing have recently been surveyed by Campbell and Ashby,[6] who conclude that the trend towards the use of microfiche in journal publishing will continue and will 'aid the development of journals as more powerful vehicles for the distribution and storage in accessible form of research material and ideas.'

SYNOPTIC JOURNALS

Microfiche is also exploited in the experimental synoptic journals now being published in Europe and the USA. One way of publishing synoptics is to issue the journal in two forms: a full form in microfiche, made either from typeset or camera-ready copy and perhaps also available in miniprint (see below) for use in libraries and other reference centres; and a synoptic form, probably typeset, in which the author summarizes the full paper in some fixed fraction of its length or a fixed number of pages (ranging from two to six). Alternatively the synoptic form alone might be published, with copies of the full original typescript available on demand from a data store. In both systems subscribers to the synoptic journal can buy microfiche, reprographic or miniprint copies of full papers if they want more detail. In the method used by the *Journal of Chemical Research (S)* and *(M)*,[7] the synopsis is accepted for publication only after the full paper has been through the complete editorial selection process.

This system could have a retrograde effect on both science itself and the editorial process. If people read synopses without obtaining full details of the work that interests them, they may acquire the habit of accepting statements without examining the evidence. Likewise, refereeing for a seldom-consulted archive may prove so unrewarding that standards in this activity too will deteriorate. And copy-editing should probably not even be attempted for the archival form, provided that the manuscript is comprehensible to readers. It is inauspicious that, in the first trials conducted by the chemical societies of the UK, France and Germany, only one out of 310 papers summarized in the synopsis part of the journal was requested in the complete version.[7] Nevertheless, the experiment continues, with the launching of the *Journal of Chemical Research* in London in 1977.[8]

A drawback of synoptics is that authors have to prepare three versions of their papers—the full text, an abstract and a synoptic. The guidelines for authors preparing synopses should be very carefully thought out and more detailed instructions than usual should be given about the presentation of typescripts (see Ref. 9).

MINIPRINT

Miniprint, which is just legible to the naked eye, is used either for complete articles or for extensive data that can usefully be printed immediately after an article. It may either be typeset in very small type or be reduced from typed pages supplied by the author. Readers need either very good sight or a magnifying glass. Use of miniprint reduces paper and mailing costs, and significant savings can be made (see Hey[10]).

SELECTIVE DISSEMINATION OF ARTICLES

The selective dissemination of articles has been discussed, tested and, to a certain extent, practised.[11] Subscribers either order articles from regularly supplied lists of titles available, or arrange for articles that match their 'interest profiles' to be sent to them direct. The profiles are based on index terms chosen by the subscribers as reflecting their interests. They are spared from receiving material they do not want. This system may be suitable for societies or publishers dealing with several different fields, but its cost-effectiveness is still in doubt. And as readers and authors are often unskilled at finding accurate keywords, even when given a thesaurus from which to select them, the system also has intellectual drawbacks.

ON-DEMAND PUBLICATION

On-demand publication sometimes refers to arrangements like those provided by selective dissemination systems, by which readers can obtain printouts of journal articles as wanted. It also refers to a service offered by a few publishers by which photoduplicates of books or typescripts can be provided on request. Copies are not cheap, and the system is not economical if more than 250 copies of a book are likely to be ordered.

ELECTRONIC JOURNALS AND OTHER NEW FORMS OF 'PUBLISHING'

Although electronic journals produced and stored in a computer and read on a video screen sound an expensive proposition, a University of Toronto study predicts that from the middle or late 1990s onwards they will become cheaper than the conventional kind;[3] and a study in Norway predicts that 1990 will see the start of the 'paperless society' there.[12] The ARPANET communication system which links computers in the USA and Europe already allows scientists to exchange information even more easily than by mail or telephone, and at least one newsletter (the *SIGART Newsletter*) was being produced through the system two or three years ago.[5] ARPANET has also proved useful for transmitting manuscripts to referees and for other editorial tasks.[5] This and similar interactive systems allow co-workers thousands of miles apart to communicate effectively when they draft joint papers, and editors can work with referees and other advisers through these systems. Audio cassettes, gramophone records, video cassettes and televised information systems are other types of process into which editors may find themselves venturing. These are also video disks which can hold many books or journals on a disk the size of an ordinary long-playing record.[5]

EARLY CAPTURE OF TEXTUAL MATERIAL ON MAGNETIC TAPE

The savings that can be made in composition costs when authors provide camera-ready copy have been mentioned several times in this book. Camera-ready copy can be prepared more easily with word processors than with conventional typewriters. Word processors record typed characters on a magnetic card, disk or cassette and allow the typist to correct, insert or delete material without retyping the rest of the manuscript. The more expensive word processors have video screens which display what has been typed and allow for changes and corrections to be made on the spot. When the copy is perfect, the tape or other magnetic record is fed into the same or a separate machine, which types the whole page or chapter flawlessly and at high speed. Some word processors can be used to control photocomposers, and various instructions can be incorporated to control the typeface, type size, format, right-margin justification, italicization, and so on; words can even be flagged for indexing later.

Another refinement is to have the original copy typed in an optical character recognition (OCR) typeface which a scanner can translate directly into a magnetic tape or other recording. The tape can be used to produce any number of copies of an article for the editor, referees, author(s) and copy editor to work on, and instructions for change from any of them can be incorporated into a corrected tape which can be used to control photocomposition. When scanners and OCR typefaces come into wider use, copy editors should be spared some of their more humdrum tasks, such as proofreading.

The existence of a magnetic tape or other record means that even before a book or journal is printed, the title, bibliographic details, key terms and abstract of a chapter or article can be fed to abstracting and current-awareness services without further keyboarding, with its almost inevitable errors. This is unquestionably an advantage in time, money and accuracy.

EDITORIAL PROCESSING CENTRES

The use of computers and scanners in editorial procedures forms part of the concept of Editorial (or Electronic) Processing Centres (EPCs), much discussed since it was first put forward in 1972.[13,14] In an EPC several learned societies would share an automated system, providing enough work to make the system financially worth while. Four levels of automation are envisaged. In all of them authors would submit manuscripts typed in an OCR typeface to the Centre, where the manuscripts would be scanned and entered into a computer system. Printouts—preferably the kind without typesetting instructions embedded in the text—would go to the editor and later to the referees. Comments would be typed in OCR type for recording via the scanner, with printouts being provided at any stage as needed. The computer would be programmed for copy-editing, with printouts going to authors before publication. If authors approved of the changes they could simply telephone the Centre and the message would be typed into the computer. If they disapproved of the changes or had more alterations to make, the manuscripts would be recycled through the EPC to the editor. Final versions of manuscripts would be transferred from the computer to a magnetic tape which the printer would use to control phototypesetting. Again, data for abstracting and indexing services would be available as by-products.

The computer could also handle the various 'housekeeping' chores described in Chapter 3: assigning manuscript numbers; providing lists of referees with their specialties matched to the key terms given in the title or assigned by the editor, together with information about referees' past performance and present workload for the journal; typing letters to referees; automatically producing reminders to referees, the editor or authors when manuscripts become overdue at any stage; and, after acceptance, providing deadline reminders to copy editors, printer and authors. Computers should not, however, be used to churn out letters to authors from the editor: no software program yet devised can cope satisfactorily with the countless different circumstances an editor should discuss individually with authors.

As well as editorial activities, an EPC-computer system should be able to handle the maintenance and upkeep of subscription lists for the societies taking part, sending invoices and reminders out as necessary.

Studies of the EPC concept funded by the National Science Foundation in the USA have indicated that the system is technically feasible and economically viable but at the moment is showing no signs of becoming an operational reality.[15] Is a system of this kind feasible in countries other than the USA? Woodward[14] has described a modified version more suitable for European and other countries where full-scale EPCs would be too expensive or are not needed. In the Cooperative Publishing Office (CPO) proposed by Woodward, editors and referees would work on authors' typescripts until final edited versions had been accepted and approved. At that stage manuscripts would be retyped in OCR type in the publishing office. Copies would go to authors for checking, and the corrected version would be scanned and stored until needed for a journal issue. Material for secondary services would also be typed by the CPO for input to the computer system, and reminders and other letters could be sent out as from an EPC. Woodward calculated that at 1976 prices in the UK the initial investment in a CPO would be about £150 000. With the capital sum discounted over five years, the operating costs would be about the same as conventional costs; at 20 000 pages a year the CPO should save about 9 % of the conventional publishing, printing and distribution costs.

EPCs and CPOs were intended to solve some of the temporal and financial problems of publishing for learned societies, but commercial publishers who invest in scanners or editing terminals are in effect already running editorial processing centres themselves. Learned societies may find it more satisfactory to have their journals published commercially than to collaborate with other societies in setting up an EPC or a CPO. For the societies they are supposed to help, the greatest drawback to EPCs or CPOs would be the initial capital costs and the extra salaries of people employed to run them. At present some of the costs of copy-editing, improvement of illustrations, and correspondence of all kinds may disappear into institutional overheads. The rest of the work is done by the editor in trains or planes, in the lunch-break, or after the children have gone to bed. Learned societies benefit from this freely donated time, and as long as dedicated people are prepared to do the work, the societies will want to encourage them.

PROFESSIONALISM IN EDITING

Many scientists edit journals and books either in their 'spare' time, as just mentioned, or in a small part of their working lives. Yet editing is clearly no job for an amateur. Editing should of course be in the hands of scholars active in the fields covered by the publications for which they are responsible, but this often means that the editors are professional scientists first and editors some way afterwards.

Editors can help themselves in several ways. One is to read appropriate journals, among them *Scholarly Publishing*, the *IEEE Transactions on Professional Communication*, the *Journal of*

Technical Writing and Communication, the *Journal of Research Communication Studies* and others, as well as the books and articles on editorial practice and policy referred to in this book. One book that is particularly valuable on technical and other innovations is Capital Systems Group's *Improving the dissemination of scientific and technical information,* a looseleaf publication that is updated from time to time.[4] A similar publication produced in the UK[16] is also helpful. DeBakey's book, *The scientific journal,*[17] is essential reading, and Grünewald's guidelines[18] provide a succinct account of the work of editors. The *Editerra editor's handbook*[19] has (or will have) three useful sections (publishing and printing; editing; standards and style) that will interest editors in all disciplines.

Another way to improve one's professionalism as an editor is to join an association of editors (some of these, such as CBE and Editerra/ELSE, have useful newsletters). The number of associations covering different disciplines and different geographical areas is increasing (see the list of associations in Appendix 10), and the First International Conference of Scientific Editors, held in Jerusalem in 1977, has given birth to IFSEA—the International Federation of Scientific Editors' Associations—as well as to a volume of proceedings.[20]

A third solution—where funds are available—is for editors to share their responsibilities with one or more scientifically trained assistants, either part-time or full-time. Assistant editors, like any professionals, should master all the details of editorial work, keep up to date with developments, and themselves make innovations.

Although assistant editors of large-circulation journals in the UK are usually scientifically trained, in the USA it is quite common for editors to send accepted papers direct to scientifically untrained copy editors, who deal with the technical editing work described in Chapters 6 and 7 but do very little rewriting. As this did not seem very satisfactory, Woodford[21] attempted to introduce a system for training 'executive editors' for biochemical journals in the USA. Those who took the course had advanced degrees and research experience in the biosciences. They were trained to assist chief editors by working in detail on publishable typescripts before their acceptance for publication. The philosophy on which the training was based was that a scientific paper is in most cases more intelligible, useful and enduring if it is the product of cooperation between the author and an executive editor: the author originates the ideas and does the work but is not necessarily good at getting it onto paper, while the executive editor, though not an expert on the subject matter, understands it and is also an experienced communicator. Clearly, there must be mutual respect in such cooperation, and both partners must be willing to learn.

Authors are not always willing to learn from copy editors who are not scientists, but executive editors are more acceptable on several counts. First, with their scientific training executive editors are less likely to make misguided changes that arise from a lack of understanding of the subject; and if these editors do misinterpret a passage, the authors should realize that other well-informed readers may do the same. Secondly, subediting of manuscripts submitted to journals can be done before the manuscripts are finally accepted, at a time when authors are more amenable to guidance. Thirdly, rank-pulling is impossible because the executive editor has high scientific status. Experienced copy editors can overcome the inherent disadvantages of their position, especially if editors back them up firmly, but they often start at a disadvantage.

For these reasons it seems sensible for a part-time chief editor with a heavy work load to persuade the sponsoring organization to employ a professional assistant editor with scientific training in the appropriate field(s).

Finding and paying for suitable copy editors may be nearly as difficult as finding executive editors. Neither a first degree in science nor one in English (for English-language journals) is any guarantee that a person without previous experience will turn out to have the necessary qualities of patience, attention to detail, an eye for spelling and typographical errors, a sound knowledge of grammar and a feeling for language, together with the sense not to antagonize authors and the wit to know when to stop comma-catching and let the book or journal get to press.

In a few large organizations copy editors receive some formal training, but many of them learn as they work. When employers can afford to break their copy editors in gently, proofreading and reference-checking are the best jobs for them to tackle first; text editing should be left until they have experience of all the other copy-editing procedures. Editors can speed up the learning process by getting new copy editors to read Judith Butcher's book on *Copy-editing*,[22] as well as *Writing scientific papers in English*[23] and any relevant disciplinary or national style manuals that are recommended to authors (*Nordic biomedical manuscripts*,[24] Dorothy Mizoguchi's book for Japanese authors,[25] and others), since style manuals and guidelines for authors show copy editors what to look for in typescripts. (Copy editors should read this book too, of course.)

Whether or not they are blessed with help from executive editors or copy editors, journal editors who take a professional attitude to editing can subject themselves and their journals to regular review and self-assessment. One mechanism for doing this is to discuss the objectives of the journal with readers, using the editorial pages as a sounding-board in the way mentioned earlier (p 136). Examples can be found in the *Journal of Medical Education*,[26] in which a new direction for the journal was announced in 1971; in *Biochimica Biophysica Acta*,[27] in which a change in editorial policy on the acceptance rate was justified on the grounds that there had been an unmanageable logarithmic growth in the number of papers submitted; and in the *New England Journal of Medicine*, whose editor confessed[28] that several innovations by the journal had not succeeded, and suggested some reasons for the failures (Ingelfinger's article,[28] incidentally, is a goldmine for the innovative editor). These three editorials are all examples of editors discussing their policies and procedures with their customers—thinking aloud and using the scientific method of hypothesis, testing of hypothesis, and deduction.

A second procedure for self-assessment is to use the *Journal Citation Reports* published by the Institute for Scientific Information.[29] The number of times a journal, as opposed to an individual paper, is cited is a fair indication of the impact—positive or negative—it is having on the scientific community. If the impact factor (average number of citations per article during the first few years after publication of each issue) of the journal falls over the years, something is certainly wrong; the editor has to discover what it is.

At present, only the full-time editors of certain large-circulation journals are accorded the status they deserve, while scientific editing in general confers little prestige on its exponents. As editors become more proficient the status of editing will rise, together with the general standard of the publications for which they are ultimately responsible. This is a highly desirable state of affairs at which to aim—but it depends partly on the continued existence of books and journals in a world where communication systems are advancing and changing very rapidly indeed.

THE OUTLOOK FOR EDITORS AND EDITING

In practice, what changes are we about to see in the scientific communication system? Will scientific articles in future always flicker at us from video screens? Are we really heading for a paperless world devoid of the pleasures of browsing? Are editors to be replaced by electronics?

The answer to all three questions is 'No', or at least 'Not for a long time yet'. In 20 or 30 year electronic journals will probably be widely used but it seems likely that journals printed on paper will exist side by side with the electronic species. Words on paper are still the most efficient and acceptable way of transmitting archival information or any material that readers have to study for any length of time. Until scientists everywhere have instant access to computer terminals, books and journals will remain the most acceptable and attractive means of packaging that information. And because the costs of entering material into computer systems and storing it are high, editors will still be needed for electronic journals for the same reasons as they are needed for paper ones—to control the quality, quantity and form of what goes into the system.

Even though this view of the future for editors and publishers is an optimistic one, a concerted effort is needed now to improve the state of the art of scientific publication.[16] Costs need to be brought down (see Ref. 15, p 27–30, on the subject of low-cost books), or prevented from rising exorbitantly, and ways should be found of drastically shrinking the publication lag for books and journals without diminishing the quality of the information offered to readers. Above all, production and distribution should be made vastly more efficient. It is many years since it became possible for newspapers to be composed in one city and for facsimile versions to be produced in other cities, hundreds of miles away: with more communications satellites circling the world, and with decreasing computer costs and ever-improving production methods, how long will it be before books and journals can be economically photocomposed in one continent and reproduced as bound copies, in any number needed, anywhere in that continent or another? The electronic era will show its achievements in this way just as surely as it already does in allowing access to one or more pages at a time on a screen.

Although many of us will be happy to look at material for which we are in a hurry on a video screen or microfiche reader before deciding whether to obtain hard copy versions, most of us—whether we are reading for pleasure or to obtain general background information —will also want to go on reading books or journals in their conventional form, however unconventional the production method may be. Even when terminals sprout in every office or laboratory, 'Who wants to go to bed with a floppy disk—or with a microform projector?'[30] All the indications are that paper publications, and their editors, will coexist happily, and for long time to come, with whatever electronic and other innovations may spread into the world of scientific publishing.

Appendix 1
A Publisher's contract with an editor

There are many possible variations in the wording of an agreement between a publisher and an editor. The clauses given below merely represent the main points usually covered. Some publishers may ask individual contributors to sign agreements not unlike this one, instead of signing a copyright assignment form.

A. MEMORANDUM OF AGREEMENT
   made this   day of   One Thousand Nine Hundred and Seventy-

   BETWEEN Millhouse Press, of 13 Stable Road, London WC1 5XX, hereinafter referred to as 'the Publishers' of the one part, and   of   hereinafter called 'the Editor' of the other part.

B. The Publishers shall publish at their own risk and expense a work consisting of essays by various contributors edited by the Editor and provisionally entitled

   (hereinafter referred to as 'the Work')

C. Copyright in individual essays shall be assigned to the Publishers by individual contributors. Copyright in the Work is hereby assigned by the Editor(s) to the Publishers on consideration of its publication and on the terms hereinafter expressed.

D. Two copies of the final typescript of the Work shall be delivered to the Publishers in good order ready for press on or before   .   the said final typescript consisting of not more than approximately
   words on the lines of the attached synopsis.

E. If in the opinion of the Publishers an index is required it shall be supplied by the editor or at his or her expense.

F. The Editor undertakes to obtain and deliver to the Publishers upon delivery under clause   hereof (or, with the agreement of the Publishers at some later date) written permissions for any textual or illustrative material which is to be included in any part of the Work written by the Editor and of which the copyright is not the Editor's and the Publishers undertake to assist and advise the Editor in this task. All relevant permission and reproduction fees shall be paid by the Editor. The Editor further undertakes to secure with the Publishers' assistance and advice such further permissions as the Publishers may from time to time require for the purpose of exercising their rights under this Agreement and to pay all relevant permission and reproduction fees. The Publishers shall themselves be entitled but not required to obtain all or any of such permissions and to deduct from any moneys due to the Editor such sums as may have been paid by them but are by virtue of this clause the responsibility of the Editor.

G. The proof sheets of the Work shall be read by the Editor and by the relevant contributor(s) but the final typescript of the Work shall be deemed to constitute the final version of the Work and corrections of substance (i.e. corrections other than those of printers' and publishers' errors) at proof stage by individual contributors or by the Editors shall be allowed only under exceptional circumstances. If the total alterations in proof (corrections of printers' and publishers' errors excepted) exceed 10 % of the cost of composition then the excess shall be paid for by the Editor.

H. During the legal period of copyright the publishers shall pay the following royalties, such royalties being divided as follows—20 % to the Editor and 80 % equally divided between the contributors to the Work.

(a) a royalty of 10 % on the English published price of all copies sold of the hardcover edition rising to 15 % after the sales of the first 5000 copies (except as hereafter provided);

(b) a royalty of $7\frac{1}{2}$ % on the English published price of any paperback edition sold (except as hereafter provided);

(c) a royalty at the appropriate rate as specified in (a) or (b) above on the net receipts from all copies sold at a discount of 45 % or greater discount.
[See p 7]

J.   (a) The Publishers shall use their best endeavours to obtain revenue from the sale of volume and subsidiary rights and shall undertake all necessary negotiations.

(b) In the event of the Publishers leasing translation or reprint rights in the volume as a whole (as distinct from the leasing rights in a part or parts of the Work) then the Publishers shall pay the Editor 50 % of the net proceeds.

K. The Publishers shall not be responsible for any accidental loss of or damage to the Work (including illustrations or other material) by fire or otherwise while it is in their custody or in course of production.

L. No royalties shall be paid in respect of the following:

(a) Copies of the Work presented to the Editor, or to others, or to the press.

(b) Copies of the Work destroyed by fire, water, enemy action, in transit or otherwise.

(c) Copies of the Work sold at or below cost of production.

M. (1) An account shall be taken annually of all sums due to the Editor hereunder in each year up to 31 December and the amount due accordingly shall be paid to the Editor (less any contra account) in the April next following.

(2) The Editor warrants to the Publishers that the Work is in no way whatever a violation of any existing copyright that it contains nothing libellous and that he or she will indemnify the Publishers from and against all claims proceedings damages losses and costs which may be taken suffered or incurred on the ground that the Work or any part thereof infringes copyright or contains anything libellous.

N. The Editor shall receive two free copies of the Work. Other contributors shall receive one free copy each of the Work. Further copies for personal use (not for resale) may be obtained at a discount of 30 % off the English published price.

O. (a) The Publishers shall have the power at their discretion to dispose of by sale (at the best obtainable price) or otherwise the residue or part of the residue of any edition after not less than two years from first publication. (In respect of copies disposed of by sale at a price greater than cost the Editor shall be entitled to receive a royalty on the net receipts of 10 % in respect of the hardcover edition of the Work and $7\frac{1}{2}$ % in respect of a paperback edition of the Work.)

(b) Where the said residue or part of the residue of any edition is to be disposed of by sale the publishers shall give the Editor the option of purchasing some or all of such stock at the said best obtainable price, such option to be deemed to have been complied with by the Publishers four weeks after they shall have given notice in writing to the Editor containing an offer of said stock and to have been refused by the Editor in the absence of notice in writing by the Publishers within the said period accepting such offer.

P. If any difference shall arise between the Editor and the Publishers touching the meaning of this agreement or the rights or liabilities of the parties hereunder the same shall be referred to the arbitration of two persons (one to be named by each party) or their umpire, in accordance with the provisions of the Arbitration Act 1950 or any statutory modification or re-enactment thereof.

Appendix 2
Form of assignment of copyright

Continuing developments in international legislation make it essential for copyright in [the book/journal] to be controlled by a central organization. This will both ensure maximum protection against unlawful use and enable [the publisher/journal] to benefit from cooperative licensing arrangements, which are already being established.

Authors are therefore asked to sign and return the statement below, keeping the duplicate copy for their records.

Please note:
1. *Authors may re-use minor parts (such as some of the tables or illustrations) of their own material after publication without seeking further permission,* subject only to full acknowledgement to [the book/journal] as the original source.

2. For commercial use by a third party the author's approval will be sought (to be assumed one month after notice has been sent to last known address).

3. Where the copyright rests with the author's employers their consent should (if possible) be obtained to [the publisher/journal] handling copyright matters for the article *with third parties* and in particular to include it in any licensing arrangements made for [the book/journal] as a whole.

Copyright assignment:

In consideration of the publication in   by   of my chapter/article/comment(s) entitled

I hereby assign to   the copyright throughout the world in the chapter/article/comment(s) on the conditions mentioned above:

Signed   _____

Date   _____

Name   _____

Address   _____

  _____

If the copyright belongs to your employers, please give their name:

and indicate whether [the publisher/journal] may register the article and part of the complete issue and handle copyright matters on their behalf with third parties: Yes/No

Please return to:
    The Editor,

_____

_____

_____

Appendix 3
Letter to potential contributors to a multi-author book

Sample letter to a potential contributor to a book on Lung liquids

14 September 1979

Dear   ,

    As you may know, I am planning to compile a book on *Lung liquids,* and I am writing to ask if you would like to contribute a chapter.

The book will deal with water and solute exchanges across capillary and alveolar epithelia—a subject less familiar than gas transfer across these membranes. Its purpose will be to show how basic research can contribute to the understanding of clinical problems, and it is directed to postgraduate research workers and clinicians in respiratory physiology, membranology and fetology. The idea is to describe basic physiological research on the properties of epithelial membranes and to point out how that work applies to what happens in the lung, particularly the fetal lung, in both normal and abnormal conditions. I hope to include recent work on other respiratory epithelia such as the fish gill.

The present plan is for the book to open with a section on some aspects of lung structure. The water and solute permeability of lung capillaries and epithelium in fetal and postnatal life and their function in controlling bulk water movements will then be considered. Next, some aspects of epithelial function and ion transport across the fish gill, amphibian lung and mammalian lung will be compared, special attention being paid to the fetus. Finally, the pathogenesis and pathophysiology of lung oedema will be discussed.

What I should very much like from you, if you are interested in contributing, is a chapter on the clinical disorders associated with lung liquids, to close the book. The chapter should be between 6000 and 8000 words, plus tables and figures as necessary.

The timetable for the book is as follows:

Manuscripts to reach me by 15 January 1980
Final revision of manuscripts to be completed not later than
    1 April 1980
Proofs to reach you by about 15 June 1980
Your corrected proofs to be returned to me by 1 July 1980
Book to be published by mid-September 1980

It will be essential for everyone to keep strictly to these deadlines. If typescripts do not reach me in time, I may have to revise the plan of the book with the omission of certain chapters, or write those chapters myself—which won't be nearly as satisfactory as if they were written by others! My own part in the book, apart from the editing and an introductory review of the present state of research on lung liquids, will be a chapter on ion transport across amphibian lung.

I am inviting as other contributors J. Brown, H. Schmidt, (etc.). D. Horn and L. Cavalli have already undertaken to provide the chapters on   .

The book will be published by the Millhouse Press, which will hold the copyright. Those who accept the invitation to contribute will be asked to assign the copyright in their chapters to the publisher. In recognition of this, you will receive 8 % of the royalties payable. Secretarial and postage costs will not be paid. Contributors will receive one copy of the book and 50 free reprints of their own chapter. Contributors will also be able to obtain further copies of the book at a discount.

I look forward to having a response from you within the next week or two, and I hope it will be positive. I should also be glad to have your comments on the general plan for the book as outlined here.

Yours sincerely,

Appendix 4
Guidelines for authors

Example (with comments in italics) of guidelines for authors contributing to a multi-author monograph entitled 'Lung liquids' (see Chapter 1 and Appendix 2)

AIMS AND SCOPE

The book will deal with water and solute exchanges across capillary and alveolar epithelium. Its purpose is to show how basic research can contribute to the understanding of clinical problems. The readers will be research-oriented clinicians working in paediatrics or general medicine and postgraduate research workers. Basic physiological research on the properties of epithelial membranes will be described, amd its application to normal and abnormal conditions in the lung—particularly the fetal lung—will be discussed. Recent work on other respiratory epithelia such as the fish gill will be included.

TYPESCRIPTS OF CHAPTERS

Length: 6000–8000 words (20–30 typescript pages; typed double-spaced).
Submission: By 15 January 1980 (ribbon copy plus one other) to [address]

PUBLISHER, COPYRIGHT AND FEE

The book will be published by Millhouse Press Ltd, London. Your acceptance of the invitation to contribute to the book will be taken to mean (a) that your chapter will be an original review of your own and others' research, not previously published elsewhere, and (b) that you agree to assign copyright to the publishers, in return for which you will receive a copy of the book and 50 free reprints of your chapter. You will also receive 8 % of the royalties paid by the publisher.

REPRODUCTION OF PREVIOUSLY PUBLISHED MATERIAL

If you use any previously published tables or illustrations, or cite lengthy passages of text, it is *your* responsibility to obtain the copyright-holder's written permission for the material to be reproduced in this book. If the copyright-holder is not the author, please obtain the author's permission too. The written permission(s) should accompany the typescript.

Many authors think that obtaining permission to reproduce material is the responsibility of the editor or publisher. It isn't. Authors should be asked to obtain such permissions themselves. Strictly speaking, they need obtain only the permission of the copyright-holder—sometimes a journal, a learned society or a publishing house rather than the original author— but the original author should be asked as well. This often leads to an unexpected bonus in the form of new information.

In the USA, publications based on work supported by public funds and which carry no copyright notice can be used freely. (See also Chapter 8.)

ETHICS

Where relevant, please provide proof that your own experiments have been conducted in accordance with named ethical guidelines, and send a copy of the approval of any relevant ethics committee. Try not to include references to ethically dubious work published by others, unless you add a comment about your reservations.

Authors are primarily responsible for considering all ethical matters before they begin work that will affect any living person or creature. In most countries there are mechanisms to ensure that they do so. The editor must assume secondary responsibility, and insert comments when appropriate (e.g. when authors discuss work, not their own, which has been published even though its ethical justification was questionable). Every time ethically dubious work is published or referred to, it acquires some degree of respectability which may encourage other investigators to follow a bad example. (See also Chapter 5.)

FORM AND STYLE

Write simply and concisely, remembering that the book will be read by people from other disciplines. Use short words rather than long ones, and concrete rather than abstract terms; where appropriate, prefer the first person singular or plural to the third person, and the active to the passive voice. Avoid vague statements, jargon and laboratory slang, and words not defined in dictionaries. Give references in the text by name and date, not by numbers (see below, under REFERENCES). Avoid footnotes and abbreviations; when these are essential, place all footnotes together on a separate page or pages, and define abbreviations in the text at first mention. Acceptable abbreviations for this book are given on the last page of these guidelines, but please use even acceptable abbreviations sparingly and with discretion. A recommended guide to form and style is *Writing Scientific Papers in English: an ELSE-Ciba Foundation Guide for Authors* (O'Connor & Woodford 1975 Elsevier/Excerpta Medica/North-Holland, Amsterdam, paperback 1978 Pitman Medical, Tunbridge Wells).

Avoidance of Footnotes. *For the reader, footnotes are distracting; for the printer they may be difficult and expensive to keep track of and to insert on the right page. Their content can usually either be worked into the text, deferred to an appendix or omitted altogether; but occasionally (for example, when an editor's comment, elucidation or cross-reference to another article is called for) a footnote can be invaluable to the reader and should not be transformed in any of these ways.*

The request to the author to type footnotes on a separate page is appropriate only if hot-metal typesetting is being used, in which the printer uses different machines to set type of different sizes (since footnotes are usually set in smaller type than the main text). When this is so, the printer must be able to give the page on which the footnote is typed to a different machine operator. The type set up elsewhere has to be reunited with the main text, on the correct page; hence the extra cost.

Avoidance of Abbreviations. *An excess of abbreviations irritates and confuses readers, especially those who are not familiar with the subject or the language.*

When a cumbersome name or phrase must be used frequently in a text, and cannot always be replaced by a pronoun or shortened ver-

sion, abbreviations are useful; but readers must be able to look up the meaning of any abbreviation easily. Some readers consult only part of a chapter or journal article, and therefore see abbreviations long after these have been first mentioned and defined. A page of abbreviations and their explanations can usefully be placed at the beginning of a book as well as at the beginning of each chapter, and a list is sometimes placed at the beginning of journal articles. The editor must also, of course, ensure consistency in use of abbreviations. For a book, it helps if the guidelines for authors include a list of permitted abbreviations, culled from the leading journals in the discipline, or (in the life sciences) from O'Connor & Woodford (Ref. 1, p 86–92) or such guides as the CBE Style manual[2] or the European Journal of Biochemistry[3]; this is preferable to a simple reference to these sources, since authors may not have easy access to them.

TITLE PAGE

Make the title accurate and informative, but not too long (up to 100 characters and spaces). Provide a short title also, if necessary (up to 45 characters), for running headlines in the book. Write your own name, with given name(s) or initial(s), and those of your co-authors, if any, in the way that you and they usually write names for by-lines. Give the name and address to which correspondence should be sent.

Names of Authors. *Many authors seem to enjoy publishing under different names at different times—or at least to specialize in including or omitting one or other initial or other part of their names on different occasions. This confuses computers (and even human indexers) terribly and is to be discouraged, as authors will end up being indexed separately under every possible version of their names.*

ABSTRACT

An abstract in English, of preferably not more than 200 words, should precede the text. It should convey the scope of the paper and give as much information as possible. It will normally *outline* the purpose and methods of the work, and *detail* important findings and conclusions. (For further information on writing the abstract see Landau & Weiss.[4]) The abstract is not an intrinsic part of the paper—it must be intelligible on its own, without reference to the main text. It should enable a reader to decide whether or not to read the paper; it should be suitable for filing and for use by abstracting journals. A good title and abstract help information services to publicize work rapidly and facilitate future retrieval. **Title and abstract are the keys to your work—write them accordingly.**

INDEX ENTRIES

On a separate page, please list about a dozen items suitable for the subject index of the book.

The indexer, who aims for consistency, may not actually use the author's terms as main entries, since different authors may choose different synonyms for the same object or concept. However, if authors bring terms they consider important to the indexer's attention these terms will at least be cross-referenced.

Index entries should not be (but frequently are) confused with keywords, which have a different function (see Chapter 5).

TEXT

Please ensure that the chapter can be understood by readers from other disciplines. Say how your chapter relates to the subject of the book.

HEADINGS IN TEXT

Please make ranking of headings and subheadings clear by marking them (in pencil) A, B, or C in the margin. Please do not use more than three orders of headings in the text.

Style of Headings. *It is useless to explain to authors that (for example) 'bold face, caps, centred' will be used for first-order headings, 'bold face, initial cap only, flush left', for second-order headings, and so on. Whatever rules are laid down, typists and authors mostly insist on underlining capitalized headings (which means to a printer 'italic capitals, please'—a heading rarely, if ever, used). Authors can, however, easily rank-order headings, though the editor has to check that this has been done properly, and that the various chapters or articles are consistent in this respect, as in others.*

ACKNOWLEDGEMENTS

Group these in a paragraph at the end of the text. Please obtain permission to make the acknowledgement, and approval of the wording, from the person thanked.

It may seem strange to ask authors to obtain permission to make acknowledgements, but it is surprising how often this is refused, or a request made to re-phrase the acknowledgement.

TABLES

Tables should be intelligible without reference to the text. Please keep their number and size to a minimum. Large tables are difficult to read and often impossible to print. Type tables double-spaced, on separate pages, and number them with arabic numerals in the order they are referred to in the text. Give each table a brief descriptive title, avoiding abbreviations if possible. Do not rule vertical lines or use ditto signs.

ILLUSTRATIONS

Keep illustrations to a minimum (not more than 10). If previously published illustrations are essential, please obtain the copyright-holder's written permission. Please supply glossy photographs in black and white only, unmounted, and of the highest possible quality (a line drawing or a written description is often preferable to a poor electrophoretogram or similar photograph). Line drawings, diagrams, graphs and formulae should be in black ink on heavy white paper or card not larger than 210×297 mm (i.e. A4 paper). (Good glossy photographic prints, unmounted and correctly lettered, are also acceptable instead of the original.) Keep lettering on illustrations to a minimum, and have it done professionally (or in pencil on an overlay), making sure that lettering is unbroken and that symbols and abbreviations correspond with those in legend and text. Lettering, axes and curves must be large and clear enough to stand any necessary reduction. Do not use lettering of greatly differing sizes, as all sizes will have to undergo the same percentage reduction. The maximum size of illustrations in the book is 115×165 mm, provided that the legend does not exceed 20 words; smaller if the legend is longer. Please keep these proportions in mind when you design the originals. Include scale bars where necessary, or (less desirable) state magnification of material submitted. Trim off or mask redundant areas of prints and indicate 'Top' in soft pencil on the back. Number illustrations with arabic numerals in the order they are referred to in the text (and, in the margin of the text, indicate the approximate positions at which you would like to see them inserted eventually). Write your name on the back of every illustration. Type legends consecutively, double-spaced, on a separate page or pages. Please do not place legends on the illustrations themselves. Do not use paperclips on any illustrations.

REFERENCES

A carefully selected list of references, not an exhaustive one, is desired. Please make sure that all citations in the text appear in the reference list, and vice versa. Names and dates should be used in the text, *not* numbers, and the reference list should be arranged alphabetically. Do not include unpublished work in the list unless the paper describing it has been accepted for publication; instead, put '(A.B. Smith, personal communication, 1978)' or '(K.S. Jørgensen, unpublished work)' in the text. Please consult Smith or Jørgensen as to the appropriateness, accuracy and acceptability of giving such a citation in the relevant passage.

Form of references. *The instructions for references given here are based on the suggestions given in full in Appendix 6.*

Unpublished work. *The citation of unpublished work which has not been through the fire of refereeing and editing can be misleading. Readers should therefore be alerted* **as they read the text** *that an argument using such a citation may rest on shaky ground; they are simultaneously warned that they will be unable to examine the evidence for themselves. Further, when authors are requested to consult the originator of the unpublished work (the 'personal communicator') before citing it, they often find that they have misremembered or misinterpreted the information or that is has in the meantime proved to be incorrect (Ref. 5, p 87–88).*

Note that the accuracy of references is the author's responsibility. Please check, with the original source if possible, that details are correct and complete, as in the examples given below.

Citations in the text

Use 'Jack & Smith (1977) and Braun et al (1978)' if the authors' names form part of the sentence; otherwise put '(Jack & Smith 1977, Braun et al 1978)'. When there are three or more authors, use the form Braun et al every time. If several papers by the same author(s) published in the same year are cited, put a, b, c, etc. after the year of publication, e.g. Smith (1971b).

The list of references

Form

Type double-spaced throughout.

Order of names

Arrange alphabetically; *but* arrange papers by three or more authors chronologically (earliest paper first) *after* all papers by the same first author alone or with one co-author. List all authors of a paper, up to and including six names; if there are seven or more authors, write 'et al' after giving the first three names. Add a, b, etc. to the date when there are two or more papers by the same author(s) in the same year. List names beginning with 'De', 'Van', 'von', etc. under 'D' or 'V/v', etc.

Order of items

Please note punctuation and order of items in these examples:

> Abel B C, Cain A D, Adam E, Eve A 1976 Bark thickness in apple trees. Tree J 12:90–99
> Bull F, Friend A 1975 Jumping over the moon. In: Jones M, Lloyd P (eds) Space travel. Galaxy Press, Houston (Soc Space Sci Symp 21) vol 3:1–24
> Zorba A, Quinn A 1976 Bone structure of early Cretans, 3rd edn. Elsevier/Excerpta Medica/North-Holland, Amsterdam

That is, give names and initials of up to six authors, year of publication, title of paper or chapter, title of book or abbreviated journal title, volume number (if any), and first and last pages of papers of chapters. For books, add edition number if second or more, editor's name and initials (if there are three or more editors, give the first name and 'et al'), publisher and place of publication, and information (if any) about the series. For journals, omit the issue or part number unless each issue, rather than each volume, begins on p 1. Abbreviate journal titles as in the *International List of Periodical Title Word Abbreviations* (the system used by *Chemical Abstracts, Biological Abstracts* and *Index Medicus*).

PROOFS

You will receive two sets of proofs of your chapter by about 15 June 1980. Further sets of proofs cannot be supplied. Please write *essential* corrections clearly in ink in the margins of the proofs, with corresponding marks in the body of the text. Answer any queries written in the margins of proofs, if only by writing 'OK as set'. Keep corrections to a minimum and do not add new material. Please make sure that your co-authors (if any) approve of any changes. Please return one set of corrected proofs by 1 July 1980 to: [name and address]. Failure to do so will result in the chapter being printed without your corrections.

REPRINTS

The publishers will send the principal author of each chapter 50 free offprints of the chapter when the book is ready. Extra reprints can be ordered from the publisher before the book is printed; an order form with prices will be sent with the proofs.

BOOKS

The principal author of one or more chapters (but not the co-authors, if any) will receive a copy of the book as soon as it is published (about mid-September 1980). Contributors may order further copies from the publisher [name and address of Sales Department] at 30% discount on the list price.

ABBREVIATIONS

Please use abbreviations sparingly, if at all. Abbreviations acceptable in this book are as follows:

(*Give the list, in alphabetical order.*)

These guidelines can be adapted for conference proceedings and journal articles (see Chapter 2).

Appendix 5
Checklist for manuscripts: questions and action on receipt in editorial office

1. Does the title page include:
   title
   keywords (if requested)
   names of all authors and their affiliations
   running title
   address for correspondence and reprint requests?
2. Is an abstract provided? Is it
   informative
   intelligible without reference to the text
   suitable for direct use by abstracting services
   of suitable form and length?
3. Are the pages numbered consecutively? Are they all present?
4. Are all tables numbered and present? Are they complete with titles and footnotes to make them intelligible without reference to the text? Are any of them too large for the format of the book or journal?
5. Are legends for illustrations separately listed? Are they typed in the correct form?
6. Are all diagrams, graphs and photographs of good quality? Are they all identified in pencil? Do they correspond to the legends?
7. Is there a separate page of references, typed double-spaced in correct form and complete with titles and inclusive pagination?
8. If a second copy of the manuscript has been requested, is it present and complete with respect to items 1–7?
9. If the paper was solicited, does the abstract indicate that the author has dealt with the subjects requested, and does the text—quickly perused—confirm this? Are any ethical problems likely to arise?
10. If anything is missing, or does not follow the guidelines, the paper

is best returned to the author immediately with a request for rectification. A copy of the guidelines for authors, marked appropriately, may help to clarify the request.

Note: At the end of the first round of refereeing and editing, items 2, 4, 5 and 6 will have to be reconsidered in the light of the editor's greater familiarity with the manuscript's contents. All the above questions can, however, be adequately judged when a manuscript first arrives, and should be checked before the manuscript is sent to the referees.

Appendix 6
Guidelines and review form for referees

See Chapter 4 for discussion of refereeing, and Chapter 1 for a further exploration of the kinds of criteria that might be used in judging the suitability of articles for publication in any particular journal.

The covering letter to the referee might read as follows.

Dear　　　　　　,

The enclosed manuscript has been submitted for publication in the Journal of Botanical Geology. I would very much appreciate your advice as to its suitability for publication. The enclosed form may be helpful in indicating the kind of advice we are seeking. If you consider the article good, excellent, or outstanding I would appreciate your comments on both major and minor aspects of the paper; otherwise, on major aspects only.

If *for any reason* you find yourself unable to review the manuscript within the next two weeks, please return it to me immediately using the return envelope provided. Alternatively, if you can suggest another referee—perhaps a colleague in your department—please discuss the possibility with me (by telephone if convenient). Refereeing by a junior colleague must be supervised, and subject to the usual constraints of confidentiality.

Please type any comments you think would be useful to the author(s) on the page provided with the enclosed form and on any continuation sheets as necessary. Harsh phraseology should be avoided. The comments may be signed or unsigned, as you prefer. Any comments intended for the editor but not for the author(s) should be sent in a covering letter when you reply. *Please do not communicate with the author(s) in any way.*

The referee's form asks for your assessments of various aspects of the paper. Please tick the appropriate comment—or N/A (not appropriate)—under each number. Use of the form is not obligatory, but the categories listed do indicate criteria the editorial board considers important for acceptance of papers for publication. Please note that we are concerned solely with whether the article is suitable for this journal, not with whether it deserves publication at all. Consequently, journal policy may dictate that I act contrary to your advice when it comes to a decision. If this happens, I hope you will not be offended; I shall try to give reasons for my decision.

For acceptable papers, we are anxious to improve clarity, succinctness and quality of presentation generally. Your suggestions to this end will be welcome if you have time to offer them in your comments. Please do not write on the manuscript itself, but on a photocopy of it if you wish to go into this degree of detail. Tables and illustrations are as important as text in the quality of presentation. Please also examine the title and abstract critically, with the needs of information retrieval in mind.

We are most grateful for your help.

Yours sincerely,

The Editor

Enc.

The enclosed referee's form might look something like the following sample (drawn up by K. Faegri as the outcome of the ELSE Working Group on refereeing practices):

REFEREEING FORM

Journal:

Manuscript:

Author(s):

1. Paper
    of general importance
    important in the field of ...
    very specialized
    outside my competence – should be submitted to ...

2. Information contained
    new
    valuable confirmation
    repetition of known results

3. Technical and experimental methods
    new
    adequate, well controlled
    inadequate, controls insufficient

4. Amount of experimental material and data
   large
   adequate
   small
   insufficient

5. Calculations
   adequate
   erroneous

6. Statistical treatment
   adequate
   erroneous

7. Interpretation
   adequate
   not warranted by data
   suffers from important omissions
   suffers from loose generalizing

8. Title
   adequately descriptive
   should be changed (to . . .)

9. Abstract
   clear and adequate
   should be rewritten
   missing

10. Language
    grammatically good
    needs revision

11. Presentation and style
    adequate
    too brief for clarity
    too comprehensive, must be shortened
    contain irrelevant material
    may cause offence
    arrangement unsuitable, should be better subdivided
    do not follow Instructions to authors

12. Illustrations
    number and quality adequate
    Fig. . . . may be left out
    A figure is desirable to illustrate . . .
    Fig. . . . need not be in half-tone/a separate plate
    Quality of prints/drawings inadequate

13. Tables
    adequate
    should be rearranged to represent data more clearly
    Table . . . may be left out

14. Abbreviations, formulas, units
    conform with accepted standards
    do not conform with accepted standards, should be changed
    should be explained

15. Literature references
    adequate
    inadequate
    to . . . cannot be located

16. The paper is graded as
    excellent
    good
    acceptable
    sound, but dull
    confirmatory
    significance not obvious
    weak
    too speculative
    too preliminary
    outside the scope of the periodical, might be suitable for . . .
and
    deserves urgent publication
    is acceptable with minor/extensive revisions as indicated
    is not acceptable (conditional/unconditional)

17. Further information necessary before decision

18. Comments – see separate page (attached)

Appendix 7
References in scientific publications: suggestions from a Ciba Foundation Workshop, London, 25 November 1977

Summary

A unified system for bibliographical references is described. The suggestions, which are in the main compatible with ISO DIS 690, allow the name/date (Harvard), the numeric-alphabetic or the sequential-numeric system to be used for references in scientific books and serials; an optional dual-access system is also outlined. The 'master typescript' system described allows numbers to be substituted for names/dates *in the text* when a paper is submitted to a publication that uses a numeric system, In *reference lists,* depending on what the author's target publication requires, references must be arranged either alphabetically or sequentially, in the order of their citation in the text. In all lists, whether alphabetic or sequential, references should contain the same elements, arranged in the same order, as follows:

> Abel B C, Cain A D, Adam E, Eve A 1976 Bark thickness in apple trees. Tree J 12:90–99

Extra punctuation marks can be added if required. Authors may leave further capitalization and italicization to be marked by editors/copy editors. Titles of articles should be included; they can be easily deleted if the publication does not require them. Journal titles should be given *either* in full *or* abbreviated in accordance with the standards named in this document.

INTRODUCTION

The suggestions made here form a two-part system dealing with the citation and arrangement of bibliographic references in scientific serials and monographs. The proposals are addressed to authors, typists, editors and copy editors, and will also interest publishers and printers. The *'master typescript'* method explained here can be easily adapted for publications using either the name/date or one of two main numeric systems for references (sequential-numeric and numeric-alphabetic). The *standard layout* suggested for references in reference lists can be used for all three systems. If there are differences between the suggestions in this document and an editor's 'Instructions to authors', the latter must take precedence in the final manuscript submitted.

The purpose of citations (in the text) and references (in the list) is the identification and retrieval of documents (usually an article or a monograph). The connection between citation and reference is made either by repetition of the author's *name* and the *year* of the publication cited, or by repetition of a reference *number*. The two most common systems that use numbers assign them either in the *sequence* in which the references appear in the text or by numbering references in an *alphabetic* list.

These suggestions are similar to the recommendations made in the draft International Standard (ISO DIS 690) on bibliographic references, except that in the system described here initials are used instead of forenames, punctuation marks are kept to a minimum, ISSNs and ISBNs are not mentioned, and (for monographs) the publisher's name precedes the place of publication.

The theme of these suggestions is uniformity. They are put forward as a compromise between the best of the innumerable systems that at present take up so much time when manuscripts are being prepared for publication.

The *master typescript method* is based on two premises: first that it is much easier to convert the text from the name/date to one of the numeric systems than vice versa, and secondly that many authors use the name/date system in preparing the early drafts of their papers. (*Note:* Authors who are sure that their papers will be accepted by a publication using a numeric system do not need to use the master typescript method but they should follow the suggestions made here in sections 3 and 4.)

The principal features of these suggestions are:

(1) a master typescript method is described that allows easy conversion of name/date citations to numeric citations;
(2) reference lists should be arranged according to the system (numeric or alphabetic) required by the author's first target journal;
(3) references should always be made up of the same elements, arranged in the same order;

(4) references should be styled with a maximum of information and should conform as closely as possible with the conventions of spelling and punctuation of ordinary text in the language concerned. However, for easier transformation between reference systems, punctuation is here kept to a minimum;

(5) other than as shown in the examples, capitalization and italicization of elements in references need not be indicated by authors but may be left for editors or copy editors to specify according to each publication's typographical style;

(6) an optional dual-access system is described that not only provides readers with a bibliography but also allows them to refer back from the reference list to find where the reference is cited in the text, using the reference list as an author index.

If a master typescript is prepared according to these recommendations, the author can—with a minimum of effort—alter copies of the master so that they conform to the requirements of individual serials or books, as follows:

(a) if the information contained in certain elements (e.g. titles of articles) that are listed here as standard parts of a reference is not wanted in a particular publication, the unwanted elements are deleted before the final typescript is submitted. If punctuation additional to that recommended in this document is required by the publication, punctuation marks are added as necessary.

(b) If the numeric-alphabetic system is required in the target publication, the list is numbered and numbers are substituted for the citations originally typed in parentheses in the text.

(c) If the sequential-numeric system is required in the target publication, the list is rearranged/retyped in order of citation (in practice, if the first journal to which an author submits a paper uses sequential numbering, the references in the list should be typed in the order of their appearance in the text). Name and date citations in the text are then changed to the relevant numbers.

SUGGESTIONS

1. Citations in the text

1.1   In the master typescript, citations should be in the name/date form.

Jack & Smith (1977) report . . .
or
. . . as was recently reported (Jack & Smith 1977, Braun et al 1978).

If the target publication uses a numeric system, several spaces should be left after each citation in the text.

After conversion to a numeric system (1.5), names of cited authors will appear in the text only if they were originally cited outside parentheses:

Jack & Smith (1977) report that . . .

becomes

Jack & Smith (22) report that . . .

But

   as was recently reported (Jack & Smith 1977)

becomes

as was recently reported (22).

1.2   For citations in the text that refer to three or more authors, the form Brown et al should be used every time such citations are made, including the first.

1.3   If citations refer to specific pages in books or in lengthy journal articles, those page numbers belong with the citations in the text, not in the reference list, and may be placed after the date. Reading is facilitated if the year or reference number is separated from the page number by adequate punctuation:

(Smith 1977 p 302), or (Smith 1977:p 302).

In a numeric system this would become:

(22:p 302) or (ref.22:p 302)

Alternatively (and perhaps preferable where superior numbers are used), a new number may be assigned each time a different page of the same book or article is cited in the text; each such reference in the list then gives the specific page number as well as the other elements of the reference.

1.4   Citations referring to communications which cannot be retrieved by readers do not belong in the reference list. If included at all, such communications should be described in the text as 'unpublished work' (*not* as 'in preparation') or as a 'personal communication' (*not* as a 'private communication') and the source should be included:

. . . as was found recently (J Smith, 1977, personal communication).

or (for a meeting without published proceedings):

This project has produced significant results (M. Brown, unpublished paper, 3rd Congr Psychol Eng, 25 November 1977).

1.5   If a numeric system is required in the publication, appropriate numbers are substituted for the name/date citations in the text of the master typescript (see 2.1.5 and 2.2.1).

1.6   Where names/dates are used in the text, and if it is desirable for readers to be able to refer back from the reference list to the text, a dual-access system (Abbott 1974) may be used. In this system, numbers are placed *between* names and dates in the text, with the numbers running consecutively through the text (as in the sequential-numeric system, but with each citation being assigned a new number, however many times a reference may be cited in the text):

Jack & Smith[1] (1977) report . . .

or

. . . as already described (Jack & Smith[5] 1977).

These numbers are then placed in parentheses at the end of each reference in the reference list in the way shown in 2.1.6.

2. Reference lists

2.1   Alphabetic lists

2.1.1   For publications requiring alphabetic reference lists, entries should be arranged in strict alphabetic order, *unless* there are several citations of articles/monographs by *three or more* different authors *with the same first author*. References of this latter kind, where 'Brown et al' (for example) is followed by several dates in the text, should be arranged chronologically in the list, regardless of the number (*above two*) of authors and regardless of the alphabetical order of the names of authors other than the first (since the names of the other authors are not known when the text is being read). References arranged in this alphabetic-chronological way should be placed after papers by Brown or by Brown & X, as shown in 2.1.2.

2.1.2   Arrangement of entries referring to the same first author (IUB-CEBJ 1973):

Citation in text	Reference list
Brown (1977)	Brown A 1977 . . .
Brown & Green (1976)	Brown A, Green B 1976 . . .
Brown & White (1975)	Brown A, White C 1975 . . .
Brown et al (1974)	Brown A, White C, Green B 1974 . . .
Brown et al (1975)	Brown A, Black D, White C, Green B 1975 . . .
Brown et al (1976)	Brown A, Black D, Green B 1976 . . .
Brown et al (1977a)	Brown A, White C, Green B 1977a Why wheels turn. Gen Eng 7:59–65
Brown et al (1977b)	Brown A, Green B, White C 1977b How wheels turn. Gen Eng 8:10–15

2.1.3 Authors' surnames should be given and alphabetized exactly as spelt, with prefixes. *Mc* and *M'* should not be alphabetized as *Mac*. Names beginning with prepositions such as *de, De, van, von, O',* etc. should be alphabetized under the first letter of the prefix. The term *Jr* or roman numerals may be added after initials. The important principle is conformity between the citation in the text and the entry in the reference list.

2.1.4 Terms such as 'ibid.', 'idem', 'op.cit.' and 'loc.cit.' should never be substituted for complete references in reference lists. In the text, if used at all, they should be used sparingly and with great caution. Later changes in the text can make such references misleading.

2.1.5 If the numeric-alphabetic system is required, the alphabetically arranged references are first numbered:

1. Adam E 1976 . . .
2. Adamson J 1975 . . .

The numbers are then substituted for the name/date citations in the text.

2.1.6 If the dual-access system described in 1.6 is used, the numbers from the text are inserted in parentheses at the end of each reference in the reference list:

Jack V F, Smith J 1977 Structure of seeds of Stellaria media (L.) Vill. J Bot 35:290–295 (1,5,149)

2.2 Sequential-numeric lists

2.2.1 If the sequential-numeric system is required, the name/date text citations are numbered sequentially in the order of citation in the text; the references in the list are numbered accordingly and the list is arranged so that the entries are in numerical order, regardless of which letter of the alphabet the (first) author's name starts with. When a reference is cited more than once in the sequential system, either (a) the reference may retain the same number, thus breaking with the strict sequential principle, or (b) it may appear as many times in the list as it is cited in the text, each time numbered according to the sequence of citation. Before conversion or preparation of the typescript the author must consult the instructions to authors of the target publication to see how it handles multiple citation of a single reference.

3. References to articles in serials

3.1 References to articles in serials should take the following forms:

Jack V F 1977 The seeds of Stellaria media (L.) Vill. J Bot 35:257–261

Abel B C, Cain A D, Adam E, Eve A 1976 Bark thickness in apple trees
Tree J 12:90–99

3.2   This system uses the minimum punctuation necessary to present
the information clearly. It also takes into consideration that punctuation marks can be added easily if the journal's style so requires, and
that words and characters can be deleted more easily than they can be
added (see 3.4). The references in 3.1 include the following features:

Surnames and initials of all authors are inverted.
The initials are spaced to permit punctuation if required.
A comma appears between the initials of one author and the surname of
   the next author.
No ampersand or 'and' is needed between authors' names but space
   should be left for its subsequent insertion, if required.
A stop is placed only at the end of titles of articles.
No elements are underlined.

3.3   The date of publication is placed immediately after the authors'
names. These two pieces of information are the most valuable in identifying or appraising a reference and are the key elements in locating a
reference in a reference list when name/date citations are used.
3.4   Titles of articles in serials should be given, as many readers consider this to be essential information. However, if the first target
publication will not print them, the articles titles can easily be deleted
or omitted.
3.5   Serial titles should *either* be given in full, *or* be abbreviated in accordance with ISO 833, ANSI Z39.5 (1969), and BS 4148 (1970, 1975)
(these standards are compatible with each other) or with lists (such as
Index Medicus, BIOSIS List of Serials, etc.) based on the principles
set out in those standards. One-word titles are never abbreviated.
3.6   First *and* last pages of articles in serials and chapters in
monographs should be given. This information tells readers the length
of the article, i.e. whether it is a short note or letter or a full-length
paper, and indicates how much a photocopy is likely to cost.
3.7   The issue number of a serial is redundant information unless
each issue is paged separately; if issues *are* paged separately, the issue
numbers should be inserted (in parentheses) immediately after the
volume number:

12. Jack V F 1967 Trees. Sci Am 17(3):38–47

For newspapers or popular weeklies the full date of the issue may be
given instead of the volume number:

Smith A 1974 Creating wealth. Times (Lond) 25 November: p 3

4. References to monographs

4.1   References to monographs should take the following basic forms:

4.1.1   Monographs by one or more authors, without an editor:

Jack V F 1977 Monograph of Stellaria media (L.) Vill. Pergamon, Oxford

Zorba A, Quinn A 1976 Bone structure of early Cretans, 3rd edn. Elsevier/Excerpta Medica/North-Holland, Amsterdam

4.1.2   Chapters or sections of edited monographs:

Jack V F 1977 Seeds of Stellaria media (L.) Vill. In: Smith J (ed) Anatomy of Caryophyllaceae. Springer, Berlin, p 250–280

or (preferred if there are references to several contributors to the same book):

Jack V F 1977 Seeds of Stellaria media (L.) Vill. In: Smith (1977) p 250–280

...

...

Smith J (ed) 1977 Anatomy of Caryophyllaceae. Springer, Berlin

4.1.3   Chapters in edited monographs forming part of a series:

Bull F, Friend A 1975 Jumping over the moon. In: Jones M, Lloyd P (eds) Space travel. Galaxy Press, Houston (Soc Space Sci Symp 21) vol 3:1–24

4.2   The references in 4.1 include the following features:

Name(s) and initials of editor(s) are given as shown in 4.1.2 and 4.1.3. 'Editor', 'editors', and 'edition', may be abbreviated as 'ed', 'eds', and 'edn' respectively.

A stop is placed at the end of the chapter titles.

The publisher's name, shortened if necessary, is placed before the place of publication. For publishers operating in several places, it is sufficient to give the name of the first place listed on the title page of the cited book as the publisher's address.

Page numbers or volume and page numbers referred to, are placed after the place of publication.

No full stop is used at the end of the entries.

No elements are underlined.

References

Abbott K M 1974 References—a new system used by CSIR. Scientiae 15:27–28

ANSI Z39.5 1969 Abbreviation of titles for periodicals. American National Standards Institute, New York

BIOSIS list of serials. BIOSIS/Biological Abstracts, Philadelphia

BS 4148 1970 The abbreviation of titles of periodicals. Part 1. Principles. British Standards Institution, London

BS 4148 1975 The abbreviation of titles of periodicals. Part 2. Word-abbreviation list. British Standards Institution, London

ELSE Working Group 1977 Recommendations on references. Earth Life Sci Ed 5:7–8

Index Medicus. US Dept of Health, Education and Welfare, Public Health Service, National Institutes of Health. US Government Printing Office, Washington, DC

ISO DIS 690 Bibliographic references to monographs and serials

ISO 833 Documentation—International list of periodical title word abbreviations

IUB-CEBJ 1973 The citation of bibliographic references in biochemical journals. Recommendations (1971). Biochem J 135:1–3 [and elsewhere]

This document evolved from discussions before, during and after an ELSE-Ciba Foundation Workshop on The Consolidation and Adoption of a Rational System for References, held at the Ciba Foundation, London, on 25 November 1977. The Workshop, funded largely by the Ciba Foundation, was held in order that the ELSE Working Group's recommendations on references (1977) and the ensuing discussions and attempts at formulating generally acceptable guidelines could be discussed by a wider group. The participants in the Workshop represented the earth sciences, life sciences, chemistry and biochemistry, physics and engineering.

ELSE-Ciba Foundation Workshop on Consolidation and Adoption of a Rational System for References held at the Ciba Foundation, London, on 25th November 1977

*List of participants**

Miriam Balaban	Editor, Desalination; and National Council for Research and Development, Jerusalem, Israel
D H M Bowen	Director, Book and Journals Division, American Chemical Society, Washington, DC, USA
L W Carter	Chief copy editor, Springer-Verlag, Heidelberg, West Germany
Anita DeVivo	Executive Editor, Journals of the American Psychological Association, Washington, DC, USA
W G Evans	Royal Society, London, UK
K Faegri (Chairman)	Editor, Naturen, University of Bergen, Norway
H Götze	President, Springer-Verlag, Heidelberg, West Germany
N Hankins	Institute of Physics, Bristol, UK
A Hopkinson	UNISIST Centre for Bibliographic Descriptions, British Library Research and Development Dept, London, UK

*N.B. Not all the participants agree with all the details of the suggestions made in this document.

E J Huth	Editor, Annals of Internal Medicine, American College of Physicians, Philadelphia, USA
C Liébecq	Chairman, IUB Committee of Editors of Biochemical Journals, Liège, Belgium
S Lock	Editor, British Medical Journal, London, UK
A Martinsson	Editor, Lethaia, Dept of Palaeobiology, University of Uppsala, Sweden
Maeve O'Connor	Senior Editor, Ciba Foundation, London, UK
D Sharp	Deputy Editor, The Lancet, London, UK
J St Aubyn	Editor in Chief, Institution of Electrical Engineers, Stevenage, Herts, UK

Appendix 8
Code of advertisement policy

This code is reproduced by kind permission of the editor of the British
Medical Journal.
*For disciplines other than medicine this code could be modified as
necessary.*

(a) The publication of advertisements has become a recognized function of
medical journals, but any advertisement may be refused without explanation.

(b) The advertisements in a journal, like the text, are a source of information for readers. This information is provided by the advertiser, who is
responsible for its accuracy; but care should be taken that no advertisement
contravenes the principles set out below.

(c) Advertisements should not imply or promise benefit which, after due
consideration and, if necessary, consultation with experts, appears highly im-
probable. Claims should be supported by trustworthy evidence.

(d) No therapeutic product should be advertised unless its essential con-
stituents, and their quantity in each dose, are disclosed to the editor of the
journal. Methods of manufacture need not be disclosed.

(e) Advertisements should not impugn the dignity of the medical profession or offend against good taste or recognized standards of medical practice.

(f) Advertisements of drugs or appliances should not contain testimonials,
anonymous or otherwise. This does not exclude dated references to reputable
medical journals, but such advertisements must not include misleading
quotations from articles.

(g) Advertisements of books may contain quoted matter from reviews so
long as a dated reference to the review is given, but not the name of the
reviewer.

(h) Opinions expressed by contributors to medical journals must not be
quoted in a way that makes them look like editorial opinions.

(i) The distinction between the advertisement columns and the text should
be kept so clear that no ordinary reader can mistake one for the other.

(j) Publication of an advertisement means that in the Editor's judgement it does not contain misleading statements: but such publication does not necessarily mean that the journal endorses the claims made, and such endorsement must not be implied in advertisements of the same product in the lay press.

(k) Medical journals should not accept advertisements of products that are improperly advertised in the lay press or elsewhere.

(l) Advertisements should be considered on their own merits. An advertisement that is otherwise acceptable is not necessarily made unacceptable by the fact that the advertiser is putting forward improper claims for other products.

(m) Disparaging references: no advertisement should be published which appears to bring discredit on the products of other manufacturers.

Appendix 9
Guidelines for book reviewers

Journal of Botanical Geology: Guidelines for book reviewers

Length and form of review: 700–1000 words, typed double-spaced starting on the attached page 1.

Date by which review should be sent in: [date within two/four weeks of book being posted to reviewer]. If for any reason you cannot review the book by this date, please telephone the book review editor (Dr X. Libris, Telephone no.   ) as soon as possible.

Fee: the editor regrets that no fee is payable for book reviews; the review copy, however, remains your property.

Anonymity: reviews in the journal are normally signed. If you have a particular reason for remaining anonymous, please discuss this with the book review editor; if he agrees to anonymity, please mark your review accordingly.

Please note that the journal requires fair and balanced reviews. Even if your review is a negative one, please use temperate language in your evaluation of the arguments in the book and avoid attacking the authors/editors personally.

There is no need to comment on the price of the book unless it is outstandingly expensive (or cheap): readers can judge for themselves, with the help of your evaluation, whether a book is worth what the publisher is charging for it. Paperbacks are not in themselves cheaper than hardbacks; when they cost less than a hardback book of the same length it is only because the publisher expects to sell a very large number of copies and can price the paperback accordingly.

In your review, please:

(1) Describe the contents briefly.
(2) Indicate the intended readership.
(3) Evaluate the book first on its own terms, saying how well you think the authors/editors have achieved their stated aims. You may then want to criticize those aims and the way the subject has been handled, taking into account the following questions (where relevant), amongst others that may occur to you:

    Is the material well selected and well organized?
    Are the arguments clear and logically correct?
    Are the statements of fact accurate?

Are the conclusions convincing, original and important for the discipline as a whole, or for the special topic of the book?

Where experimental work is discussed, is the experimental design satisfactory?

Is the style clear, concise and readable?

(4) Comment briefly on any or all of the following:

the general appearance of the book,

the legibility of the typeface,

the incidence of typographical errors,

the clarity of the illustrations,

the accuracy, up-to-dateness and coverage of the references, and

the usefulness of the index (if there is one).

(5) Please return the review (which should include your name and address) to:

Dr X. Libris,

Dept of Geobotany,

The University,

Capital City,

UK

Book review for Journal of Botanical Geology, page 1

From (name): . . . .

Address: . . . .

. . . .

. . . .

. . . .

Title and subtitle of
book reviewed: . . . .

. . . .

Edition no. (if other than 1st): . . . .

Name(s) and initials of
author(s) or editor(s): . . . .

. . . .

Year of publication: . . . .

Publisher: . . . .

Place of publication: . . . .

Name of series: . . . .

No. of pages: . . . .

No. of tables and illustrations: . . . .

Price: . . . .

(Above to be filled in by editorial office)

Appendix 10
List of editors' associations

(The addresses below apply to July 1978)

LIFE SCIENCES

CBE—Council of Biology Editors (North America)
President: Dr H Edward Kennedy, Executive Director, Biosciences Information Service, 2100 Arch Street, Philadelphia, Pa. 19103
Secretary: Prof A J Ladman, Department of Anatomy, University of New Mexico Medical School
Treasurer: Gisella Pollack

ELSE—European Association of Editors of Biological Periodicals
President: Herbert J Kramer, Medizinische Univ. Poliklinik, 5300 Bonn, Wilhelmstr. 35–37, FRG
Vice President: Gillian Page, Director of Journals, Cambridge University Press, 200 Euston Road, London NW1 2DB, UK
Secretary: Nancy Morris, Bruins, 30 Longdown Road, Lower Bourne, Farnham, Surrey, GU10 3JL, UK
Treasurer: Miriam Balaban, National Council for Research and Development, POB 4059, Jerusalem, Israel

FOOD AND AGRICULTURE

Association of Food and Agriculture Journals (in formation)
Ernest Mann, Commonwealth Bureau of Dairy Science & Technology, Shinfield, Reading RG2, UK

EARTH SCIENCES

Editerra—(Europe and adjoining areas)
President: Prof. Svend Saxov, Laboratory of Geophysics, 6–8 Finlandsgade, DK–8200 Aarhus–N, Denmark
Secretary: Nancy Morris, Bruins, 30 Longdown Road, Lower Bourne, Farnham, Surrey GU10 3JL, UK
Treasurer: Anthony P Harvey, Ragstones, Broadoak, Heathfield, Sussex TN21 8UD, UK

AESE—Association of Earth Science Editors (North America)
President: Dr Stuart E Jenness, POB 7376, Ottawa, Ontario KiL 8E4, Canada

Secretary-Treasurer: Mr John Heller, US Geological Survey, Denver Federal Center, Stop 303, Box 25046, Denver, Colo. 80225

IUGS—Advisory Board for Publication
Chairman: Michael G Bassett, Department of Geology, National Museum of Wales, Cardiff CF1 3NP, UK

Alegeo—(Latin America)
Dr Cecily Petzall, Dirección de Geología MMH, Centro Simón Bolívar, Torre Norte, piso 19, Caracas, Venezuela

BIOCHEMISTRY

CEBJ—IUB Committee of Editors of Biochemical Journals (International)
Prof. Claude Liébecq, 69/054 Bd. de la Constitution, B-4020 Liège, Belgium

CHEMISTRY

ACS-CAS—American Chemical Society and Chemical Abstracts (US)
There is no association, but Dr D H Michael Bowen is on IFSEA organizing committee, and ACS-CAS is actively involved in editors' affairs.

IUPAC—International Union of Pure and Applied Chemistry
Considering formation of editors' committee
Executive Secretary: Dr Maurice Williams, IUPAC Secretariat, 2–3 Pound Way, Cowley Centre, Oxford

EdEuChem—Editors of European Chemistry
President: Prof. E Cherbuliez, Fossard 48, CH-1231 Conches/Geneva
Secretary: Dr Edwin Kisman, Sigma Chemie, Publishing Foundation, Riouwstraat 153, POB 1767, The Hague

IFCC—International Federation of Clinical Chemistry

CEJCCC—Commission of Editors of Journals Concerned with Clinical Chemistry
Chairman: Dr R Dybkaer, Dept of Clinical Chemistry, de Gamles By, Nørre Allee 41, DK-2200, Copenhagen N, Denmark
Secretary: Mr P M G Broughton, Wolfson Research Laboratories, Department of Clinical Chemistry, Queen Elizabeth Medical Centre, Birmingham B15 2TH, UK

PHYSICS

There is no editors' association but the European Physical Society has a scheme for standards for the Europhysics journals and the American Institute of Physics is an active publications centre.

IUPAP—Prof. B R Coles, Department of Solid State Physics, Imperial College, Prince Consort Road, London SW7, UK

EPS—Publications Advisory Committee
Chairman: Prof. E R Dobbs, Bedford College, London

EPS Secretariat, POB 39, CH-1213 Petit Lancy 2, Switzerland

UK IP–Executive Secretary: Dr Louis Cohen, The Institute of Physics, 47 Belgrave Sq., London SW1X 8QX

Prof. J Ziman, University of Bristol, H H Wills Physics Laboratory, BS8 1TL

Vice-President: Prof. R G Chambers, University of Bristol

Director of Publications: C I Pedersen, Techno House, Redcliffe Way, BS1 6NX, Bristol

USA AIP—Dr A W Kenneth Metzner, Director, Publications Division, American Institute of Physics, 335 E 45th St., New York, NY 10017

Dr William Koch, Director of American Institute of Physics

CRYSTALLOGRAPHY

International Union of Crystallography

Executive Secretary: Dr J N King, 13 White Friars, Chester CH1 1NZ

Former Editor: Prof. A J C Wilson, Dept of Physics, University of Birmingham, POB 363, Birmingham, UK

Editor, Acta Crystallographica, Prof. S C Abrahams, Bell Labs., 600 Mountain Ave., Murray Hill, NJ 07974

Prof. Andre Guinier, Laboratoire de Physique des Solides, Université Paris Sud Orsay, France

MATHEMATICS

No editors' association but Mathematical Association of America (MAA) and American Mathematical Society (AMS) active and interested.

MAA—Mathematical Association of America

Executive Director: Dr Alfred B. Willcox, 1225 Connecticut Ave., NW, Washington, DC 20036

Prof. Earl J Taft, Rutgers, The State University of New Jersey, Department of Mathematics, Hill Center for Mathematical Sciences, Busch Campus, New Brunswick, NJ 08903

AMS—American Mathematical Society

Dr William J Leveque, POB 6248, Providence, RI 02940

ANTHROPOLOGY

CIPA—Committee on International Publication in Anthropology (International)

Prof. Cyril S. Belshaw, Editor, Current Anthropology, Dept of Anthropology and Sociology, University of British Columbia, Vancouver, BC V6T 1W5

Dr Isaac Chivas, Laboratoire d'Anthropologie Sociale, Collège de France, 11 Place Marcelin Berthelot, Paris 5e

SOCIOLOGY

Ad hoc Council of Social Science Editors (international)
Prof. James L McCartney, Department of Sociology, University of Missouri, Columbia, MO 65201

PHILOSOPHY

Association of Philosophy Journal Editors
President: Prof. Robert N Beck, Department of Philosophy, Clark University, Worcester, MA 01610

HUMANITIES

CELJ—Conference of Editors of Learned Journals
President: Marilyn Gaull, Department of English, Temple University, College of Liberal Arts, Philadelphia, Pa. 19122

PSYCHOLOGY

Anita DeVivo, American Psychological Association, 1200 Seventeenth St., NW, Washington, DC 20036

WATER RESOURCES KNOWLEDGE TRANSFER

Dr Neil Grigg, Water Resources Research Institute, 124 Riddick Bldg., North Carolina State University, Raleigh, NC 27607

ENGINEERING

IEEE—Institute of Electrical and Electronics Engineers (North America)
Elwood Gannett, Institute of Electrical and Electronics Engineers, 345 E. 47th St., New York, NY 10017

Institution of Electrical Engineers (UK)
Editor in Chief: J D St. Aubyn, Institution of Electrical Engineers, Stevenage, Herts., SG1 1HQ, UK

GENERAL

ASJ—Association of Scientific Journals (North America) (US Association of Scholarly Publishing contemplated—John Strawhorn, Capital Systems Group, 6110 Executive Blvd., Rockville, Maryland 20852)

James Lufkin, G2118 Honeywell Plaza, Minneapolis MN 55408

Editeast—Association of Editors in Science in Southeast Asia, Australia and Oceania
President: Dr Santokh Singh, Geological Survey of Malaysia, Jalan Guerney, Kuala Lumpur, Malaysia
Treasurer: Dr Amando M Dalisay, Exec. Dir., National Research Council of the Philippines, PTRI Building, Bicutan, Tagig, Rizal, Philippines
Secretary: Dr Bakri Abbas, LIPI. Medan Merdeka Selatan II, Jakarta, Malaysia

ALPSP—Association of Learned and Professional Society Publishers, c/o Institution of Mechanical Engineers, 1 Birdcage Walk, London SW1H 9JJ, UK
Secretary: R J Millson

IFSEA—International Federation of Scientific Editors' Associations

Organizing Committee

Miriam Balaban, National Council for Research & Development, POB 4059, Jerusalem (for correspondence)
D H Michael Bowen, American Chemical Society, 1155 Sixteenth St., Washington, DC 20036
Martin Cremer, Gesellschaft für Information und Dokumentation MBH, 6000 Frankfurt/Main 71 (Niederrad), Herriotstrasse 5, W. Germany
Louis Cohen, Institute of Physics, 47 Belgrave Sq., London SW1X 8QX
Knut Faegri, Botanical Museum, Bergen University, N 5014 Bergen, Norway
H Edward Kennedy, Biological Abstracts, 2100 Arch St., Phila, Pa. 19103
Wolfgang Löhner, UNESCO, 7 place de Fontenoy, 75700 Paris
Ernest Mann, Commonwealth Bureau of Dairy Science and Technology, Shinfield, Reading RG2
Anders Martinsson, Department of Palaeobiology, University of Uppsala, POB 564, S-751, 22 Uppsala
Jacques Michel, Bureau National de l'Information Scientifique et Technique, 8–10 rue Crillon, Paris Cedex 04
Gillian Page, Cambridge University Press, POB 92, London NW1 2DB
Udo Schützsack, Gesellschaft für Information und Dokumentation MBH, 6000 Frankfurt/Main 71 (Niederrad) Herriotstrasse 5

Organizations interested in editors' affairs—either members or observers

UNESCO—Division of the General Information Programme
UNESCO, 7 place de Fontenoy, 75700 Paris
Dr Adam Wysocki
Dr Wolfgang Löhner

Commission of the European Communities, Directorate General for Scientific and Technical Information and Information Management
J Michel Gibb, DG XIII, European Centre, Kirchberg, Luxembourg
ICSU—International Council of Scientific Unions

F W G Baker, Executive Secretary, ICSU, 51 Blvd. de Montmorency, 75016 Paris

GID (formerly IDW)—Gesellschaft für Information und Dokumentation MBH
Dr Martin Cremer, Bischofsweg 31, Frankfurt/Main

BNIST—Bureau National de l'Information Scientifique et Technique, Ministère de l'Industrie et de la Recherche, 8–10 rue Crillon, Paris, Cedex 04
Jacques Michel
Lucette Degail

ISSC—International Social Science Council
Dr Samy Friedman, International Social Science Council, 1, rue Miollis, 75015 Paris

NSF—National Science Foundation, Division of Science Information Services, 18th & G Streets, Washington DC 20550
Sarah Rhodes
William Savin

STM—International Group of Scientific, Technical and Medical Publishers
Paul Nijhoff Asser, Secretary General, 462 Keizersgracht, Amsterdam

ISI—Institute for Scientific Information
Dr Eugene Garfield, President, ISI, 325 Chestnut St., Philadelphia, Pa. 19106

Ciba Foundation
Maeve O'Connor, Senior Editor, The Ciba Foundation, 41 Portland Place, London W1N 4BN

NOP—Nordic Publishing Board in Science (Denmark, Finland, Norway, Sweden)
Dr Walter Schytt, Mrs Synnøve Irgens-Jensen, NOP, NAVG, Munthes gt. 29, Oslo 2, Norway

NOP (M)—NOP for Medicine, Karolinska Institutet S-104 01 Stockholm 60, Sweden

Pacific Science Association—a regional body consisting of the National Research Councils and Academies of the Pacific region—primarily concerned with scientific communication
Dr Roland Force, Secretary General, The British Museum, Honolulu

STC—Society for Technical Communication
H Kenneth Hansen, Chairman of STC International Liaison Committee, 9500 N. Oliver Avenue, Minneapolis, MN 55444

NAS—National Academy of Sciences USA (International Information Policy)
Joel Lloyd, National Academy of Sciences, 2101 Constitution Ave., Washington, DC 20418

Royal Society UK
Dr R Keay, 6 Carlton House Terrace, London SW1

National Enquiry into Scholarly Communication
(Sponsored by the American Council of Learned Societies)
Edward E Booher, Director, POB 2067, Princeton, NJ 08540

Codata
Prof. Edgar F Westrum Jr, Department of Chemistry, University of Michigan, Ann Arbor, Mich. 48109
Codata Secretariat, 51 Blvd de Montmorency, 75016 Paris

ICSU AB POGSI
Jeanne Poyen, Secretary General, 17 rue Mirabeau, 75016 Paris

ISO—International Organization for Standardization
Central Secretariat, 1 rue de Varembe, C.P. 56, CH-1211 Geneva
Mr B Norbrink, Director, Information and Public Relations
Mrs Johanna Eggert, Secretary, ISO/TC-46, DIN Deutsches Institut für Normung, Burggrafenstrasse 4/7, 1 Berlin 30, W. Germany

IDRC—International Development Research Centre, Box 8500, Ottawa K1G 3H9
Reginald MacIntyre, Associate Director, Publication Division

CSG—Capital Systems Group
John Strawhorn, 6110 Executive Blvd., Rockville, Maryland 20852

INSPEC—D Barlow, The Institution of Electrical Engineers, Savoy Place, London WC2R 0BL

ESA—European Space Agency, ESTEC (European Space Research and Technology Centre), Noordwijke, The Netherlands
William Burke

PUDOC—Centre for Agricultural Publishing and Documentation
POB 4, Wageningen, The Netherlands
Aart Rutgers, Director

PCRC—Primary Communications Research Centre, University of Leicester, Leicester LE1 7RH, UK
Prof. A J Meadows, Director

References

Preface

1. Mann P H 1978 'Neurotic, often boneheaded, rarely rational': scholarly authors and their publishers. Bookseller. April 22: 2408–2409 [See also Mann P H 1978 Author-publisher relationships in scholarly publishing. British Library Research & Development Department Report No. 5416. BLRDD, London]
2. DeBakey L 1976 The scientific journal: editorial policies and practices. Mosby, St Louis, Mo.

Chapter 1 Editing outlined

1. Chase J M 1970 Normative criteria for scientific publication. American Sociologist 5:262–265
2. Mollon J D 1976 [Book review of Handbook of perception.] Nature 206:1293–1295
3. DeBakey L 1976 The scientific journal: editoral policies and practices. Mosby, St Louis, Mo.
4. ANSI Z39.1-1967 American national standard for periodicals: format and arrangement. American National Standards Institute, New York

Chapter 2 Guiding authors

1. Nathan D 1977 Franz Ingelfinger retires: a thank-you note from a *Journal* contributor. New England Journal of Medicine 297:285
2. Woodford F P 1968 Scientific writing for graduate students. Rockefeller University Press, New York. Re-issue (1976) available from FASEB, Bethesda, Md.
3. Evans M 1978 The abuse of slides. British Medical Journal 1:905–908
4. Anon 1978 Next slide please. Nature 272:743
5. O'Connor M, Woodford F P 1975 Writing scientific papers in English. Elsevier/Excerpta Medica/North-Holland, Amsterdam
6. DeBakey L 1976 The scientific journal: editorial policies and practices. Mosby, St Louis, Mo.

Chapter 3 Keeping papers moving

1. Glen J W 1977 Editorial processing of manuscripts and proofs. In: Glen J W (ed) Editerra editors' handbook. Editerra, Farnham, Surrey

2. Guidelines for APA Journal Editors 1977 American Psychological Association, Washington, DC

Chapter 4 Working with referees

1. Ingelfinger F J 1974 Peer review in biomedical publication. American Journal of Medicine 56:686–692
2. Kochen M, Perkel B 1978 Improving referee-selection and manuscript evaluation. In: Balaban M (ed) Scientific information transfer: the editor's role. Reidel, Dordrecht (1st Int Conf Sci Ed, Jerusalem, 1977)
3. Pyke D A 1976 How I referee. British Medical Journal 2:1117–1118
4. DeBakey L 1976 The scientific journal: editorial policies and practices. Mosby, St Louis, Mo.
5. Neufeld J 1970 To amend refereeing (letter). Physics Today 23:9–10
6. Prinz G A 1970 More ideas on refereeing (letter). Physics Today 23:11–12

Chapter 5 Manuscript editing: creative and substantive editing

1. DeBakey L, Woodford F P 1973 Extensive revision of scientific articles: whose job? Scholarly Publishing 3:147–151
2. Anon 1970 The craft of shortening. Lancet 2:1077–1078
3. O'Connor M, Woodford F P 1975 Writing scientific papers in English. Elsevier/Excerpta Medica/North-Holland, Amsterdam
4. ANSI Z39.14 1971 American national standard for writing abstracts. American National Standards Institute, New York
5. Landau N, Weiss R B 1976 Information flow between primary journals and secondary services in the biological field. British Library Research & Development Report 5239, British Library Lending Division, Wetherby, West Yorkshire
6. Eisenhart C 1968 Expression of the uncertainties of final results. Science 160:1201–1204
7. Swinscow T D V 1976 Statistics at square one. British Medical Association, London
8. Burg C 1977 As reported in Earth and Life Science Editing No. 4:8
9. Editorial Board 1977 Policy of the Journal and instructions to authors: amendments (1977). Biochemical Journal 161:1–2
10. Kirkman A J 1965 Turning scientists into free thinkers. Nature 206:1293–1295
11. Woodford F P 1967 Sounder thinking through clearer writing. Science 156:743–745
12. Wilson J H Jr 1969 Better written journal papers—who wants them? Science 165:986–987. Rebuttals in Science 166:454–455
13. APA 1977 Publication manual change sheet 2. American Psychological Association, Washington, DC
14. Anon 1976 [Book review of Complications in foot surgery: prevention and management.] Lancet 2:1120
15. McEldowney D 1976 An editor's reading. Scholarly Publishing 7:315–320

16. Strunk W Jr 1918 The elements of style. [Second edition by Strunk W, White E B. Macmillan, New York, 1972]

17. Gowers Sir Ernest 1948 Plain words. [Combined with The ABC of plain words 1951 as The complete plain words 1954 and revised by Sir Bruce Fraser in 1973.] HMSO, London

18. Trelease S F 1958 How to write scientific and technical papers. Williams & Wilkins, Baltimore [and 1969, M.I.T. Press, Cambridge, Mass.]

19. Barzun J, Dunbar G 1976 Simple and direct: a rhetoric for writers. Harper & Row, New York

20. Thorne C 1970 Better medical writing. Pitman Medical, London. [Second edition: Lock S 1977 Thorne's better medical writing. Pitman Medical, Tunbridge Wells, Kent]

21. Booth V 1977 Writing a scientific paper, 4th edn. [Available from Biochemical Society Book Depot, Colchester, Essex]

22. Woodford F P (ed.) 1968 Scientific writing for graduate students. Rockefeller University Press, New York and 1969 Macmillan, London [Reprinted as a paperback in 1976 by Council for Biology Editors and available from FASEB, 9650 Rockville Pike, Bethesda, Md. 20014, USA]

23. Tichy H J 1967 Effective writing for engineers, managers, scientists. Wiley, New York

24. ANSI Z39.16—1972 American national standard for the preparation of scientific papers for written or oral presentation. American National Standards Institute, New York

25. Howard-Jones N 1976 Study of WHO editing. Unpublished WHO report PUB/76.3 [Single copies may be obtained from the Chief, Office of Publications, World Health Organization, 1211 Geneva 27, by persons professionally interested in the subject]

26. Fowler H W 1926 A dictionary of modern English usage. [Second edition revised by Sir Ernest Gowers 1965.] Clarendon Press/Oxford University Press, Oxford

27. Follett W 1977 Modern American usage. Warner Books, New York

28. Random House College dictionary 1975 Random House Inc., New York

29. Ingelfinger F J 1976 Seduction by citation (editorial). New England Journal of Medicine 295:1075–1076

30. DeBakey L 1976 The scientific journal: editorial policies and practices. Mosby, St Louis, Mo.

31. ELSE Working Group on Medical Ethics 1972 ELSE Newsletter No. 4:2–3

32. Anon 1971 Publish and be damned a second time (editorial). Nature 233:294

33. Hess E L 1975 Effects of the review process. IEEE Transactions on Professional Communication PC-18:196–197

Chapter 6 Manuscript editing: technical editing

1. Graham J 1975 A new look at cold comp. IEEE Transactions on Professional Communication. PC-18:135–138

2. Butcher J 1975 Copy-editing: the Cambridge handbook. Cambridge University Press, London
3. Manual of style 1969 12th edn. University of Chicago Press, Chicago
4. CBE Style manual 1978 4th edn. American Institute of Biological Sciences, Washington, DC
5. APA 1974 Publication manual, 2nd edn. American Psychological Association, Washington, DC
6. O'Connor M, Woodford F P 1975 Writing scientific papers in English. Elsevier/Excerpta Medica/North-Holland, Amsterdam
7. Editorial Office 1977 Abbreviations and symbols. European Journal of Biochemistry 74:1–6
8. O'Connor M 1978 Standardisation of bibliographical reference systems. British Medical Journal 1:31–32
9. DeBakey L 1976 The scientific journal: editorial policies and practices. Mosby, St Louis, Mo.
10. Wilkinson G 1978 Referencing (letter). New Scientist March 16: 788

Chapter 7 Completing books and journal issues

1. Cavendish J M 1974 A handbook of copyright in British publishing practice. Cassell, London
2. Wagner S 1977 New copyright law primer. Part 1: the basics. Publishers Weekly 212(25):37–42 (26 December)
3. Wagner S 1978 New copyright law primer. Part 2: the formalities. Publishers Weekly 213(5):65–70 (30 January)
4. Anon 1978 New copyright law: effects on Science, contributors and users. Science 199:10
5. ISO 2108 1972 Documentation—International Standard Book Numbering (ISBN)
6. CBE Style manual 1978 4th edn. American Institute of Biological Sciences, Washington, DC
7. Anderson M D 1971 Book indexing. Cambridge University Press, London
8. O'Connor M, Woodford F P 1975 Writing scientific papers in English. Elsevier/Excerpta Medica/North-Holland, Amsterdam
9. AAP/STM Copyright Clearance Center Task Force 1977 A handbook for serial publishers: procedures for using the programs of the Copyright Clearance Center Inc. STM Copyright Bulletin 11, STM Publishers, Amsterdam
10. Capital Systems Group 1975 (and updated) Improving the dissemination of scientific and technical information: a practitioner's guide to innovation. Obtainable from Capital Systems Group Inc., 6110 Executive Boulevard, Suite 850, Rockville, Maryland 20852
11. Smith C A 1975 Second thoughts on medical writing. American Journal of Diseases of Children 129:91, 171, 386, 418, 548, 741, 870, 900, 1034, 1140, 1356, 1386
12. ANSI Z.39.1 1967 American national standard for periodicals: format and arrangement. American National Standards Institute, New York
13. ISO DIS 30 Bibliographical identification (biblid) of serial publications

14. DeBakey L 1976 The scientific journal: editorial policies and practices. Mosby, St Louis, Mo.

Chapter 8 Printing

1. Harman E 1976 A reconsideration of manuscript editing. Scholarly Publishing 7:146–156
2. Butcher J 1975 Copy-editing: the Cambridge handbook. Cambridge University Press, London
3. Jennett S 1973 The making of books, 5th edn. Faber & Faber, London
4. Varley H L 1973 Composition and type design. In: Day R A et al (eds) Economics of scientific publications. Council of Biology Editors, Washington, DC
5. Dessauer J P 1974 Book publishing: what it is, what it does. Bowker, New York
6. Seybold J W 1977 Fundamentals of modern composition. Seybold publications, Media, Pennsylvania
7. Capital Systems Group 1975 (and updated) Improving the dissemination of scientific and technical information: a practitioner's guide to innovation. Obtainable from Capital Systems Group Inc., 6110 Executive Boulevard, Suite 850, Rockville, Maryland 20852
8. O'Connor M, Woodford F P 1975 Writing scientific papers in English. Elsevier/Excerpta Medica/North-Holland, Amsterdam

Chapter 9 Reading Proofs

1. Di Battista M A 1975 Tape proofreading: an adaptation for part-time staff. Scholarly Publishing 6:147–150
2. BS 5261 1976 Guide to copy preparation and proof correction, part 2. Specification for typographic requirements, marks for copy preparation and proof correction, proofing procedure. British Standards Institute, London
3. ANSI Z39.22 1974 American standard for proof corrections. American National Standards Institute, New York
4. O'Connor M, Woodford F P 1975 Writing scientific papers in English. Elsevier/Excerpta Medica/North-Holland, Amsterdam

Chapter 10 Editing conference proceedings: a closer look

1. Capes M (ed) 1960 Communication or conflict: conferences: their nature, dynamics and planning. Tavistock Publications, London
2. Bieber M 1968 How to run a conference. Allen & Unwin, London
3. Mead M, Byers P 1968 The small conference. Mouton, Paris
4. Manten A A 1976 Symposia and symposium publications. A guide for organisers, lecturers and editors of scientific meetings. Elsevier, Amsterdam
5. Wolstenholme G E W 1964 Obese degeneration of scientific congresses. Science 145:1337–1339
6. Woodford F P 1974 The Ciba Foundation: an analytic history. Elsevier/Excerpta Medica/North-Holland, Amsterdam

7. Appleton D R, Kerr D N S 1978 Choosing the programme for an international congress. British Medical Journal 1:421–423
8. Weiss R 1977 [Review of Animal virology.] Nature 267:84
9. Martinsson A 1976 Editor's column: symposia and congresses. Lethaia 9:107–109
10. Hall J E 1977 [Review of Electrical phenomena at the biological membrane level. Proceedings of a meeting.] Science 198:499–500
11. Chamberlain G 1978 [Review of The fetus and birth: Ciba Foundation Symposium 47] Journal of the Royal Society of Medicine 71:157–158
12. Etzioni A 1976 Scientists' meetings: collegial versus positional. Science 193:361
13. Martinsson A 1974 The symposium—a criticism of its implications for publication and a review of I.U.G.S. policy. Editerra Circular Letter 31:1–7
14. Cooper R 1976 The value of large international congresses: round table meetings. Trends in Biochemical Sciences 1:275

Chapter 11 Starting a new journal: financial aspects

1. Wittmann A 1977 Birth of a journal: the need. IEEE Transactions on Professional Communication PC-20:79–81
2. Langley J H 1970 Starting a new journal? Scholarly Publishing 2:75–86
3. Russak B 1977 Starting a new journal (part one). Information Reports and Bibliographies 6(3):3–5
4. Grossmann B 1977 Starting a new journal (part two). Information Reports and Bibliographies 6(3):5–7
5. Wittmann A 1977 Monitoring journal profitability. Information Reports and Bibliographies 6(3):10–11
6. Scal M 1973 Page charges: who should pay for primary journal publication? In: Ref. 16, p 22–27
7. Martinsson A 1974 Changing our package. Lethaia 7:1–4
8. Mound L A 1976 Commercial or learned society publication? Earth Science Editing No. 3:4
9. Chan W 1975 Reprint requests abolished. New Scientist 67:597–598
10. Deal W J 1976 Reprints. New Scientist 68:353–354
11. Hare E H 1978 Surviving inflation? Some recent financial problems of a specialist medical journal. In: Balaban M (ed) Scientific information transfer: the editor's role. Reidel, Dordrecht, p 391–400
12. Abelson P H, Ormes R V 1976 Supporting society journals. Science 193:9
13. Astrup P 1970 Voltairean principle. New England Journal of Medicine 283:204, 206
14. Ingelfinger F J 1969 Swinging copy and sober science. New England Journal of Medicine 281:526–532
15. Ingelfinger F J 1970 Drug display. New England Journal of Medicine 282:507–508

16. Day R A et al (eds) 1973 Economics of scientific publications. Council of Biology Editors, Washington, DC
17. Reville C O Jr 1977 Profit and loss: balance sheet of an ongoing journal. Information Reports and Bibliographies 6(3):7–10
18. Schulman J 1977 Concluding remarks [seminar on Economics of journal publishing]. Information Reports and Bibliographies 6(3):16–17
19. Beck R N, Lineback R H 1978 Page composition costs of philosophy journals: a report on a study. In: Balaban M (ed) Scientific information transfer: the editor's role. Reidel, Dordrecht, p 405–412
20. Metcalfe J R 1976 Are modern methods necessarily the best? Earth Science Editing No. 3:9

Chapter 12 Editing a successful journal

1. Gordon M D 1978 Disciplinary differences, editorial practices and the patterning of rejection rates for UK research journals. Journal of Research Communication Studies 1(2): in press
2. Schwartz B, Dubin S C 1978 Manuscript queues and editorial reorganization. Scholarly Publishing 9:253–259
3. Fox Sir Theodore 1965 Crisis in communication. Athlone Press, London
4. Ingelfinger F J 1968 To impart the precepts and the instruction. Lancet 2:766–767
5. Maddox J 1967 Is the literature dead or alive? Nature 214:1077–1079
6. Walster G W, Cleary T A 1970 A proposal for a new editorial policy in the social sciences. American Statistician 24:16–19
7. Mason A S 1968 Apologia. Lancet 2:864–865
8. Jesse A 1978 On the information transfer from primary to secondary sources and from secondary to primary sources—an editing experiment in an interdisciplinary field (Automatic Image Analysis). In: Balaban M (ed) Scientific information transfer: the editor's role. Reidel, Dordrecht, p 559–564
9. DeBakey L 1976 The scientific journal: editorial policies and practices. Mosby, St Louis, Mo.
10. Martinsson A 1976 Editor's column: dates of scientific publications. Lethaia 9:219–220
11. Anon 1976 New features. British Medical Journal 2:836
12. Ingelfinger F J 1976 Specialty journals in philosophy and ethics. New England Journal of Medicine 295:1317–1318
13. Anon 1978 To sign or not to sign? British Medical Journal 1:598
14. Anon 1977 Bladder cancer and saccharin. Lancet 2:592–593
15. Conference of Editors 1959 Handbook for editors of learned journals. Modern Language Association of America, New York
16. Macrae G W 1972 Report of the task force on scholarly communication and publication. Council on the Study of Religion, Waterloo Lutheran University, Ontario
17. Anon 1971 Delinquent reviews. American Sociological Review 36:595
18. Chen C-C 1976 Biomedical, scientific and technical book reviewing. Scarecrow Press, Metuchen, N.J.

19. Manten A A 1975 Book reviews in primary journals. Journal of Technical Writing and Communication 5:227–236

20. Bewley T 1977 Only connect! [A non-review of PN Furbank's E. M. Forster: A Life.] British Medical Journal 2:1131–1132

Chapter 13 Editing in the Future: innovation and education

1. Bush V 1945 As we may think. Atlantic Monthly Magazine 176 (July): 101–108

2. Baker W O, Brown W S, Mathews M V et al 1977 Computers and research. Science 195:1134–1139

3. Senders J W 1977 An on-line scientific journal. The Information Scientist 11(1):3–9

4. Capital Systems Group 1975 (and updated) Improving the dissemination of scientific and technical information: a practitioner's guide to innovation. Obtainable from Capital Systems Group Inc., 6110 Executive Boulevard, Suite 850, Rockville, Maryland 20852

5. Greaser C U 1976 Alternatives to traditional forms of scientific communication. Scholarly Publishing 8:54–66

6. Campbell R, Ashby P 1978 Microforms and journal publishing. STM Innovation Bulletin 1:14–15. In: STM Newsletter 45. International Group of Scientific, Technical & Medical Publishers, Amsterdam

7. Anon 1977 Instructions for authors. Journal of Chemical Research (S) Issue 2:i–xi

8. Grünewald H 1976 A rational system of publication and retrieval. As reported in Earth Science Editing No. 3:5

9. Williams I A 1977 Editorial. Journal of Chemical Research (S) Issue 9: no page number

10. Hey M H 1978 Miniprint in the Mineralogical Magazine. Earth & Life Science Editing No. 7–8

11. Lea P W 1976 Trends in scientific and technical primary journal publishing in the USA. British Library Research and Developing Report No. 5272HC, British Library Lending Division, Wetherby, West Yorkshire

12. Kewney G 1977 Publishing's future pivots on the data base. New Scientist 22/29 December: p 769

13. Bamford H E Jr 1972 A concept for applying computer technology to the publication of scientific journals. Journal of the Washington Academy of Science 6:306–314 (cited by Woodward, Ref. 14)

14. Woodward A M 1976 Editorial Processing Centres: scope in the United Kingdom. British Library Research and Development Report No. 5271HC, British Lending Division, Wetherby, West Yorkshire

15. Rhodes S N 1977 Editorial Processing Center—prelude to phase III. IEEE Transactions on Professional Communication PC-20:102–105

16. Primary Communications Research Centre 1977 Scholarly publishers guide: new methods and techniques. PCRC, University of Leicester

17. DeBakey L 1976 The Scientific journal: editorial policies and practices. Mosby, St Louis, Mo.
18. Grünewald H 1977 Draft guidelines for editors of scientific and technical journals. Unesco, Paris (limited distribution, Division of the General Information Programme)
19. Glen J W (ed) 1977 Editerra editors' handbook. Editerra, Farnham, Surrey
20. Balaban M (ed) 1978 Scientific information transfer: the editor's role. Reidel, Dordrecht (Proceedings of the first international conference of scientific editors, April 24–29, 1977, Jerusalem)
21. Woodford F P 1970 Training professional editors for scientific journals. Scholarly Publishing 2:41–46
22. Butcher J 1975 Copy-editing: the Cambridge handbook. Cambridge University Press, London
23. O'Connor M, Woodford F P 1975 Writing scientific papers in English. Elsevier/Excerpta Medica/North-Holland, Amsterdam
24. Svartz-Malmberg G, Goldmann R (eds) 1978 Nordic biomedical manuscripts: instructions & guidelines. Universitetsforlaget, Oslo
25. Mizoguchi D U 1976 (In Japanese) [English papers in life sciences]. Kodansha, Tokyo
26. Editorial Board 1971 A new direction for the Journal of Medical Education. Journal of Medical Education 46:641–642
27. Anon 1966 A statement of policy by the Managing Editors of Biochimica et Biophysica Acta. Biochimica Biophysica Acta 121:223–227
28. Ingelfinger F J 1976 Journal ventures that flopped. New England Journal of Medicine. 295:727–729
29. Garfield E 1976 Significant journals of science. Nature 264:609–615
30. Bailey H S Jr 1977 The traditional book in the electronic age. Publishers Weekly Dec 5:24–29

Appendix 4 Guidelines for authors

1. O'Connor M, Woodford F P 1975 Writing scientific papers in English. Elsevier/Excerpta Medica/North-Holland, Amsterdam
2. Council of Biology Editors 1978 CBE Style manual, 4th edn. American Institute of Biological Sciences, Washington, DC
3. European Journal of Biochemistry 1977 Abbreviations and symbols. 74:1–6
4. Landau N, Weiss R B 1976 Information flow between primary journals and secondary services in the biological field. British Library Research and Development Report 5239, British Library Lending Division, Wetherby, West Yorkshire
5. DeBakey L 1976 The scientific journal: editorial policies and practices. Mosby, St Louis, Mo.

Acknowledgements

Of all those who gave time and thought to the preparation of this book, none deserves more thanks than Dr F. Peter Woodford, who wrote most of the first draft and provided critical guidance on much of the second. He is a co-author in fact if not in appearance on the title page, and but for the pressures of his other work he would have been named as the first author of this book. My debt to him is very great.

I also want to thank very warmly indeed all those who read and commented on the first draft, and who shared their professional expertise with great kindness and generosity. The advice of the members of the informal but dedicated panel of referees named here has improved the book enormously, and their encouragement in the earlier stages of writing this book was invaluable:

Ms Miriam Balaban
(Jerusalem)
Dr Alexander G. Bearn
(New York, NY)
Dr Lois DeBakey
(Houston, Texas)
Miss Selma DeBakey
(Houston, Texas)
Dr John T. Edsall
(Cambridge, Mass.)
Professor Knut Faegri
(Bergen)

Dr J. Stanton King
(Winston-Salem, NC)
Dr Stephen Lock
(London)
Professor Anders Martinsson
(Uppsala)
Dr John Metcalfe
(Farnham Royal, Slough, Bucks.)
Miss Gillian Page
(London)
Mrs Julie Whelan
(London)

Others whose help I much appreciate include Ms Joanna Marx (Pretoria), Mr Philip Vuysje (Amsterdam) and Mr Basil Walby (Melbourne); the members of a British Medical Journal/ELSE Workshop for technical editors held in Winchester on 17 and 18 November 1977, who commented on Chapters 5 and 6; and Miss Gillian Clack and Miss Sandra Davis, who patiently typed and retyped the chapters as they changed.

Finally, I want to thank the Ciba Foundation, Editerra, ELSE, IFSEA, IUBS and IUGS for the moral support each of these organizations provided during the preparation of this book.

Index*

* Index compiled with the assistance of William Hill.